DEC 2009

810.9928 SHAPING
Shaping memories
:REFLECTIONS OF AFRICA

D1554964

WITHDRAWN

Shaping
Memories

Shaping
Memories

Shaping Memories

REFLECTIONS OF

AFRICAN AMERICAN

WOMEN WRITERS

EDITED BY
JOANNE VEAL GABBIN

UNIVERSITY PRESS OF MISSISSIPPI / JACKSON

Alameda Free Library
1550 Oak Street
Alameda, CA 94501

www.upress.state.ms.us

The University Press of Mississippi is a member of the
Association of American University Presses.

Copyright © 2009 by University Press of Mississippi
All rights reserved
Manufactured in the United States of America

First printing 2009
∞
Library of Congress Cataloging-in-Publication Data

Shaping memories : reflections of African American
women writers / edited by Joanne Veal Gabbin.
     p. cm.
 ISBN 978-1-60473-274-0 (alk. paper)
 1. African American women authors—20th century—
Biography. 2. Authorship. I. Gabbin, Joanne V. II. Wintergreen Women Writers' Collective.
 PS153.N5S46 2009
 810.9'928708996073—dc22
  [B]   2008055184

British Library Cataloging-in-Publication Data available

To the memory of Margaret Walker, who was
never able to attend Wintergreen but affirmed
the greening of the spirit that it represents.

To Alexander, Dorothy Mae's oldest child,
with whom I have shaped a lifetime of memories.

CONTENTS

Silence . . . A Dangerous Luxury

Spirit Houses

What Roots Us

A Sanctuary of Words

ACKNOWLEDGMENTS

In 1987 when I invited a group of women to the Wintergreen Resort nestled in the Blue Ridge Mountains to welcome Nikki Giovanni to Virginia, I could not have known that we would become the Wintergreen Women Writers' Collective, a gathering of writers who gain strength and direction from communion with one another. For more than twenty years we have shared our writing, traded teaching strategies, unburdened our minds, and renewed our spirits in the intimacy of conversations around the dining table. Those conversations provided the impetus for this collection. I am grateful to more than fifty Wintergreen Women who have made their journey up the mountain and have given so richly of themselves by sharing their stories.

I am also grateful to the writers who contributed their essays to this collection, and I thank them for giving me permission to publish their work. I appreciate the continuing kindness and encouragement of Nikki Giovanni, who was the catalyst for the founding of this collective. I especially want to thank Sandra Govan for her dedication in keeping the history of the group in her own inimitable way. I want to acknowledge Daryl Dance for her help in doing the first review of the manuscript and Opal Moore for writing the book's inspirational Coda. My thanks go to all the Wintergreen Women who took the time to review the manuscript and offer suggestions.

So many people have helped to make this collection possible. I want to thank the editorial assistants in the Furious Flower Poetry Center for their invaluable contribution. Julie Caran, Natalia Bradshaw-Parson, and Clarissa Shoecraft saw many iterations of the manuscript which has become *Shaping Memories: Reflections of African American Women Writers*. Their administrative and organizational support was essential in producing this collection. I would also like to thank Karen Risch and Jessica Lewis for their consultation and encouragement in reviewing the manuscript. I am indebted to Marie Brown, who has shepherded several landmark collections of women's writing, for her wise counsel. I am grateful to Seetha Srinivasan, Director Emerita of the University Press of Mississippi. Over the years, she encouraged me to be a UPM author, and I am delighted that we were able to work together on this book before her well-deserved retirement. Her enthusiasm for this project has bolstered me during the long process of preparation and review. I want to thank Walter Biggins, editor at UPM, for his clear and helpful guidelines for the preparation of the manuscript. It has been a pleasure to work with Director Leila Salisbury and the entire University Press of Mississippi staff in publishing this book.

As I think back to days in 1987 before I found my way to the Peddler's Edge house at Wintergreen, I remember that my husband, Alexander, first convinced me to host the gathering in a place where I would enjoy myself as well. For more than forty years of marriage, he has been my encourager, my champion, my consultant, and my adviser. He has happily sent me off to do my work and celebrated my successes. I am grateful for his love. I also feel blessed that I have been able to share the Wintergreen experience with my daughter, Jessea Nayo. She has been nurtured and inspired by these women she affectionately calls her "Literary Aunties."

INTRODUCTION

She pulled in her horizon like a great fish-net. Pulled it from around
the waist of the world and draped it over her shoulder. So much of life
in its meshes! She called in her soul to come and see.

—ZORA NEALE HURSTON

Every time I read the closing lines of Zora Neale Hurston's *Their
Eyes Were Watching God*, I marvel at their goose-pimple-giving perfection.
Janie Crawford, a forty-year-old widow, has returned home after being
away for more than a year. The only man she has ever loved is dead, and
she is left alone to live with her memories. As she walks past her judg-
mental neighbors, "the sitters and the talkers," she senses their indignation,
their tongues ripe with curiosity and speculation. At once, they resist and
need the intimacy of her company. Yet, only Pheoby, Janie's best friend, is
allowed to hear the experiences that have led to this moment in her life.
Hurston tells us in the beginning of this novel, in her classic metaphor for
the life of women, "Now, women forget all those things they don't want to
remember, and remember everything they don't want to forget. The dream
is the truth. Then they act and do things accordingly."

In this collection, *Shaping Memories: Reflections of African American
Women Writers*, we get to share in the intimacy of women writers who are
remembering "everything they don't want to forget," the things that define
them as women, as writers, as teachers, as scholars, and as sister-travelers.
These women have a deep association with the hard work of self-discovery,
with turning difficult challenges into opportunities for growth and change,
with refusing to collude with principalities in their own silence.

These women know how to tell the truth. They do it because sharing
is integral to being in relationship. This collection is rich with personal

reflections that show significant experiences in their development, defining moments that shaped the women that they have become. In the opening section, "Women in Community," Nikki Giovanni tells how strong friendship can bring logic to the world. Remembering her parents' chronic arguments and the care of women who helped to dissipate her anger and resentment, Giovanni writes: "Theresa [my mother's friend] didn't try to explain; she just kept pointing out it was not something I had any control over. Which when you are ten or twelve is a powerful thing to know."

Paule Marshall extends our understanding of community as she shines a light on the tradition of conversation among her mother's friends that she said, more than any other single factor, shaped her art: "I didn't realize it then but those long afternoon rap sessions were highly functional, therapeutic; they were, you might say, a kind of magic rite, a form of juju, for it was their way to exorcise the day's humiliations and restore them to themselves."

Many of the women in this collection share their experiences of being part of the academy; they talk vividly of their challenges in, as Sandra Govan puts it, "the white noise" of institutions of education. Kendra Hamilton depicts her desperation with the prejudices of the rarefied space of her private school, an interior struggle that only surfaced in the pages of her private journal. "I said nothing—those days were teaching me to listen—but smoothly, silently, a door inside me cracked open and a thread of cool air began to stir . . . "

Others recognize in their lives the dangers of silence. Linda Nelson in "On My Return from Exile" tells us that her purpose "is to wage war against an imposition of silence" and confesses that her mother's insistence that she censor herself when she was young stalled her writing for years. In her memoir, Janus Adams chronicles her own sacrifices in being "the first," a situation that characterized the lives of many black women during the late 1960s and the 1970s, and the psychological pain of ignoring injustices in order to maintain safety. When she eventually emerges from the "bunker" of her own creation, she writes, "When, at last, I ventured out, I went back—mentally, emotionally—retracing the years that had brought me to that day I'd sunk so low that I crawled into a closet and almost died inside."

In the pages of this book we meet women in community with one another and the nurturing and responsibility that community demands, women negotiating educational institutions at all levels of development, women finding their voices despite societal gags such as racism and religious chauvinism. The memoirs offer a window into the literary and familial influences in the writers' lives and a view of the reverence they place in the power of words to heal, transform, and renew lives.

In their company, we see women who find the words to speak of birth and death, of formative years shaped by pervasive segregation, of loves supreme. Yet, in all, their writing is central, for writing is sanctuary; it is the art of discovering a safe space in which to be. Writing is also a memorial; it is like the *Ibeji* that Yoruba carved out of wood to preserve the memory of lost twins; they take on their own life as spirit houses. Writing is still, even in this age of super-technology, what can be made with the hands. It is like Nikky Finney's grandmother's ambrosia, delicately crafted for its tart/sweetness. It is redemptive like Eugenia Collier's account of her mother's paranoia and the pain it inflicted on her and the rest of the family. For ultimately, even the most tragic memories root us; they are braided into the texture of our lives.

The essayists featured here are members of the Wintergreen Women Writers' Collective. Being writers drew them to this group, but their friendship kept them in communion with one another for more than twenty years. For this collection, they have cast their nets wide to draw in childhood remembrances, the kind that sting like a freshly stripped limb off the mulberry bush or soothe like a grandmother's laying-on-of-hands. They reveal to us a love of books and the people who shaped them and their art. Sometimes the memories are torturous, but they cannot be jettisoned because they have within them the power of salvation and redemption. These narratives pull into view the decades that saw African Americans emerge from a storied invisibility through struggle and tumult to palpable freedom. They make us remember when we raged against an imposition of silence because we were women or because we were black. They make us remember all those moments that urged us into self-expression.

For all of the women writers gathered here, their prose is the prize catch, as it is their own gesture of civil disobedience, their act of grabbing the power that they know is theirs, and their salvation. Gloria Naylor told Nikki Giovanni at the 1997 Wintergreen Retreat, "I didn't understand . . . at first when people told me, you've got to do your work, your work is your salvation. I didn't understand it, but . . . it turned out to be the case." Like Hurston's Janie, the women featured in *Shaping Memories* have pulled in their horizons like great fish-nets and beckoned us to come and see what has been caught in their meshes. As you encounter their twenty-five distinct voices, you will hear how the soul grows to accommodate new experiences, how women who have so much creativity and vision continue to tell the truth as they see it and dare to expect the dream.

—JOANNE VEAL GABBIN

Women in Community

A Distant Star Called Possibility

Wintergreen

—NIKKI GIOVANNI

I always envied my mother her friends. Well, I guess that's not quite true. I did envy my mother her friends but not *always*. When I was a little girl, I didn't envy, though I did think something extraordinary was going on. Mommy had four friends and they were always around. One was Flora Alexander, whom Mommy and Gus had helped send to college. Flora's parents had no money and didn't think she could go to Knoxville College let alone any other school of higher education. Gus, my father, talked with Mr. and Mrs. Fletcher (Flora's parents) and convinced them Flora should go. Then he convinced Uncle Lee, Attorney Leon Render, to find a scholarship; then he convinced Brett Pendleton that he should help, too. It worked. Flora got to college and graduated. To show her appreciation, Flora used to babysit Gary, my sister, and me. She said she hated it. Gary was cool, competent, and always on top of things. I was a rather whiney child. I wanted my Mommy. I cried almost from the time Mommy and Gus walked out the door until I either fell asleep or they came home. I think Flora, after a time, learned to like me, and I know I learned not to cry all the time, but I did cry a lot and I was always wanting my Mommy. Clearly, Flora was Gary's good friend. Gary's son, Christopher, is Christopher *Alexander* Black for Flora Fletcher Alexander. Gary was always a shopper. And she loved clothes. Flora was the sharpest dresser, too, and always had the latest records. I loved records and books but didn't care a fig what I had on. Flora and Gary bonded. I needed something else.

My heart belonged to Theresa Elliot. Theresa was always there when we needed her. My father was one of those people who give liquor a bad name. No one ever had to wonder, or at least I never had to wonder, what I would be doing on Friday and Saturday nights: I would be listening to arguments. Well, that's not exactly true. I would be listening to my father cursing and hitting and my mother, who was silent and taking it. It's a bad thing to hit your wife. Number one: you will grow old and need someone to take care of you. Number two: it taints your daughter's view of marriage and the place of men in her life. And number three: it teaches your son bad habits that get repeated and repeated and repeated. But Theresa was always there. If it got really crazy, we would go to her house. My godmother, Edna Westfield, used to try to explain the craziness, but there is no explanation for craziness. Theresa didn't try to explain; she just kept pointing out it was not something I had any control over. Which when you are ten or twelve is a powerful thing to know. I went to live with my grandmother.

I recently, through the exegesis of my aunt Ann, learned that I also had done a good job. I had thought only of my need to escape, not at all of my grandparents' need to be needed. Anto, which is what we called her, kept all Grandpapa's letters. I cry as I read them even now. They were glad to have me. I didn't know that then. I only knew it was important to be smart, to make good grades, to not get into any trouble, and to carry my own weight, since I knew Mommy had no money and Gus, who made a decent living, wasn't going to give me anything. I still have the rug he bought me when I went to college. He was dying before I realized he loved me. Such a waste.

Girlfriends are the most precious things on earth. I took a test, which was probably the most important test I ever took, to leave high school early and go to college. Good for me. One more year of high school and I'm sure I would have been a secret alcoholic or some sort of crazy something. I passed the test and was accepted into Fisk University. Fisk was special to me because Grandpapa had graduated Fisk in 1905. I had hoped to follow in his footsteps. It was not to be. I had too much anger, too much hurt, and not enough sense of myself. I was kicked out. And that was good. That allowed me to recognize that the dean who kicked me out was wrong, but

I was wrong, too, and it let me meet Jackie Cowan. Dean Cowan was a lifeline. She was neither intimidated nor competitive. She let me sit in her office for hours on end. Sometimes I was reading a book; sometimes I was just sitting. But the anger was leaving and the love was coming through. She gave me responsibilities and I would do anything to keep from letting her down. I felt the same way about my grandmother, though I let my grandmother down when I got kicked out. Jackie might not have understood me, but she and I traveled that road to graduation and grad school. She had a brain tumor ten years later. I remember sitting in her hospital room. When she was lucid she was surprised to see me. How could that be? I adored the ground she walked on. There was no other place for me to be.

So I was building my girlfriends, but Mommy was luckier than I was. Mine were dying. Jeanne Noble was my friend. So was Lillian Benbow. Both were succumbing to cancers. And you feel so alone. I had my mother and my aunts. I had a wonderful friend who is, in fact, my oldest friend, Sister Althea, a black Episcopalian nun. Sister Althea always says I don't believe anyone loves me. I probably don't. But she does. And I love her. And I'm glad.

When I went back to Fisk it was Mommy's friend, Lauretta Kinnard, who sent me for one semester. Mommy paid for fall; Lauretta for spring. Then I finally got a scholarship and that was good. Attitude. They kept saying I had a bad attitude. And some people wonder why I learned to hate Theodore Currier. He was very kind to John Hope Franklin and many others, but by the time I encountered him he was old and, in my opinion, corrupt. He refused to give me a recommendation for a Woodrow Wilson. "Chicken," he said, (he called everyone either Chicken or Chief), "your hair is so rebellious." I had an Afro and he did not approve of that. *Mr. Currier*, I wanted to say, *Go Fuck Yourself*. I didn't say that, but Jackie didn't like the way he treated me either, and she gave me a dynamite recommendation to the University of Pennsylvania School of Social Work, and I was off to grad school.

What I knew, what I know, is that friends are essential. Mommy's friend Dorothy Twitty is precious to me. I took Ron, her son, to get his first driver's license. Ron rose to be the second highest officer in the Cincinnati Police Department. A part of the Cincinnati riots was the refusal of the department to make Ron Twitty chief. The city deserved the riots.

But we were talking about friends. And there is nothing without friendship. I had been invited to speak at James Madison University where I met Joanne Gabbin. She and I and some students were having dinner after my speaking. We talked about *Strawberry Summers*, cooking good food, and I shared with Joanne that I just accepted an invitation from Virginia Tech to be a Visiting Professor. I was looking forward to our universities working together. Joanne with glee said: *We must get together to welcome you to Virginia*. And it was set.

I came to Virginia in my son's car, which was in really bad shape. Thomas and his friends had sat on the roof at the drive-in one night and the roof had caved in. Needless to say, when it rained the rain came in. The car smelled like a wet, dead skunk. I left Blacksburg and went back to Cincinnati. Mommy went with me to purchase a car. I simply could not go to a girlfriends' weekend in a stinky, wet automobile. I purchased a candy-apple-red, five-speed Toyota MR2. Joanne had invited me and about ten other women to Wintergreen for a weekend of girl-friend-getting-to-know-each-other. Some of us were famous; some not. Some were students; some faculty. Some poets and writers; some critics. Some white; some black. All reaching out to that wonderful world of friendship.

It was great. We played cards, swam, walked in the woods (dodging the bears), read poetry to the group, cooked and ate, and it was great. It was supposed to be a onetime thing, but we all said: *Let's do it again*. And we have been doing it for the last twenty years. We have had new members; we have had daughters and friends. I took both my mother and my sister and my sister's friend to Wintergreen. My friend Linda was taking her daughter Kim. It is a safe place. To relax. To be surrounded by love. To be. A haven. Where we cheer each other on. Not my mother's friends, for sure, but riding the night winds, our hearts skip across the clouds, coming to rest on a distant star called *possibility*; we arrive at Wintergreen. Good for us.

Wintergreen and Alaga Syrup

A Writer's Reflections on Memory,
Writing, and Place

—CARMEN R. GILLESPIE

As a child, every time I heard the song "I'll Take You There," with its amazing guitar lead-in, followed by the call of its opening line, "I know a place," and then the easy assured response, "I'll take you there," I used to envy the Staple Sisters—as a child in the backseat of my parents' car, and later in dark, dancing spaces. With Pop Staples's bass guitar line for air, surely their house must have contained everything necessary. Now, during nights like this one, while I try to understand, try to make meaning by putting words to paper, I put the song on repeat as I confront the specter of a blank screen and an impending deadline.

When I mention the soulful, stabilizing presence of Pop Staples's repetitive, reassuring bass in the song, my friends, my acquaintances, and even strangers never remember the guitar riff, only the fervent, soulful singing, but for me the bass was the heartbeat I imagined in the Staples' home. Not their actual home, but the one I constructed, tore down, and rebuilt again and again. It conjured chords, hair curlers, and sisters singing in the sheltering arms of that beat—fictional foundations unfamiliar to my memory and unearthed by desire, the hunger of a child who never felt safe as a girl, for whom the idea of creating harmony with a father who intuitively led the way *and* had the confidence and self-assurance to follow the pathway created by his daughter's voice was a dream out of reach. Of course, his daughter, Mavis Staples, knew the way. How could she not?

There are spaces and places that are curiously, unexpectedly generative, and, for me, driving a car, particularly on a long trip, has always been that space—to listen, think, imagine, remember. One such trip, through Thomas Jefferson/Sally Hemings country in Virginia, unbeknownst to me at the time, marked one of the beginnings of my life as a writer. That trip took place during the spring of 1987. I was headed to the first of what would become an annual writers' retreat for African American women living in the Virginia, Carolina, and D.C. regions. The retreat was held that year and for several years after at the Wintergreen Resort outside of Charlottesville, Virginia.

"I'll Take You There" was one of the songs I played over and over again during my first journey up the Wintergreen Mountain more than twenty years ago. At the time, I was in the first fall of a master's degree in English at James Madison University, the same university that had hired its first African American literature professor only two years before. The arrival of Joanne Gabbin at James Madison signaled for me a visitation by Papa Legba, god of the crossroads. Joanne's classes and her invitation to attend the first Wintergreen retreat changed my life forever.

The membrane between the fictional and the factual is frequently quite thin for those of us who intercourse with language and narrative for a living. My life has always been peopled with phantasms that reside only in the imagination and in the canyons and crevasses of a book. At times, the world created by written words has been more navigable and palatable than the often unmarked and untraceable universe of interpersonal relationships. As a child I was often confused and isolated by the rage that my father brought back with him from Vietnam and directed at me, sometimes verbally, sometimes physically. I often retreated to books and found sanctuary in them—a safety and understanding that seemed inaccessible in reality. My family cast my reading and writing as an idiosyncratic oddity—another characteristic that set me apart in an unflattering and unproductive way. As a result, it never occurred to me that I could keep one foot in the familiar soil of the written word *and* make a living, until I took African American literature during college with Joanne.

Before taking that class, the world of African American writing was virtually unknown to me. For the first time, I sympathized with Phillis Wheatley, fell in love with David Walker, journeyed with Janie Crawford, went underground with the Invisible Man, dreamt in purple with Celie, and soared with Milkman Dead. Not only did I live these formative texts, Joanne graced each class with an informal and personal introduction as the conductor and guide, illuminating the generative darkness. When we read Sterling Brown's poetry, she became Ma Rainey and sang to us. We became Tuskegee grads and NAACP members in order to debate the merits of nationalism and integration. On her invitation, James Farmer visited the campus and we all sat mesmerized as he told us of the Freedom Riders and his work in CORE. I could not know it then, but many years later I would enjoy the great privilege of teaching on the same faculty with Dr. Farmer; however, I still do not forget my first acquaintance with this gentle man in Joanne's class. The texts she taught and my encounters with them were living; this reading was about my history, my people, *my* life. This literature became affirmation of my perceptions of the world; these texts became my place, my home, a place that was not abusive and silencing but was full of energy, passion, and grace. I knew that I had discovered my calling. I wanted to teach literature and to write.

By the time of the first Wintergreen retreat in 1987, I had committed to becoming a professor of African American literature. The retreats have always been small, consisting of groups of about thirteen or so women. That first year the group included Opal Moore, Nikki Giovanni, Sandy Govan, Trudier Harris, Daryl Dance, and Paule Marshall. Other writers who have attended through the years include Sonia Sanchez, Joyce Pettis, Eugenia Collier, Val Gray Ward, Toi Derricotte, Karla Holloway, Marilyn Mobley, Maryemma Graham, Pinkie Gordon Lane, Mari Evans and, of course, always, Joanne Gabbin. When I have been blessed to visit the mountain, these annual respites have become to me like the familiar smell of my grandmother's house, reassuring, familial, and evocative—a ritual time for reflection and renewal—to quote Toni Morrison, "a place with a doorway never needing to be closed, snug and wide open—home" (Morrison, "Home" 13).

Serendipitously, the plant wintergreen is purported to be a curative for both internal and external wounds and is described as a creeping root that proliferates in forested areas such as in the mountains and valleys of

Virginia's Blue Ridge, the site of the annual Wintergreen retreats. Such a curative is often essential to those of us who aspire to create with language. Wintergreen has come to represent for me a communion—a balm for the brutality of the dangerous spaces women writers occupy—the often urgent need for repair of our bodies and spirits. Like the beat of Pop Staples's guitar, I like to think of Wintergreen as a representation, a trace, nearly imperceptible and yet essential, an element in a healing ritual—in, to quote Joanne, the "laying-on-of-hands."

In Toni Morrison's *The Bluest Eye*, the protagonist/narrator Claudia recalls the abrasive quality of her mother's hands as the overworked woman anxiously applies balm to her ailing daughter . . . "it was a productive and fructifying pain. Love thick and dark as Alaga syrup eased into that cracked window. I could smell it—taste it—sweet, musty, with an edge of wintergreen in its base—everywhere in that house" (Morrison 12). Although the experience is painful for Claudia, she recognizes that the discomfort her mother's efforts engender is rooted in a sincere urgency and a zealous, if hasty and abrasive, compassion.

I am grateful that I am old enough to know what Alaga syrup is. I can remember that my grandmother always had a bottle of it in her pantry, although I never saw her use it in anything she was cooking; its dark color and its viscosity never failed to hold my attention. It is that lovely sweet deep darkness, perhaps as an ironic result of its sugarcane source, which colors and coats my memories of Wintergreen as well as my feelings about the women who have participated in this gathering throughout the years and have spent their lives as scholars and writers. This intangible but real mortar helps form the passing years into an incongruous, yet dependable, mosaic.

The Wintergreen experience resists the eroding flow of antagonism and hostility African American women writers and scholars often face in our professional and personal lives. Through the lush landscape Jefferson *and* Sally Hemings called home, we gather to speak our truths, to share our experiences and our stories—to distill that edge, that hint of wintergreen that fills our imaginative surroundings and enchants us. Thus anointed, we return to the places we call home and to the classrooms, computers, conferences, and committees that are the tools and terrains of the academic and creative lives we have chosen. In these spaces we inhabit, there is often a need for the Alaga, the thick dark richness of community, friendship, and love, to impede the cold.

Many of us serve in an academy often icy with resistance to what we bring, what we believe, what we teach, who we are. But my journey along this way was not the harsh confrontation many of the women who come to Wintergreen faced and who often were the first African American women to challenge the exclusivity of both the constituency and the content of this profession.

Over the years, I have heard the stories of petty viciousness and even brutality these women experienced as they began their careers in the 1960s and '70s. Daryl Dance's tales of her experiences as one of the first African American doctoral students at the University of Virginia resonate and sustain me as I encounter the transformed but still virulent resistance to my own credibility, my presence—like the colleague who took me out to dinner during the first month of my first tenure-track job (also in Virginia) and told me that she wanted to discover for herself if I was a fraud. Later that year, during the wiring of English department offices for on-line computers, the technicians discovered a box in the ceiling crawl space above a department office. After the contents had been examined, the department chair gave the box to me. As I sat in my office sifting through the package, I wondered what it was about the contents of this box that had so threatened its original owner as to warrant its relocation in the small, dusty space above the English department. The box discovered in the ceiling tiles above the English department contained about forty or fifty copies of an African American anthology from 1970. Apparently someone in the department, in an attempt to prevent the dissemination of these texts, had climbed up on his or her chair or desk and shoved the heavy box into the ceiling, hoping against hope that this action would delay or prevent the introduction of African American literature to these Virginia classrooms in the capital of the Confederacy. Although Wintergreen and all the work that the women who attend have produced represent the futility of that person's efforts, my own work as a teacher, scholar, and writer sometimes seems small compensation for the symbolic weight of those books and all of that work lying overhead for so many years undiscovered. Although this work is a passion, it is also and often painful and depleting. But having the seemingly tireless examples of Joanne, Daryl, Sandy, Trudier, Marilyn, Toi, Opal, Nikki, Paule, and all of the remarkable women who do this work with shocking brilliance, helps to fill in and warm the spaces—the Alaga hardens like mortar and holds the pieces . . . Even now there are other boxes silently hidden away in the darkness waiting to be found and opened, and this is the work that we do.

Part of the work of African American women writers is "gathering the pieces," the fragments of past and present so diffuse, scattered, and hidden in the wake of diaspora, slavery, migration, and perhaps, ironically, integration. The ability to know a place—know and claim it as home—is often illusive for us. As the daughter of a Vietnam vet army officer, my childhood was defined by a series of moves, physical and verbal violence, and emotionally fraught relocations from one generic military base to another. When I was ten, my father left the army to work as the personal pilot for the prime minister of Guyana and as director of the country's helicopter program. Guyana is now well known as the site of the Jonestown massacres, but in 1975 that country was fairly obscure to most Americans. This move to the "land of many rivers," as Guyana is called, was to write itself indelibly on my imagination and my future.

In Georgetown, the city we called home for three years, three muddy tumultuous rivers converge. Guyana's landscape, so different from anything I had ever known, flooded the banks of my imagination. Water is everywhere; so much so that the houses stand stilted, stories above the grass, perched as if on tiptoe. The Demerara, Essequibo, and Berbice rivers, born deep in the rainforests of the Amazon, finger through Georgetown and, eager to escape into the sea, burnish the ocean with earthen silt for nearly a mile offshore. Here I first found the ocean and by its shores, on the seawall that barred its encroach, watched women with enormous round wicker baskets on their heads sell shrimp—sell on shores where so many ancestors were brought to be sold—sold to grow sugar cane on plantations where, fed by the lives and labor of brown men and women, windmills ground the green into brown sugar to be sold.

While Guyana was home, occasionally we would trade Guyana's lush greens and muddy sugary browns for the iridescent blues of the Caribbean islands. During one visit, we flew to nearby Barbados. Later I would learn about the centrality of this island to the history of the North American slave trade and about the ways that it formed the template for colonization and sugar production and, horrifyingly, for breaking—seasoning—slaves. The first experience of life in enslaved exile for many Africans occurred in Barbados.

During my first arrival, the translucent Barbados blues and greens, magnetic even from the air, gave me no hint these same shores staged such suffering. In Bridgetown, we walked through the market shopping for tourist trifles in the same space where slaves were once sold. As a child, I was oblivious to the complexity of this history and to the nearly sacrilegious seduction of the island's beauty.

On that trip, I made my first visit to one of the highest points on the island, Farley Hill. I remember asking my mother for a pen and paper, and there I wrote one of my first poems. I don't remember what I wrote, but there in Barbados I understood that home transcends both geography and time, and that there is great and ancient power in the human attempt to translate experience into language. Farley Hill is a windswept landscape perch—profligate now only with curvaceous mahogany trees. From there I could see the sea. The trees are never still and thus, caressed by the fragrant warm air, they cannot help but whisper. It is cool and dark, even at noon. Beyond the trees, there is a cane field, the main source of income for all of the previous owners of the plantation, its house now roofless and occupied only by occasional tourists, pastel-uniformed school children, Sunday picnics, and national celebrations. This place metaphorizes my scholarly, theoretical, artistic, and personal engagement with American, African American, and African diasporic literatures and cultures. Farley Hill epitomizes many of the foci of these literatures as well as my primary concerns as an artist: the displacements and losses of slavery, the realities of homelessness and the search for home, the struggle for selfhood and ownership, the desire for and acquisition of voice. Living in Guyana and visiting Barbados introduced me to some of the complex questions of home. Eventually the currents of these experiences carried me to graduate school and up the mountain to Wintergreen. Proving that occasionally real life mirrors the curvaceous arcs of fiction, in 2007, the twentieth-anniversary Wintergreen retreat was held in Barbados.

Wintergreen has been for me an opportunity to listen—to listen to the wisdom of the women who generously share their work and life stories each year. They invite me into the house and, although hesitant, I know that I too have stories to tell and work to do, lost boxes to discover and to open. Indeed, I know a place.

From "Shaping the World of My Art"

—PAULE MARSHALL

In order to talk about what I believe to be some of the important early influences which shape my work, it will be necessary to take a giant step back to that stage in life when, without being conscious of it, I began the never-ending apprenticeship which is writing. It began in of all places the ground-floor kitchen of a brownstone house in Brooklyn. Let me try to recreate the setting for you. Picture if you will a large old-fashioned kitchen with a secondhand refrigerator, the kind they used to have back then in the thirties with the motor on top, a coal stove that in its blackness, girth, and the heat it threw off during the winter overwhelmed the gas range next to it, a sink whose pipes never ceased their rusty cough, and a large table covered in flowered oilcloth set like an altar in the middle of the room.

It was at this table that the faithful, my mother and her women friends, would gather almost every afternoon upon returning from their jobs as domestics—or to use their term for the work they did "scrubbing Jew floor." Their workday had begun practically at dawn with the long train ride out to the white sections of Brooklyn. There, the ones who weren't lucky enough to have a steady job would stand on the street corners waiting in the cold— if it was winter—for the white, mainly Jewish housewives to come along and hire them for a half day's work cleaning their houses. The auction block was still very real for them.

Later, armed with the few dollars they had earned, my mother and her friends would make the long trip back to our part of town and there, in the sanctuary of our kitchen, talk endlessly, passionately. I didn't realize it then but those long afternoon rap sessions were highly functional, therapeutic; they were, you might say, a kind of magic rite, a form of juju, for it was their way to exorcise the day's humiliations and restore them to themselves.

The people they worked for were usually the first thing to come under the whiplash of their tongues. For hours at a stretch they would subject their employers to an acute and merciless analysis. And they were shrewd students of psychology. They knew those Jewish housewives far better than the latter would ever know them. But then this has long been a standard phenomenon in Black-white relations in America. The oppressed has to know the enemy—his survival depends on it. While the oppressor, to defend against his guilt, usually chooses not to know us. Baldwin writes eloquently of this. I never saw any of these women they spoke of—and had no wish to; it was bad enough that I was forced to wear their children's cast-off clothes—which my mother sometimes brought home in a brown paper bag—yet my mother and her friends made them visible to me with their deft and often devastating descriptions. In doing so, they began to teach me all the way back then what is perhaps the most invaluable lesson for a writer of fiction; i.e., the importance of skillful characterization, the novelist's responsibility to make his people live and have their being on the printed page.

Then, because my mother and her friends were poor peasant women who had emigrated from Barbados just shortly after World War I, they often spoke of home: the people, places, and events that had been so much a part of their former lives. The people: "C'dear, how I could forget Eunice Ford from Rock Hall, and that woman had a face like an accident before it happens." The events: "Remember old Mr. Steed's funeral. Poor soul, he had a hard life, but a sweet-sweet funeral. They put him away proper." They would describe the weddings they had attended in great and loving, if biting, detail:

"Soul, lemme tell you bout the time that young girl Birdie Worrell marry that old-old man by the name of Mr. Gay Lisle Pembroke. You remember old Mr. Gay Lisle, an old man been down here since God said let us make man. Well, Birdie and old Mr. Gay Lisle had this big wedding. Wha'lah, it was a wedding to end all weddings. Birdie was in a gown with more lace than the law allowed, and old Mr. Gay Lisle who was old enough to be her great-grandfather call heself stylin in a high collar and tux. Birdie mother spend money she din have hiring fancy cars from town, and the little flower girls (I was one them) was hanging out the window of the cars puking and crying for their foot hurt in the shoe 'cause they wasn't used to either car nor shoe . . .

"And the reception! Jesus-Mary-and-Joseph. It was a reception to end all reception. After the guest had done yam up everything in sight then they had to perform. It seems somebody passed a remark about Birdie looks (she was another accident) that old Mr. Gay Lisle heard. Well, he up and give the person one! And soon the whole place was like federation. The chairs tumbling. *Bruggadung.* The women and children falling over each other like bombs were falling. *Buggadung bung.* Some jealous somebody went and smash the windows of the fancy cars from town. And the women that had been living with old Mr. Gay Lisle long long years before he met Birdie, and had seven children for him, went and near tore the gown clean-clean off Birdie . . .

"And what—after all the money spent on the beautiful-ugly wedding the honeymoon didn't last the night. They wasn't in the house no time before old Mr. Gay Lisle come flying out in the road with not a stitch on and Birdie pelting rock-stone at he."

"What she was running him for?" Virgie Farnum asked.

"Now you mean, nuh! That man was too old to raise up a finger never mind anything else."

As part of the late afternoon ritual they also recounted endless tales of obeah, which was the name they gave to their form of conjure or roots or mojo or vodun or what have you; their way of dealing with the inexplicable and unknown: like true Africans they had great respect for the powers that pass man's understanding.

"Lemma tell you, Soul, when I was a girl home I did see obeah work on somebody and the person is dead-dead today . . . You did know Affie Cumberbatch? A good-looking clear-skin girl from up Hillaby with hair halfway down she back. You know the person I talking 'bout?"

The other nodded.

"That girl die when she was only twenty and in perfect health. Now tell me what she die from?"

"Woman, how we could remember and that thing happen donkey years."

"Then lemme tell you and listen and believe, oh ye of little faith. This Affie was running with my wuthless uncle, and when his wife, my dear-aunt Dorie found out she swear she was gon work obeah and kill Affie Cumberbatch dead-dead. She took me with her to the obeah man. I hear she tell him she want to work obeah on Affie and she pay him good-good money. And I see the bag of the obeah man . . . "

"Yuh lying now."

"Who tell you I lying? I see the bag, muh. It had in some rusty nails and feathers and broken glass and thing. He took some out and put in a bottle and bury it, and all the time he doing this he chanting. He give my dear-aunt duppy dust to put in my uncle food so he would pass it on to Affie when he was in bed with she. He told my dear-aunt not to worry, that Affie Cumberbatch was as good as dead. And I kiss my right hand to God, when you hear the shout, Affie Cumberbatch had took in sick. Her people spend money enough on doctors and still cun find what was wrong with the girl. They even boil lizard soup and all and give she, but it din' do no good. Affie said she felt like crawling under the skin and she continue cry for a pain. She said she heard the duppies walking pon the roof at night and a hand cold as death 'pon she body. And by-Jees, before the year out Affie Cumberbatch was in she grave. Now tell me that's some game-cock bring ram-goat story?"

And they often spoke about the sea, which hemmed in their tiny island and which they said was visible from every point on the land. "The sea," they used to say with great respect, "ain't got no back door." Meaning it was not like a house where you might escape out the back way in case of a fire. Meaning it was not to be played with. Many years later when I visited Barbados and actually saw the sea at Bathsheba, Walker's Bay, and Cattlewash,—places that had been familiar to them,—I echoed their sentiments. It was not to be played with. I tried capturing the feeling and thoughts it aroused in me in my last novel, thoughts and feelings about the Middle Passage:

> It was the Atlantic this side of the island, a wild-eyed, marauding sea,
> full of dangerous currents, lined with row upon row of barrier reefs,
> and with a sound like that of the combined voices of the drowned
> raised in an unceasing lament—all those, the nine million and more
> who in their enforced exile, their Diaspora, had gone down between

this point and the homeland lying out of sight to the east. This sea
mourned them. Aggrieved, outraged, unappeased, it hurled itself
upon each of the reefs in turn and then upon the beach, sending
up the spume in an angry froth which the wind took and drove like
smoke in over the land.

(*The Chosen Place, The Timeless People*, 106)

The sea, the old sod, their former friends and family—all these formed
the nostalgic content of their talk. But mixed in with those memories, tem-
pering the nostalgia were the bitter, angry recollections of the poverty and
the peculiar brand of colonial oppression and exploitation they had known
on the island. "You know what it is to work hard and still never make a
headway?" one of the characters in my first novel bitterly asks, and it could
well have been my mother or one of her friends speaking on those long
ago days. "That's Bubados. One crop. People having to work for next skin
to nothing. The white people treating we like slaves and we taking it. The
rum shop and the church join together to keep we pacify and in ignorance.
That's Bubados. It's a terrible thing to know that you gon be poor all your
life, no matter how hard you work. You does stop trying after a time. People
does see you so and call you lazy. But it ain' laziness. It just you does give
up. You does kind of die inside . . . that's why I wun let my mother know
peace till she borrow the money and send me to this man country."

And of course they talked about "this man country," as they somewhat
contemptuously referred to America, the blatant racism they encountered
here, the Depression which was still very much with us at the time, and
their sometimes troubled relations with American Blacks who called them
monkey chaser and Black Jews, and whom they in turn labeled shiftless
and servile. The white man had succeeded in dividing our house. Econom-
ics, sociology, psychology,—and politics. Roosevelt, who had rescued the
country from the economic morass of the Depression, was their hero but
so, too, I remember, was Marcus Garvey. His name was constantly being
invoked, for he had been their leader in the early twenties, the revolutionary who had said the end to white domination, the deliverer who had urged
the black and poor like themselves to rise up: "Rise up you mighty race,"
who had declared Black is beautiful to women like themselves who had
been brainwashed into believing they did not possess beauty. Garvey who

had said economic self-sufficiency and Black nationhood. Who had said Africa . . .

Because of their constant reference to him, he became a living legend for me, so that although, when I was a little girl, he had been stripped of his power and was an old man living out his last days in obscurity in England, he was still an impressive figure, a Black radical and freedom fighter whose life and example had more than a little to do with moving me toward what I see as an essentially political perspective in my work.

All this then made up the content of their exhaustive and vivid discussions. For me, listening unnoticed in a corner of the kitchen (seen but not heard as was the rule then), it wasn't only what the women talked about, the content; but the way they put things, the style. The insight, irony, wit, and their own special force which they brought to everything they discussed; above all, their poet's skill with words. They had taken a language imposed upon them, and infused it with their own incisive rhythms and syntax, brought to bear upon it the few African words and sounds that had been retained. In a word, transformed it, made it their own. I was impressed, without being able to define it, by the seemingly effortless way they had mastered the form of the storytelling. They didn't know it, nor did I at the time, but they were carrying on a tradition as ancient as Africa, a centuries-old oral mode by which the culture and history, the wisdom of the race had been transmitted. Theirs was the palaver in the men's quarters and the stories the old women told the children seated outside the round houses as the sun declined. They were, in other words, practicing art of a high order, and in the process revealing at a level beyond words their understanding of and commitment to an aesthetic which recognizes that art is inseparable from life, and form and content are one.

Moreover, all that freewheeling talk together with the sometimes bawdy jokes and the laughter which often swept the kitchen was, at its deepest level, an affirmation of their own worth; it said that they could not be either demeaned or defeated by the daily trip out to Flatbush. It declared that they had retained and always would a sense of their special and unique Black identity.

I could understand little of this at the time. Those mysterious elements I heard resonating behind the words, which held me spellbound, came across mainly as a feeling which entered me it seemed not only through my ears but through the pores of my skin (I used to get goose pimples listening to them at times) to become part of my blood. It sings there to this day. I couldn't define it then, but I know now that contained in that feeling were those qualities which Black people possess no matter where you find them in the hemisphere—and which to my mind make us of one people. Ralph Ellison in *Shadow and Act* defines them for us: "The faith," he cites first of all, "the humor, sense of timing, the rugged sense of life and our manner of expressing it." The qualities are part of our force as a people; they derive from the emotional core deep at the center of Black life, and which perhaps has its source in our archetypal African memory. The Black critic and scholar, Esther Jackson, refers to it as "the underground aspect of our experience." Larry Neal, the poet and editor of *Black Fire*, has termed it "our emotional history." Amamu Baraka, in a beautiful poem about his mother, simply calls it "that nigger feeling." "I wanted to know my mother," he says in the poem, "when she sat looking sad across the campus in the late 20's into the future of the soul. There were Black angels straining above her head, carrying life from our ancestors, and knowledge, and the strong nigger feeling."

It was this "nigger feeling"—Afro-Caribbean perhaps, in its particulars, but solidly Black at its base—which informed what those women at the kitchen table had to say. In turn, it was this marvelously complex expressive quality, this energy as Baraka refers to it, along with their skill with language and the strongly political cast to their talk, which I believe helped to shape me as a writer at that unconscious level where it must always begin. For instance, it was they who taught me, without either one of us being aware of what was going on, my first lessons in the narrative of art. From them I learned that the primary responsibility of the fiction writer, if he would be a storyteller in the African tradition, is to tell an interesting tale on that first level, no matter what else he is about in the book. It was this perhaps which led to my love of the novel as a literary form, a love which was later reinforced when I came to read Hardy and Mann, Conrad and Wright. I realize that it is fashionable now to dismiss the traditional novel as something of an anachronism, but to me it is still a vital form. Not only does it allow for the kind of full-blown, richly detailed, visual writing that I love (I want the reader to see the people and places about which I am writing), but it permits me to operate on many levels and to explore both the inner state of my characters as well as the larger world beyond them.

Essentially, then, you might say that it was those women long ago, perhaps more than any other single factor, who were responsible for laying the foundation of the aesthetic—aesthetic taken to mean here the themes and techniques—which most characterize my work. Because of this, the best of my writing, where it is strongest and most truthful, is really a celebration of them.

One of the principal objectives of that aesthetic as I see it is to give expression to those qualities Ellison defined for us above. For example, it was the desire to capture the special poetry of Barbadian speech and the rugged sense of life it conveyed which prompted me to attempt my first novel. Ellison also says there are other qualities, equally as impressive, which describe us as a people. He names them: "Our inner strength" (that strength that comes from suffering), intellect, will (that will to survive), and cunning; all those attributes which have enabled us, no matter where we found ourselves, to keep on keeping on despite the trauma of the Diaspora, the enslavement that followed, and the oppression of one kind or another which is still with us today. And not only survive, but to remain responsive, creative beings whose ability to transform our suffering into art—listen to the blues, to the wit and irony of the earlier Sparrow calypsos—attests to the fact that we have kept our humanity intact. "Here you done treat me like a dog and I come out a human being," John Anderson, the blues singer, declares in "Mose." We are forever transcending our condition. It is this I want to celebrate.

On another level, one of the themes which absorbs me so that I find myself returning to it again and again is the question of identity. And as part of this, a concern for the role the past—both the personal and historical past—plays in this whole question. How much the women long ago can be said to be responsible for this I cannot say. But I do know that their need to reestablish a sense of themselves each afternoon by recalling their past life nurtured in me a desire to understand that combined heritage which was at once Afro-American, Afro-Caribbean, and to a much lesser degree American, that was mine. There was always the desire—only vaguely acknowledged for a long time—to bring together all the various strands (the word is synthesis) and thus make of that diverse heritage a whole.

From: Marshall, Paule. "Shaping the World of My Art." *New Letters* 40 (Autumn 1973): 97–112.

Outside of Dreams

—ETHEL MORGAN SMITH

I met Alice Bookman when we lived in Atlanta. She was a student in my screenwriting class at a writer's conference on St. Simon in Georgia and was completing a graduate degree in English at the University of Georgia in Athens. Alice was energetic and full of dreams about her writing. I knew right away that I wanted her to be my friend.

I was headed to graduate school at Hollins College in Roanoke, Virginia. My son, Marcus, was a first-year student at Wesleyan University in Connecticut. During my last three months in Atlanta, my fast friendship with Alice had flourished into lunches and talking on the telephone daily about books and writing. I preferred women writers who used the landscape of the American South, like Zora Neale Hurston, Flannery O'Connor, and Alice Walker, who taught me to claim what belonged to me—the South. Other than Toni Morrison, my friend Alice liked what she called *the classics*. Our friendship was easy since Alice was charming, funny, and positive. She and her husband had a beautiful daughter whom they named Gracie.

When I finally moved to Roanoke we continued to be in touch by way of telephone, and sometimes quick notes or cards. Alice even suggested that we write an epistolary novel.

"Like *The Color Purple*?" I asked.

"I was thinking more like *Pamela* or *Pride and Prejudice*. Even *Dangerous Liaisons*," she responded.

I had read all of those books, but had no affinity for them.

During the middle of my first semester Alice announced she was pregnant again. She was overjoyed with the hope of having a baby boy. When she told me she was planning to drop out of school, I told her graduate school was a way for her to keep writing, and it was important that she complete her degree. Alice had been a flight attendant at TWA for twenty years before marriage, family, and writing. She was working on a novel called *Soul Plane*, which was about her experience as a flight attendant.

Alice rang my phone less and less. I assumed she was busy with a toddler and a new baby on the way. My life was changing too. Preparing to look for a job after graduate school and keeping my son in college occupied much of my time. The demands of graduate school were difficult in the beginning since it had been more than fifteen years since I had been a formal student. Life challenged me in other ways. A twenty-eight-year-old friend died from ovarian cancer. While I was on the telephone receiving that awful news, another call came in from a friend to tell me that a thirty-five-year-old friend of ours had committed suicide.

For weeks I walked around in a haze, burning candles and listening to Billie Holiday, which depressed me even more. I read novels about suicide—*The Awakening, Madame Bovary*, and *Anna Karenina.* Both friends had already been buried by the time I was notified. I felt cheated out of a good-bye to them. Finding closure on my own was difficult. I spent weeks trying to get their families to talk to me about how they had spent their last days. I was afraid that I wasn't going to find my way out of the darkness. Feeling alone and isolated, I buried myself in my work. Friends worried about me. I worried about me.

Late one night Alice called; she had miscarried. I added her loss to my own and felt unable to comfort her. Later, I wrote to her trying to encourage her—that she was alive with a lovely baby daughter. Many of my friends had no children and weren't going to have any. I, myself, had only one child, but had dreamed of having more. But the script of my life had changed. We were all living outside of our dreams. Talking on the telephone never seemed to be the correct venue to have such a conversation.

I wasn't able to concentrate on my schoolwork. My mental and financial states were a mess. In my graduate seminar on Toni Morrison I was struggling with my professor who knew less about the novels than I did.

My professor thought the character Jade in *Tar Baby* was the tar baby in the novel.

Telephone calls from Alice Bookman increased over the next weeks. But the positive high-spirited woman I had known earlier was gone. She wanted out of her marriage; she hated the South, and she wanted nothing more than to move to New York. Those lines of conversation challenged me. I had been out of my marriage for longer than I cared to remember. And by moving to Roanoke, I had cut myself off from other bad relationships that had drained me. Spending ten years in therapy had made me stronger; Alice made me feel vulnerable. I knew that Alice's negative attitude about life had to do with what happens when you try to change and nothing seems to work. I had been in those places too many times and had no interest in returning. "If I could just get my novel published," Alice always said. "Writers still have to work for a living, even authors as famous as Russell Banks and Joyce Carol Oates," I said. Alice resented me for saying this. I distanced myself more.

Sometimes, she would call, always late at night, with another idea about how to get published in the *New Yorker*. There are no tricks to writing. Writers write because we have to, whether we get published or not. I tried to convey that to her. "I understand you are going through a difficult time," I told her one night. "But if you want me for a friend, you've got to find a way to get into my life. And I don't mean asking me how my son is doing. I am not your therapist." Later she apologized and said she appreciated my saying that, and knew that I cared enough to say such a thing. Of course, I cared about her, but I cared more about me. I mailed her a sappy card about "hanging in there." I knew her pain, but it was her pain, and I couldn't allow it to explode in my life.

After graduation I was offered a position as a full-time instructor at Virginia Tech in Blacksburg, Virginia. I felt fortunate to have a job with health insurance and a retirement plan. And I wouldn't have to move again. I wasn't bothered at the time that I would be teaching four classes per semester for less than twenty thousand dollars a year. Alice sent me a card of congratulations for having received my graduate degree. I telephoned her and thanked her. We chatted as if the months hadn't slipped by. I was pleased. She was back in school but still unhappy in the marriage.

"What are you going to do after graduation?"

"I was offered a job teaching at Virginia Tech."

"I guess anyone can get one of those jobs if they are willing to stay in the South."

"Alice, these jobs are hard to come by anywhere. I feel fortunate."

"I can't wait to get out of this God-awful place myself. In New York there are so many more choices of work."

"Yeah, but there are a lot more people too." I tried not to take her comments personally, but sometimes such talk was too painful.

After that conversation I decided not to talk to Alice anymore. I couldn't allow myself to be at such risk by her unhappiness. But when she graduated, I telephoned to offer congratulations. Our conversation was pleasant. She thanked me for encouraging her to stay in school. I told her she had done the work and should be proud of herself, but more important she had offered her daughter a fine role model.

Alice got a job teaching as an instructor at Morehouse College, which gave her confidence, but she still complained about the workload and the pay. I was well aware of these disadvantages since I had been teaching well over a year by then. I tried to tell her about my challenges, but Alice insisted that her situation was worse than mine. She had to be at her college every day of the week and had to get her daughter to daycare as well. On the other hand, I only had to be at work two to three days a week, and I didn't have a small child. I wasn't going to argue with her. At that moment my situation seemed less complicated to her. But I didn't have a husband or any other financial support to help me keep my son in a university, where tuition, room, and board cost more than I earned in a year.

When I heard from Alice Bookman again it was the spring of 1994. She had moved to New York City and rented two rooms from a woman who lived on West Seventy-Ninth Street. Her daughter Gracie had received a scholarship from the day school on the Upper Eastside, and Alice was teaching at a Brooklyn high school.

"Finally, I am happy. I love it here. Never again will I move. This place has so much to offer to Gracie and me."

I was delighted for her and told her she was courageous to move with a small child to support and without a job. But after a while Alice found those days difficult too. She changed jobs because the students at the high school were undisciplined, and the principal wasn't supportive of her. She then taught at the day school where Gracie attended. But she was unhappy there as well. She faced issues of class and wanted to talk about her problems constantly.

"Alice, this is what it's like rearing a child on your own—lonely and isolated. And single mothers get treated like they've committed a crime. The more upper class they are, the worse people behave sometimes," I said to her one evening.

"Was it like this when you were rearing your son?"

"Of course. Even your friends aren't interested in you if you have problems. Some are even threatened that you are single." I tried to point that out to her.

"Does it get any better?"

"Probably not."

"How did you cope?"

"Think of them as brief and necessary encounters. You can't allow yourself to care about them so much. Remember, you're trying to get the best education for your child."

"You're tougher than I thought."

"When it comes to Marcus, I am steel. Gracie is your number one goal. Just remember that nothing else matters."

On a stunning summer afternoon in 1996, I drove home feeling free and excited. I had moved one state over for a tenure-track position two years earlier at West Virginia University. My meeting with one of my graduate students who was going to take over my classes for the first two weeks of the semester, while I attended a writer's conference in Kasteel Well, Holland, had gone well. It was to be an exciting year. Alice was going to a similar conference in Spoleto, Italy. Another writer friend was going to Prague. We were going to compare notes about our international experience at the end of the summer.

At home my answering machine blinked. A writer I knew had called. I assumed he was an editor of a journal that had promised to publish the first chapter of my novel. My stomach tightened. Damn them, they've kept my work for nearly a year. I couldn't believe how they could be playing with my life. I was in a tenure-track job and needed publications. The journal had a notorious reputation for dangling and reneging, then withholding promises to publish. I telephoned him immediately.

"Ethel, I have some bad news," he said.

Damn that journal. They've decided not to publish my work. Why had I believed that new assistant? "Yes."

"Alice Bookman was on TWA Flight 800."

I was ready to argue about my writing, but there was no way anyone could have prepared me for what he said. "What?" I gasped, choking for breath.

"I am sorry to have to call you with such bad news." I seemed to hear from a distance. "And Ethel, its gets worse, Gracie was with her."

He didn't have to say that; I knew it. Gracie was to be with her father for the summer, but he had a job out of the country, and they had decided that it would be best if Gracie remained with Alice.

"No. No. This can't be true."

"Ethel, listen."

"You don't know what you're talking about. No. No," I sobbed.

"I know how hard this is, but listen."

"How can you be sure?"

"Ethel, I had such a bad feeling about the crash, I started checking the *New York Times* every day for the list of passengers. Yesterday, the name A. Bookman was listed. I called TWA, and they confirmed that it was our Alice traveling with an unknown passenger."

"There must be a million folks named Alice Bookman. Plus, she was on her way to Rome and was to leave on Thursday. I just spoke to her. There would have been no reason for her to fly to Paris." I knew if I could just reason with him that he would know that it wasn't our Alice Bookman.

I insisted that he was wrong. Alice had flown more than anyone I knew.

"Listen to me Ethel. Sit down. Just listen. I called her family. At the last minute the Rome flight was canceled, and Alice and Gracie were bumped to the Paris flight."

My breathing accelerated and the room seemed to crash around me. I had to get off of the telephone and find someone who made sense. "Thank you for calling. I can't talk anymore. But you're wrong. This can't be true. No. No."

I sobbed into my tear-soaked T-shirt. I was shaking and my eyes were stinging. I ran to the bathroom and washed my face. I threw up and rinsed my mouth and washed my face again. I tried to call my son, but I wasn't able to reach him. I just dialed every number I knew. I needed life and to be reassured that I was experiencing a horrible nightmare. Finally, I telephoned Alice's house. If I could only hear her voice, then she couldn't have been on that plane. "This machine has no room for any more calls. Please hang up and try again later." I continued to dial numbers as I wept in between calls. I left messages; it was the middle of the day and most folks weren't home. After the fifth telephone call, I cried into someone's machine, hoping that they would be there and pick up the phone. No one did.

Finally, I reached a friend in Philadelphia who knew Alice too. "I am so thankful to hear your voice." I spat out shaking.

"What's the matter?"

"Alice Bookman and her daughter were on the TWA flight last week."

"Ethel, this is terrible. I am so sorry."

"What should I do? What can I do?"

"Do you know any of her family?"

"Her ex-husband is in Africa."

"What about others?"

"She has two brothers. One in Texas and the other one is in Maine. Or is it New Hampshire."

"What about parents?"

"They're both dead."

"What a world we live in. We're closer to our friends than our families."

"Thank God, you're there."

"Ethel, I am always here for you."

"Thank you."

"Please let me call you back tomorrow. I was on my way to a meeting."

After I hung up the telephone, I needed to be close to something that belonged to Alice Bookman. I kept all of my personal letters in old milk crates that my son had given me when he worked at a restaurant one summer. Over the years I had dumped the letters into the crates until one filled up and then I would move to the next one. I had always wondered what it would take for me to go through the boxes of my life. I pulled them out of my closet to the middle of my bedroom floor. I walked downstairs and played Mahalia Jackson's "Just a Closer Walk with Thee." Upstairs I lit candles and cried.

Two hours later, muddling through the crates, I had only found two cards from Alice, saying she was swamped and we'd talk soon. I tied a red ribbon around them and placed them on my dresser.

I fell asleep at some point. I awoke to the ringing of my telephone with Mahalia Jackson's strong voice in the background . . . I thought I heard Alice Bookman. "I know you thought I was on that plane, but I wasn't. I am here in beautiful Italy working with Rosellen Brown on my novel. She thinks it's going to be a real hit. And Gracie just loves it here."

The music had stopped and the ringing telephone was Marcus. He tried to comfort me by telling me that he understood how shocking this was for me, but all we could do was hope that they were in a better place. He reminded me that Alice and Gracie would always live in my heart, and that it was a privilege to have shared their lives. Marcus had seen so much death. As a student at Harvard Divinity School he had been required to develop a relationship with a dying person. His experience with death continued at the Hole-in-the-Wall Camp where he worked during summers as a counselor with young people with blood diseases and several of them died.

I thanked him. Then I felt guilty. Why did I have such a wonderful son? Gracie would never grow up to be the fine woman she could have been. She would never receive an acceptance letter from Harvard. Or go to the prom. Or wear a bra. Or laugh anymore. She was dead. Gone.

The next day I telephoned the day school in New York City where Alice taught and Gracie was enrolled. I spoke to a pleasant woman who confirmed that they knew Alice and Gracie had been on TWA Flight 800. She thanked me for calling and told me that an article had been written about them in the school newsletter. My heart sped faster. Other folks knew this. It was no mistake. I asked her to please send me a copy of the newsletter. After I hung up I telephoned Alice's house again. "This machine is full and cannot take any more messages. Please hang up and try your call later."

I flipped through my Rolodex, trying to think of others who knew Alice but had no way of knowing that she and Gracie had been on the flight. I telephoned a woman in Indianapolis who had taught with Alice at Morehouse College, and finally another writer in Arizona who knew and loved Alice and Gracie. I felt thankful to have someone to share my grief.

I couldn't think of my own trip to Holland. I tried to convince myself that I didn't have that much to do. I needed answers to questions I didn't even know. The news media speculated that terrorists had bombed TWA Flight 800, like the Lockerbee, Scotland, plane had been bombed in 1988. Our government was asking citizens not to jump to conclusions, to wait and see what investigators would find. Families and friends of the victims demanded answers, supported by an aggressive outcry from the general public. I was scared and silent.

The next day, the writer who had called to tell me about Alice and Gracie, called again to say he had been thinking about me and knew I was suffering.

"How are your plans for your trip?"

"Fine," I lied.

"Now, you wouldn't be thinking about not going?"

"Not at all. I'm just having a hard time putting my heart into it."

"I know what you mean. But remember, Alice died doing what she believed in."

"Yeah, making her dreams come true."

"No, she died believing in her writing."

"I know. Thank you."

"I'll call you before you leave."

With less than a week to get ready to fly to Holland for my conference, two friends drove up from Roanoke to help me. They packed my bags, wrote lists of things for me to do, and bought cat food. A few friends wanted to get together and wish me well. I invited them over for a small cookout. The nice gathering helped me to gear my focus in another direction. Everyone talked about their European travels. No one mentioned TWA Flight 800.

I woke up at 4:00 a.m. sweating. I remembered that I hadn't called Alice's house that day. Maybe someone would actually be there. I might wake them was my first thought, but I called anyway. "The number you've called has been disconnected. There is no further information about this number." I was never going to speak to anyone at Alice's house because no one was ever going to be there. I wondered about all of the other calls that had been on her machine. Who were those people? I wish I could talk to them. I thought about her books. What would happen to her autographed copy of Nikki Giovanni's *Racism 101* that I had given her last year for her birthday? What would happen to the quilt that my mother had quilted for Gracie's fifth birthday? Where was Alice's novel?

Three days before I left for Holland, I received the newsletter from the day school with a photograph of Alice and Gracie titled "Teacher's Dream Downed With Jet." I stared at the photos. Gracie looked so proper in her private school uniform. I wondered what they were wearing on the plane. Alice's eyes sparkled with pride. I cried until I ached all over. I tried to remember the last time I had seen them. Did it matter? They were dead. Blown into pieces. Never to live on this earth again. Was life so fragile that in a matter of seconds we're here and then not? I read and reread the article. Then, I photocopied it and mailed it to the people I had spoken with over the telephone. Was this all I could do? I felt that if I cried any more my heart would float out of my body. How much would my suffering help me to survive? My friendship with Alice was over. There wouldn't be another telephone call or a funny card to make things easier between us.

The day before I left for Europe, the writer called me again. "Ethel, I have news. Alice's ex-husband is back from Africa. He's devastated, particularly since he just lost his mother three months ago."

"Poor man."

"The other reason I called was to let you know that Alice's body has been found, but not Gracie's."

I hadn't heard the word *body* before. It was so final. Alice and Gracie were the late, the departed, the lifeless, the no more. No one was going to call me and say that this was some horrible nightmare. Alice couldn't call and say she was in Italy. She was gone forever. The writer allowed me to cry. "Thank you," was all that I was able to say.

"I am here for you."

"And, I for you."

"You were important to her, Ethel."

"I know."

"Will we ever get through this?"

"I hope so."

Toward the middle of 1995, Alice Bookman was finding her way. Finally, her retirement funds from TWA, which had been tied up in a legal battle, were about to be awarded to her. She had bought a house. We were talking about our dreams again—our children, our writing, and the future. Her heart and head were once again on her novel. The conference in Spoleto was to be a new beginning. Alice was also thinking of a different kind of job. Like so many women after a divorce, Alice found herself outside of her dreams, but she was making it work. She was unquestionably a good mother who took the challenge of rearing her daughter seriously. Alice had learned some hard and painful lessons, but she had built a healthy life for herself and her daughter. Getting her novel published was always close and dear to her heart. TWA Flight 800 robbed us all of so many dreams.

Negotiating the Academy

The Case of the Reluctant Reader

She Who Reads Last...

—SANDRA Y. GOVAN

As might be expected of a college English teacher, from my childhood through my early adolescence through my adult life, I have *almost* always loved to read. Books were not simply my magic door, my escape, or the staples of my diet; they were my soul mates, my obsessive compulsion. Through the portals of a book I could flee Chicago's far South Side and pound through the surf on the back of Walter Farley's Black Stallion. I could replace young Alec Ramsey and it would be me tangling my brown hands in the magnificent Arabian stallion's flowing mane, feeling his huge rippling muscles gripped tightly between my thighs as I rode the Black bareback, closing my eyes against the cutting wind while we raced across the deserted beach, horse and rider merging into one fast blur of tiny brown girl and huge black horse become one.

Furthermore, books were the reason that at age twelve, old enough to "most certainly know better" as my parents later insisted, I nearly went to jail, almost got sent down to the Joliet, Illinois, Reform School for Wayward Children. A nearly maniacal urge compelled me to complete the *Rick Brant* saga of science-adventure tales that I had purchased one by one for $1.25 each. The fact that these books were not available in the local public library, coupled with the fact that I desperately needed to own all twenty-two books in the series, forced me to steal. To abbreviate a much longer story, I got busted boosting books at the neighborhood general department

store because at 50¢ an hour, babysitting money did not stretch far enough
nor accumulate fast enough. In 1962, due entirely to my effort to possess all
the Rick Brant books and to read them sooner rather than later, I designed
a current, wildly popular, sales promotion campaign dozens of department
stores employ fecklessly today. Admittedly, my method proved a bit more
unorthodox, as I would purchase one hardcover novel for $1.25 and then
slide a second one into the thin brown bag beneath the first (without help
from the salesclerk), but without question, I initiated an early variant of
"Buy one, get one free"!

The imprint books held on my imagination was such that even as an
adult, driving from Chicago to Decorah on a long semi-deserted stretch
of I-90, heading north and west through Wisconsin toward my very first
official teaching post at Luther College, in the northern hinterlands of
Iowa, I suddenly felt as if I were no longer constrained behind the wheel
of my beloved, if ordinary, Samantha Louise LeMans Pontiac Govan (the
trim sleek silver two-door bullet-car my parents had bought me two
months earlier when I obtained my master's degree). Mysteriously, I had
somehow been freed and was now driving an entirely different car. Magi-
cally, my body and my skills had also been transformed. I morphed into
Parnella Jones, a celebrated Indy 500 driver. Somehow, I became the designated driver behind the wheel of the fast-back sister car of the Black
Tiger—the swift stylish Formula I race car that ruled the track at the
Bonneville Salt Flats. There on I-90, unknown forces ruled, compelling
me to see if normally sweet Samantha Louise could actually match the
demonic red-trimmed figure posted at the high end of the speedometer.
The red number read 120 mph. The cop who caught me clocked me, he
said, at over 90. But by the time he saw me, though he did not at first have
his lights flashing, I had seen him coming in the rearview mirror and so
had slowed up to see who the fool was who was trying to race with me,
the great Parnella Jones.

Thanks largely to Agatha Christie, and the influence of my mother who
loved both a good mystery and the stories of intrigue, as a teenager I traveled to Istanbul, courtesy of *Murder on the Orient Express*, and sojourned in
the Middle East via *They Came to Baghdad*. I served as a spy in the Second
World War courtesy of *Two Eggs on my Plate* (even the title engaged me),
and I helped Nero Wolfe and Archie Goodwin solve such mysteries as *Fer-

de-Lance, *Death of a Doxie*, and *Too Many Cooks*. From Rex Stout's Nero Wolfe I learned about the vicissitudes of gourmet cooking and the thousands of varieties of orchids; Wolfe also advanced my vocabulary. From the great detective I not only learned to read for the clues but I learned words like "flummoxed" and "flummery," though I had no place to try out these treasures. At night, as a youngster, I'd go to bed reading *365 Bedtime Stories* or Alcott's *Eight Cousins* or maybe *Archie and Jughead*, or *Betty and Veronica*. Some nights, after Daddy called "lights out upstairs" and before he could thunder up the stairs to confiscate any illicit stuff, under the covers of darkness with the aid of a concealed flashlight, I'd peruse my Marvel Comics collection and mull over the strange temperament of the hot-headed Johnny Storm in the *Fantastic Four*, or the peculiar angst of schoolboy Peter Parker as his heroic alter ego, *Spiderman*. On those proverbial dark and stormy nights when I was home alone, I either read Pearl Buck's *The Good Earth*, or I would curl up on the living-room couch with Cubby, my teddy bear, and every light in the living room, the dining room, and the kitchen lit; both TV and radio blaring; and only then could I tackle the horror stories encased within my mother's prized gold-trimmed red-leather bound *Collected Stories of Edgar Allan Poe*—"The Tale-Tell Heart," "The Pit and the Pendulum," and "The Fall of the House of Usher."

From these revelations of such eclectic tastes you might be inclined to think I have always been enamored of reading. But you would be mistaken. I came to love reading through the back door—through the pain of a teacher's scorn and the humiliation of not recognizing my own name. Bear with me. Because I went through primary school in Chicago in the nineteen fifties and early sixties, and because I came into the world with dislocated hips, an impairment that forced my parents to place me in several of the public specialized schools servicing handicapped children before I could be transferred (when I entered the fifth grade) to my neighborhood public school, I had vast experience with a number of different kinds of teachers, those controlling deities or demons (white and black) who paced or prowled the aisles, who cajoled or counseled, who bullied or corralled the children in their charge with total authority. Here is my story.

I am eight years old and every morning before dawn cracks, I ride the yellow school bus to Jane L. Neil School. Jane Neil sits on Eighty-Sixth and

Indiana, worlds away from Morgan Park, the secure lower-middle-class Negro community where I live. Jane Neil lies across several neighborhood zones, if not actual time zones. I am in the third grade. I am in my seat, a too large lift-top desk second row from the window, fifth seat back. I am one of four Negro children (we were Negroes then—no longer "Colored" but not yet African American and decidedly not the much more aggressive "Black"). Present in our classroom are three quiet handicapped brown boys and me—a petite brown girl in a room seemingly filled with twenty-one shining plump and placid white crippled children, their crutches stowed beneath their seats, their unreliable limbs braced, their polio unseen and the muscle twitches caused by cerebral palsy momentarily stilled while they sit. It is late Friday afternoon in Miss Vigor's class. In fact, it is nearly two o'clock, almost time for the bell to ring and for Miss Vigor to dismiss the class so that we can all line up to move outside to the bus dock, where we are to line up again to board the buses that will carry us home.

Though I have gone outside and beyond the closed window, daydreaming, and thus have been absent for a few moments of precious class time, I do know the correct time for I have just glanced at the clock and attempted to force my will on the mechanical universe: "Ring bell, ring! I want to go home now!" I shout silently to the clock. Though I do not read words well, I have learned to read the clock and so I know when it is nearly time to go. The clock, however, moves like Mississippi following *Brown v. Board of Education*—with all deliberate speed.

While she does not actually hear the subversive silent wish, Miss Vigor evidently reads the errant thought on my face, catches a quick glimpse of it half-hidden beneath my eyes. She is a fortyish, graying, stocky woman who can move with the speed of a snake in high grass. Sensing sedition, she strikes. She stoops at my desk, her hard stubby white fingers grabbing at my chin. She pulls her puffy gray heavy-jowled face within inches from mine. I smell the garlic on her breath, see her broad nostrils flare and her tiny gray eyes narrow more as she attacks, pinching my cheeks, twisting my face around to meet hers.

"Why are you staring at that clock?" she demands. "You need every minute in this class to learn! Why, you still can't even read."

And then she adds what was meant to be the devastating blow designed to crush me should I ever again think about rebellion. "You," she hisses venomously to me and the listening class, "are dumb and stupid. You will never amount to anything because *you cannot read.*"

Certain of her victory, Miss Vigor then turned loose her grip on my face and slithered back to the front of the room.

Actually, I am not now sure whether I could not read at that point, or whether I simply *chose* not to read for her. Perhaps, because I truly did not like her, I unconsciously selected the role of the quintessential resisting reader. Or, perhaps because I was, as family oral history has repeatedly maintained, a maddeningly deliberate child—slow to move, slow to dress, slow to eat—I was also slow to read in so discomforting a setting.

You need to understand: My vaunted temperate pace at home attained the status of legend. Daddy, who needed to be at the CTA bus barn by five thirty every morning, was also assigned the job of waking me up, helping me to dress, and giving me breakfast before the school bus arrived every morning. One day, totally frustrated by my capacity to drift away while dressing, he shifted the task back to Mama, declaring with exasperation, "She could drive a crazy man crazy." It wasn't that I was a terribly willful child; rather it was more that I simply was not encumbered by the urgencies of the present moment, and so I had the capacity to wander into interior space while pulling on my socks. Other adults were equally perplexed by my pace.

"My God," they marveled, "she's as slow as molasses in January." A phrase that haunted me like a ghost knocks the walls of a haunted house.

I may well have been exceedingly relaxed with respect to movement, eating and dressing at a snail's pace, but I was neither "dumb" nor "stupid." Had that been the case, why would my second-grade teacher, the pretty, vivacious Miss Johnson, select me as the chosen one, the trusted designated runner with permission to leave the class to deliver messages to the front office or to other teachers? (Now, it could also have been that I was less encumbered than many of my peers, having neither wheelchair, crutches, nor leg braces to impede my progress. All things being relative, I was, therefore, despite my much maligned lack of speed, much faster than anyone else there!) Did I merely deduce my destination by the number on an office or classroom door, or by the colorful placards and bulletin boards that lined the halls? How could I, in the second grade, determine where I was to go with my valuable messages *if I could not read*? I had certainly developed a system of successfully finding my way, but whole word recognition seemed to play only a muted part. Rather, I employed memory, intuition, basic instinct, or plain interrogation. "Where is Miss Dawkins' room?" I might ask a hall monitor who saw me casually meandering down the wide spacious halls.

So yes. There may well have been some truth to the initial charge, "you cannot read." Or, careful attention to reading may well have been a convenience for me, a skill (I liked phonics), I either employed or ignored as circumstances warranted.

Take, for instance, the strained Christmas that my mother, brother, and I spent in Los Angeles, at my grandmother's home, the year I turned seven. This particular Christmas, which ended in abject disaster for the both of us, was spent away from my daddy, our friends, and Chicago's Christmas Eve snow. How, my brother and I fretted, could Santa Claus *land* without snow? Grandmother's magnificent Washington Square home, to us a huge and spacious mansion complete with servants' quarters and four bathrooms, if no actual servants, was the center, the hive of Christmas Day activity for her extended family. Grandmother was the queen bee and all of her sons, with all of their children, would come for Christmas dinner and to celebrate the joy of the day that very afternoon. The day before, my mother, Grandmother's oldest child, had been shopping and baking and otherwise helping Grandmother and my Aunt Louvenia, my mama's only sister, prepare for a family Christmas. My brother and I had been told to be good, to be on our "best behavior." We had been instructed to always say "Grandmother," and never to slip and say "Grandma" or "Granny" when our many cousins arrived. We were specifically instructed to not "behave like barbarians" but as respectful guests in Grandmother's home. To ease our tremendous worry, Mama had also explained that Santa would know where to find us and the mystery of how he could land on snowless roofs had been cleared up. "See, Sweetie," Mama said, "Old Santa puts wheels on the sleigh to make visits in California." (This was vital information which I promptly communicated to my brother.) On Christmas Eve, we had been firmly told to go to bed and not to wake the whole house up when we rose on Christmas morning.

That fateful morning, at about five thirty, we slipped out of bed and crept down the wide paneled staircase, silently as ordered. The towering white-flocked Christmas tree in Grandmother's large but snug sitting area/ den, which had been empty the night before, was now positively overburdened with stacks and stacks of gaily wrapped presents in all kinds of vivid colors and tinseled foil ribbons with attached paper tags. Not at all like the modest assortment of basic red and green colored packages Santa left under the tiny tree, wrapped around our presents in Chicago. Tanny, my brother, had always gotten red packages while mine were always wrapped in green. But here in Los Angeles, at Grandmother's house, presents spilled from beneath that giant tree from all sides in tumultuous cascades of vivid color. We had never seen so much loot! And it was all ours! We were the only kids in the house! Santa had really missed us in Chicago and was making up for it here!

It wasn't until I unwrapped the fourth doll that I began to sense that something was wrong. Santa had never before left me more than one doll at a time. And although I appreciated his newfound generosity, I began to suspect that something wasn't quite right. Suppose Santa had made a mistake? My suspicions raised, I put the question aloud to my big brother. More cautious now, he too began to slow the frantic, heroic effort to quietly, quickly, but efficiently tear open every package beneath the beautiful tree.

When the adults in the house, my grandmother, my stylish Hollywood aunt, and my mother, finally came downstairs later that morning, they took in the collateral damage to the tree (white flocking scattered in clumps around the room), the ripped and torn wrapping paper in mounds, the multitude of opened presents strewn haphazardly about the room while others lay half-stripped under the denuded tree, very much resembling debris from a hurricane—and promptly hit the ceiling.

"How could you?!" my aunt almost screamed.

"What made you two do such a thing?" Grandmother demanded sternly with wig askew, both hands on her hips, and gray-brown eyes hardening in shock.

"Why didn't you just look at the name tags and take only your gifts?" Aunt Lou wanted to know.

"Some of these gifts are for your cousins. They're going to be so hurt," Aunt Lou dramatically proclaimed.

At the end of the first salvo they all wearily declaimed in unison, "You've made a huge mess!" Then they continued to glare and berate us for an eternity while stooping to pick up tissue paper, wrapping paper, bedraggled ribbons and bows. In truth, my grandmother and aunt were far more distraught than Mama. She just looked at the mess we'd made, her Chicago gangsters come to call, shook her head with that familiar look of disgusted resignation, and murmured, "I told you, I told you." To whom her comment was directed was never quite clear.

Under fire from the stinging barrage of questions and accusations, I felt unfairly attacked; after all, wasn't I the one who had stopped the stripping frenzy, sensing Santa had made an error? After bombardment for what seemed like hours, and the constant picking at our souls with the charge, "if they hadn't been so selfish and just read the name tags," from the corner where I had retreated I finally raised a tear-streaked face and struggled to defend myself with all the defiance I could summon.

"I don't know why you all are picking on me," I declared. "You know I can't read!"

The Christmas debacle wounded me. But the experience with Miss Vigor, the vicious accusations she launched, truly made me mad. It was the kind of hard-held anger that as a child I could hold and stoke until, like an iron falling upon soft skin, it scorched. Miss Vigor, who, with her squat menacing storm-cloud demeanor, had clearly crossed the line, belittling me in front of the entire class. And though she spat her insults through clenched teeth, I heard them clearly as did everyone else. This woman would have to be shown. I was my mother's daughter; my daddy's baby; I had heard since I could hear Mama's abiding precept that you never let anybody walk on you; you always gave 'em, as Mama always gave her adversaries, "a piece of my mind."

But I would have to "bide my time," as Mama also said, for I could not launch a frontal attack. My teacher had pronounced me dumb; she had insisted that I could not read and therefore was destined to remain dumb. She must have this lie thrown back in her face. The next week, our class began yet another boring educational treatise—*Fun With Dick and Jane*—featuring Sister Sally; Spot, the dog; and Puff, the cat, as supporting cast. This time, however, when called upon to read aloud to the class, I invested the voices of those limited blond stick children with a resonance and vibrancy they never before had held. While other children still haltingly hunted and pecked, stumbling over each declarative simple sentence heavy on the action verbs of "see," "look," and "run" ("Sally said, 'See-the-cookies. Cookies-for Puff and Spot'"), I infused each line with voice, giving each individual character and paragraph an expressive, if histrionic, potential. Sometimes I even reversed word order or injected other lines, interpolating the "action" to add what warmth and color one could to a sorry ass Dick and Jane, those limited sagas of supposed white domestic bliss. I'd read: "Sally said, 'See the cookies, Puff. Cookies for Puff and Spot. Cookies for Baby Tim. The big cookie is for Sally. Look and see Sally's cookie. See Sally's big, big cookie.' It is so, so good. [Then] Jane said, 'See the pets. See the pets come to the house. See Sally's family run.'"

When I completed my assigned reading that day, neither Miss Vigor, nor anyone else in my class, could challenge me, laugh at me, or pick at me again. And though I believe it pained her, Miss Vigor moved me from the "C" list to the "A" list in reading. She gave me a gold star to carry home to my mama, and she had to put my name on the bulletin board ahead of everyone else's for I had become the top class reader, the one called upon to demonstrate how it should be done when adults came to visit. With the passage of time, particularly on those occasions when I struggle to understand why the Credit Union and I never can agree on my bank balance; or when I am trapped in a mind-numbing "budget adjustment" meeting with three other people, knowing I have little to offer beyond the pained plea, "Just tell me the bottom line? How much can I spend?" my mind goes back to when I was eight.

Knowing with certainty that there is no math marker on my DNA, I often think of Miss Vigor. In these rare moments of reflection, I catch myself occasionally wishing the woman had shaken me twice, reflecting that had she just attacked my total disregard for basic addition, or the intricacies of the times-tables once past the fives, perhaps I might have overcome my reluctance to multiplication or the challenges presented by long-division or fractions. Had Miss Vigor assailed my pride one more time, it's conceivable that the dreaded "word problems" that tortured me in the seventh grade might have become as comfortably familiar as Sherlock Holmes with Watson or Nero Wolfe with Archie. Perhaps I might even have developed some aptitude for algebra, some more intellectually suitable feeling for geometry or trigonometry that moves beyond simple repulsion or abject fear. As it stands, however, math remains my one true handicap.

Parting the Blue Miasma

—KENDRA HAMILTON

In 1971, I was a whip-thin tomboy, often splashed with mud, twigs in my hair, brash and trash talking, always in trouble with someone over something. I loved Barbies and the *Black Stallion* novels, *Flash Gordon* reruns, the adventures of Lassie and Rin Tin Tin. Not pretty in any conventional way, though not ugly either, I was the kind of kid who makes church ladies cuss in the parish hall. I ripped my stockings and scuffed my shoes, created complex role-playing games (Superheroes! Molemen!) with the neighbor boys, got whipped for fighting and climbing trees, got roundly teased by one and all for being so hopelessly, unrepentantly odd . . . and I was, in the main, blazingly, ridiculously happy.

I lived in a tiny little suburb, two concentric circles of houses within sight and sound and smell of deep woods and a wide river where we fished and crabbed and even (though it was strictly forbidden) swam. I knew every mother, grandmother, child was welcome in every door at any time of the day or evening, was scolded and fed, spoiled or sent home, was, in short, part of a large, brawling, warm, extended family. This was my experience of home.

By 1973, I had developed symptoms that, at first, my parents put down to adolescent growing pains, but that began to puzzle and, finally, alarm them. I hardly spoke, retreating into books and daydreams. I developed headaches. Every single day after school, I suffered migraines so intense that I moaned and thrashed on my narrow twin bed in the grip of a pain so blinding that spots danced before my eyes in the darkened room.

My mother and father were frightened. Earlier that year, my cousin Rita had suddenly, inexplicably died. She was a year and a day older than me and had been, until stricken ill two summers before, healthy and active as any child of twelve. I think the word "cancer" might have been said in the hallway as my parents discussed in panicked whispers what they were facing. But they didn't have so far to seek for answers as all that. My symptoms, which I know now corresponded to those of clinical depression, had nothing to do with any physical cause and everything to do with the fact that I had ceased to be part of a large extended family and become, well, a social experiment.

Every morning, I rose and bathed and dressed, allowed my mother to coax a few bites of breakfast past my unwilling lips, and got in the car for a twelve-mile drive south to the peninsula of Charleston. I'd exit the car amid kisses and admonitions and books and paper bags full of chicken sandwiches to enter the wrought iron gates of my new school. Ashley Hall, School for Girls.

Within those gates, on the east side of Rutledge Avenue, was an enormous house shaded by oaks and flanked by a bamboo grotto. We called it McBee House after our founder, but it was in fact an antebellum mansion known as the Spring-Witte estate before its purchase in 1909. Across a drive of river pebbles and a wide, manicured lawn was a modern building, housing the Upper School, where I had my daily classes in Latin, ancient and modern history, geometry, biology, and French.

To enter those buildings every day, I had to turn my back on a stream of brown children laughing, joking, loud-talking as they walked down the west side of Rutledge Avenue to *their* school, Charleston High. Girls I had known from eighth grade were among that number: Norma Lango and Teal Garvin and Sandra Whaley, to name just a few of the girls who had closed me out of their circle, once I entered Ashley Hall, as neatly as a wounded body mobilizes its processes of repair—constricting blood vessels and forming clots to halt the loss of blood, injecting collagen to fill the hole and form the scab. Funny thing about scabs. When they fall off the body, much of the initial process of repair is complete, but depending on the depth of the initial injury, it can take years for the process of healing and recovery to be complete.

I was a walking wound in 1973, but no one around me had noticed it. The scab had fallen off, there was an angry red scar, but everyone behaved as if nothing whatsoever had changed.

It's odd that we call what children endured in the sixties and seventies in the South "integration." I think many of us experienced the process as a violent severing—of loves and hatreds, home truths and settled routines that we had long relied on and taken for granted. And some of us—the addicts, the burnouts, the embittered—never recovered. Of course, compared to the insults and assaults that my parents and their parents had endured, what had changed probably seemed a small enough thing. I was going to a new school, a process that required not marches nor speeches but merely an application and an aptitude test which I had passed with flying colors. My mother and father couldn't know that in leaving Immaculate Conception, an all-black school served by all-black nuns and the odd white priest, to move ten blocks south to a school that educated the magnolia-tender girl children of the old Confederacy, I faced an enemy they had never imagined. Not waving fists, flying spit, and country sheriffs in wraparound shades, but a blank wall of whiteness, an ideology that made no room for me, an absent presence that threatened to consume everything I knew, everything that I was. Nor did I, a girl of thirteen going on fourteen, know this. All I knew was a word I had discovered in a homework assignment on "the four humors" my freshman year. The word was melancholy. I fingered it on the page, tasted it on my lips, and it felt right. The color of melancholy was blue. I was blue. I'd trudge between classes, each step heavier than the one before, surrounded by pale girls flying flags of center-parted hair, feeling blue. I'd stare out the window into skies like an autumn aster, hearing not one word in three, feeling blue.

My teachers noticed—one teacher in particular. About the third time she'd had to ask me a question twice before I heard her, Mrs. Trouche, the English teacher who was leading me on my first excursion through the New England Transcendentalists, asked if I'd stay after class. I warily agreed. Mrs. Trouche was a tiny thing with shocking red curls and wise young eyes. She dithered a bit, asking the usual questions about school and classes and teachers, then got to the point: "Are your parents getting divorced?" she asked me, careful of probing a tender spot. I looked at her with surprise. "No!" Then remembering the arguments, over my headaches—over, it seemed lately, anything at all: "At least I don't think so." She paused, baffled. "Is there anything bothering you? Something with your family, your friends?" I could feel the planes of my face flattening to a studied, schooled blankness as I answered, just as carefully as she had asked: "No. Nothing. Nothing at all."

It's not as if I could have told her about that moment of sheer terror I had experienced just weeks before, when I entered the hallway after the class buzzer had rung and felt myself cut off from shore and fighting the current, gasping, sinking, drowning in a sea of pale arms, paler faces that suddenly seemed feral—or the dread that had stalked me in those halls ever since. It's not as if I could have told her about Fern, who had turned to me as we shaped pots in ceramics class and artlessly said, "I don't think there was anything wrong with slavery, Kendra—do you? My grandfather told me our slaves were well taken care of and never mistreated. I think I'd rather be a slave and never have to worry about not having a warm bed or something to eat than to have to work and take care of myself." It's not as if I could have told her about the girl who had slipped and said "nigger" while we ate our sandwiches at lunch. She'd stopped short, turned poison-apple red, and babbled an apology: "I'm so sorry—I forgot. But really, Kendra, I don't think of you as black." I'm sure she thought it was a compliment she was giving. I felt bereft, too empty for anger, like a word erased from a whiteboard leaving nothing behind but a gleaming absence.

I knew no one with whom I could have shared these amorphous experiences. This was, after all, the seventies and racists were people whom we all could identify. They were the angry men on television wielding bricks and bombs against children and spitting defiance from the courthouse steps when caught. They were the polite men on the phone at election time saying, sorry, they couldn't vote for my father because they never voted for "colored." They were the scary men in hoods I encountered on a winding road in rural Goose Creek on my way to a pizza date and a sleepover with my girlfriend Babe. Their figures loomed up into the headlights out of nowhere, as what we assumed to be a routine license check devolved into two men with flashlights directing a stream of cars to a large, empty field. Instinctively, I ducked to the floorboards, heart hammering as I imagined the cross burning that was to come, and allowed Babe's white face to win us a pass. And though there was probably never any danger—later, it was something we'd even joke about—our reactions, on both sides of the color line, were identical that night. We, the hunted, sought the camouflage of night and fled into it.

So these were the racists, the identifiably bad people, of my world. Perfectly nice, perfectly friendly girls whose guileless words and unaffected deeds wounded me day after day after day? I had no word for the thing that they were, or the pain that they inflicted and, thus, no way to complain of it. And I know, too, now that I wondered if anyone would listen. My parents were thrilled at my grades and bragged so extravagantly to all their friends that I was left feeling ungrateful and vaguely humiliated by my secret misery. The neighborhood kids, consumed with cheerleader tryouts and the cute new boy at school, simply laughed at me. Art classes? The symphony orchestra? What did I think I was? White? My aunt and uncle and cousins were burning in the flames of their own guilt and loss at Rita's inexplicable death. *Why didn't we know? Why couldn't we help?* Dinners at their house were exhausting affairs that erupted into tears and acrimony at the smallest infraction of rules or lapse in behavior. When I couldn't escape the weight of the accumulating sadness by burying my nose in a book, I'd close the door to the living room, lie on the crackling plastic that encased the ivory couch, put a vinyl disc on the record player, and turn off all the lights. There was only one side of one record that I was interested in hearing: the first movement of Tchaikovsky's Fourth, and I'd play it two, three, four times—until someone slammed into my inner sanctum and demanded that I stop, stop, stop! with that depressing music and play some Al Green. There seemed to be no one to whom I could confide.

It was Mrs. Trouche who saved me.

She did so quite by accident, and when I saw her nearly ten years ago and thanked her, she'd looked at me with blank-faced surprise. And indeed, her means were utterly mundane. There were no hair-raising rescues, no showdowns with Ashley Hall's mean girls, no dramatic phone calls to or conferences with my parents—just a six-week writing assignment, the kind tenth-grade English teachers hand out every day. Mrs. Trouche asked us to keep a daily journal. To write down all our thoughts and all our experiences. To write poems, if we wanted, or stories, or songs. To draw if we had an aptitude for that—or just make squiggles with our pens. The idea was that we were to exercise the daily discipline of putting pen to paper, forming words into complete and (she hoped) complex thoughts. We would be graded on quantity not quality—we need confide no secrets nor strain ourselves to offer blazing insights. All we needed to do was put pen to paper. And write.

I remember that some of the girls groaned at the assignment, while others, the bright competitive "A" students and the dreamy artsy girls who liked to write, shot their hands into the air and began peppering Mrs. Trouche with questions. I said nothing—those days were teaching me to listen—but smoothly, silently, a door inside me cracked open and a thread of cool air began to stir the solid blue miasma that had clouded my days. At lunch, instead of lingering to listen to Karla Cox play Cat Stevens songs on her guitar down in the bamboo grotto, I wolfed my sandwich down in what seemed only three bites and drank my daily lemonade in a single gulp. Then, with about ten minutes to spare before the next class period was to start, I hurried over the pebbled walk to the school store. There, I walked right past the purple-and-white T-shirts and the pennants and coffee mugs with our school's insignia to the writing supplies. A skinny spiral notebook with a bright green cover and the narrow rules I favored seemed to leap into my hand. I picked out a brand new pen, also green, for good measure, too, and signed my name to the credit register. By that time, the buzzer had sounded, so I had to race to my locker to grab what I needed for my afternoon class. I hardly heard a word that was said the rest of the day, but not this time because of the tom-tom of misery that was beating in my ears, but because my stomach was taut with anticipation.

I couldn't wait to get home.

I couldn't wait to close the door to my room and sit down with that green spiral notebook and that new green pen.

Somewhere in my mother's attic there's a dusty box full of the detritus of my years in school: my Immaculate Conception diploma, ribbons from spelling contests, scholarship award letters, newspaper clippings, old photos. There's a notebook with a tattered green cover in that box, too. I've seen it, handled it—though not for many, many years. Flipping through the pages, I noted that the ink had faded, and my rounded cursives, the i's dotted with hearts, looked like a stranger's: or perhaps more like the ghost-child of the sharp, precise lines I make on paper today. Try as I might, I can't bring to mind a single entry—though I believe some of those entries were reborn as the poems and stories and drawings that I later published in the school's literary magazine, the *Cerberus* (which, I think I've been told, was named after someone's dog).

But I know more certainly than I know many things that I was born as a writer through the pages of that notebook. I was lost when Mrs. Trouche gave the class that writing assignment—lost in the carnival mirror of my family's trauma and the crazily mixed messages I was receiving at Ashley Hall about race and identity and belonging. Writing in that notebook was a way of writing myself back into existence one halting word, one hard-won sentence at a time.

Most of the girls to whom Mrs. Trouche gave that assignment gave it up with relief after the initial six weeks had passed. Not so with me. I kept writing. The exercise of the craft became so central to my identity at Ashley Hall that my graduation present from Babe, the only close friend I've kept from those years, was a hardbound journal suitable for sketching—and also for writing. Thirty-four years later, I've never lost the discipline. Indeed, it's fair to say that my relationship with the Word is the longest single relationship, outside of family ties, of my life.

Nowadays, my letter to the world takes public form in poetry, newspaper and magazine articles, essays, blogs, and the nonfiction book I'm struggling through. But thousands more pages are private—letters written to myself in the journals I've been keeping since tenth grade that will likely never see the light of day. Despite many moves—what I've called "my all-South tour" from South to North back to South Carolina, to Texas, then Louisiana, and now to Virginia—I still have most of these books, twenty-five years' worth of perfect- and spiral-bound pages, in a closet beneath my stair. I pay a call on these youthful selves from time to time, and every visit leaves me astonished anew at the riches I find there: dreams, poems, short stories, complete plays and screenplays, ideas for novels, dialogues, character sketches, jokes, research notes, rants. It's an entire archive of my intellectual development and creative life, and I gladly credit a red-haired woman with wise young eyes for guiding me to the labyrinth's thread.

New Kid on the Block

—JOANNE VEAL GABBIN

Everything I needed to know about negotiating the streets of the academy I learned when I was four. Well, almost everything . . . My family and I had just moved from 2019 East Chase Street in a predominately black neighborhood in East Baltimore to 1804 North Broadway in a neighborhood that was in transition from white to black. We were the first black family on the block of this tree-lined boulevard that the internationally known Johns Hopkins Hospital had made famous. My parents were proud of our three-story, red-brick row house with ornamental marble facades and marble steps. On any given day, my mother would be outside with her pail, scrub brush, and scouring stone making the blue-veined marble steps gleam. On one such day, after she had cleaned the steps and swept the sidewalk, she dressed me in one of those frilly little girl dresses with the crinoline attached, plaited my hair and put a pink ribbon on the top braid, and sat me on the front steps. Soon I moved from the steps to the tree in front of the house. It was not long before a little white boy came out of his house only two doors up the street from mine. He was taller than I was, with short brown hair and short pants. I was happy to see another child that I could play with, so when he came close to the tree, I said, "Hi, what's your name?" He said simply, "Wait right there."

I thought in my excitement at meeting the new boy that he had gone back into his house to get a toy or perhaps some candy that we could share. So when he returned with his hands behind his back and a curious smile lighting up his face, I could not have seen the metal pipe that he took from behind his back and crashed into my head. It was hours later, when I awoke with a concussion at Johns Hopkins Hospital, that my mother and father told me what had happened. My head was bandaged, and I saw the blood-spattered pink and white dress on the chair next to the curtain petition. Daddy stood at the foot of the bed. I remember that his eyes were red and the lines in his forehead were deep and wrinkled. Mama rubbed my arm and squeezed my hand over and over again. Then we went home.

Shortly after the incident the boy's family moved from the house. I never saw the boy again, so I could not ask him why he had hurt me. Nothing more came of it. My parents never thought about filing a lawsuit. It was 1950, and they had not expected redress or justice. I healed, but the scar remains on a portion of my scalp where hair doesn't grow.

In 1969 when I realized that I wanted to go to graduate school, it did not occur to me that there would be any barriers that I could not scale. I did not have money to pay tuition; I had not been accepted into a graduate program; I did not even know where my education would lead me if I accomplished the other steps. However, I was determined to attend and convinced that I would be successful.

Perhaps my confidence issued from the optimism of an age in which idealistic men and women sought to better their society by holding it accountable to its Constitution. Perhaps my determination lay in my awareness that enough people had suffered and sacrificed to allow me and others like me equal access to education. Or maybe my youth convinced me that there was time enough to try this new experiment called graduate school. Whatever my reasons, I proceeded to the office of the secretary of the English department at the University of Chicago and said, "I want to go to school. Could you help me?"

A kind, officious woman by the name of Catherine Ham was on the receiving end of this question. She had worked at the University of Chicago for many years and had rarely encountered a black student in an advanced program in literature and languages. She was aware of the uneasy truce that existed between the university and the black people who lived in the communities bordering Hyde Park. She understood better than most the great psychological distance between those privileged, well-heeled intellectuals at the University of Chicago and the people who resided just across the Midway Pliasance in Woodlawn. Like many other whites from the

university, she avoided Woodlawn where burned-out buildings and business establishments evidenced the self-destructive fury that was unleashed
just a year earlier in the wake of the assassination of Martin Luther King.
The Black Peace Stone Nation ran Woodlawn; led by Jeff Stone, they con-
trolled their turf just as surely as Richard Daley held reigns over the political and economic affairs of the rest of Chicago. I am not certain that any
of this had any bearing on her response to me, but when I left her office I
had her assurance that I would be admitted to the M.A. program in English
with a full academic scholarship.

When I enrolled at the university in September of 1969, I was eager
to learn and even more concerned about proving that what I was doing
was relevant. "Relevant," that was an important word in the late sixties
because so many of us carried with us the weight of being "firsts," and with
that came the uncomfortable realization that we could not betray or forget
those blacks who had paid very dearly for the benefits that we were reap-
ing. The Little Rock Nine and Daisy Bates, the Greensboro students who
endured the harassment and violence of hostile whites in nonviolent sit-
ins, the Freedom Riders who rode from Alabama to Mississippi amid the
threats of beatings and fire bombings were carried with me as I entered
those classrooms where I studied Mark Twain with Hamlin Hill and made
Shakespeare and George Bernard Shaw a part of my vocabulary because
of the incomparable teaching of Elder Olson. My already tortured sense of
double consciousness received another jolt when shortly after I began my
studies Fred Hampton, Mark Clark, and the members of the Black Panthers
were brutally murdered in a predawn raid masterminded by the state attorney's police. The realization of these and other sacrifices kept me humble
and vigilant.

I soon discovered that some professors did not know what to make of
me. After my first semester, one man who acted as my academic adviser
asked, "Why aren't you having trouble here?" His question not only registered his curiosity about my better-than-average performance but also
his dismay. All that he knew about the superior education boasted by the
university, all the assumptions that he harbored about the limited ability of
black students from small, historically black institutions were being upset
by what he saw as a troubling exception. Unfortunately, his myopia would
not allow him to realize that I was not an exception. I had simply gotten a

good education at Morgan State College where my professors were excellent teachers and scholars. Nick Aaron Ford, who headed the English department at Morgan, was a noted critic of African American literature. Waters Turpin, who taught me the poetry of the Romantics, was a respected novelist and chronicled the lives of blacks living on the eastern shore of Maryland. I was also taught by Ulysses Lee who, along with Sterling A. Brown and Arthur P. Davis, edited the groundbreaking anthology *Negro Caravan*. Eugenia Collier and Ruthe Sheffey, challenging teachers, were making names for themselves as critics and scholars in the field of African American literature. This kind of education was outside of his understanding, and it was much easier to dismiss me, as well as my academic background, as a perplexing aberration.

In truth, the university was no less perplexed by the question of what to do with its black faculty. Its temporary answer to the problem of attracting black scholars was to bring one or two in for a semester or year. At the end of their visit these scholars would return to their colleges, and the host department would congratulate itself for having a black in its faculty, without making a long-term commitment to black scholarship. This certainly would have been the case for George E. Kent, the man who became my mentor, had it not been for a fortuitous string of events. George Kent had come to the University of Chicago in 1969 as a visiting scholar from Quinnipiac College in Hamden, Connecticut. His classes on the Harlem Renaissance, Wright, Baldwin, and Ellison, Faulkner, the writers of the Black Arts Movement drew students from all over the campus. His strong commitment to Black literature and his insistence that it must be seen in light of its ability to bear the full weight of Western culture and the Black folk tradition encouraged in me a deep respect for the discipline.

Therefore, when I heard that Professor Kent was nearing the end of his stay and realized that no one had offered him the option of remaining at the university, I was disturbed. I demanded to know why this man with impeccable academic credentials was not being considered for a full-time position at the university. After talking with the head of the English department, I knew that I was powerless alone to persuade him or the rest of the faculty to offer a position to George Kent. So I organized a petition campaign in which I got signatures from black students all over the campus. It really did not matter that they were not students in English. I convinced students in the medical school, in business, history, religion, and social work that signing the petition would send a message to the administration that blacks demanded a serious commitment to black studies and to a black presence at the university. Needless to say when I met with the English department with petition in hand, we students prevailed. George Kent was offered the position of full professor with tenure. Now there would be a permanent scholar in Afro-American literature, making serious scholarship in the field possible.

This was the real beginning of my education at the University of Chicago. I began to take charge of my own learning. Although there was no black studies curriculum, I decided that I would be the architect of my own. Although the English department faculty suggested that I confine my study to courses in literature, I took courses from two outstanding black scholars who taught at the University of Chicago. I had a memorable class with historian John Hope Franklin, who taught a class in the Antebellum South. I remember this man, author of the monumental study, *From Slavery to Freedom*, coming into the class with a stack of legal pad pages. He would sit down and proceed to talk for an hour without one reference to his notes. With the most obscure dates at hand and with an uncanny grasp of the nuances of the psychology of the South, he held us spellbound with his insights. I also took a seminar with theologian Charles Long, whose classes were an incredible mix of sermonettes, homiletics, camp meeting drama, and hermeneutics. His witty and challenging style, combined with the energy produced by my fellow students such as Jeremiah Wright, McKinley Young, and Homer Ashley, made the class a model of what a courageous teacher could do when he or she trusted in the potential that resides in every classroom.

However, without a doubt, George Kent was the greatest influence on my development as a scholar. Under his mentorship I studied Langston Hughes, Zora Neale Hurston, Gwendolyn Brooks, and Sterling A. Brown. He not only encouraged me to read widely in the field of African American literature and folklore, but he also exposed me to the dynamic world of writing and publishing that flourished in Chicago during the late sixties. Through Kent I met Gwendolyn Brooks, the renowned poet laureate of Illinois; poet Don L. Lee (Haki Madhubuti), the founder and editor of *Third World Press*; Hoyt Fuller, the editor of *Black World*; Lerone Bennett, popular historian and writer for *Black World*; and poet Margaret Burroughs, then curator for the Du Sable Museum. I found myself in the midst of a New Black Renaissance where artists, musicians, poets, and political theorists came together to produce an outpouring of literature that affirmed Black life and culture.

My forays outside the classroom inevitably led me to another kind of school, Operation Breadbasket, now called PUSH. Along with hundreds of other Chicagoans, I went each Saturday morning to a renovated synagogue to hear Jesse L. Jackson, the charismatic leader known as the "Country Preacher." As he intoned his "I Am Somebody" battle cry, those of us in the audience stood a little straighter and believed, at least for that moment, in the vision of this man who knew intimately of black struggle. "I am— black—beautiful—proud—I must be respected—I must be protected—I am—God's child." Whether he made parallels between Moses and Dr. King or talked about the patterns of sacrifice and nurture of black women, each Saturday we were convinced again and again of his extraordinary ability to articulate our most private pain, our fears, and our most expansive hopes and expectations.

It was also during this period that I got my first opportunity to teach. The civil rights movement of the sixties, the martyrdom of King and Medgar Evers and others, the national rage at rights long withheld and promises long unkept had begun to open many doors in the early seventies. One such door was to Roosevelt University. Students there were now clamoring for courses in black literature. I, a newly made M.A. in English, was hired to teach a course called "Revolutionary Self-Conscious Literature." Never having taught before, I found myself in a classroom telling my students— many of whom were older and far wiser than I—about the anger that was endemic in the works of Amiri Baraka, the principles of the Black Arts Movement espoused by Ron Karenga, and the works of struggle written by activists from Frederick Douglass to Malcolm X. While teaching at Roosevelt, I invited Gwendolyn Brooks to read her poetry. It was then that I learned that in 1962 Frank London Brown had tried to get her a teaching position at Roosevelt. Apparently, Roosevelt had considered her, had her fill out application papers, and then denied her the position on the grounds that she did not have a degree. This revelation led me to vow that no matter where I taught, I would invite Gwendolyn Brooks, the first African American to win the Pulitzer Prize, to share her many gifts.

What I learned during my first years as a student at the University of Chicago provided me a lifetime of insights. I was one of the first fruits of the civil rights struggle, which opened the nation's universities to black scholarship. Never before, and unfortunately never since, were so many talented black students enrolled in graduate studies. I sensed even then that I was a pioneer, that what I learned, what I wrote, what I taught would have some significance.

Once I completed my course work and comps for the Ph.D., I achieved that expectant status called ABD. I was ready to take on a full-time position as an assistant professor. It was 1972 and the first crop of black scholars who had integrated the nation's universities was on the job market. At Chicago State University, students had protested the absence of black professors to teach Black literature courses. I am certain that my hiring was a direct result of their efforts. I came into an English department where I was the only black teacher. I developed the curriculum for a survey of black literature course, questioned the lack of inclusion of black authors in the American literature courses, and urged my colleagues to change the composition book that had no readings by anyone black with the exception of Booker T. Washington's *Up From Slavery*.

Although I had a real sense of accomplishment in this position, my tenure there was often disappointing. Colleagues appeared threatened by my relationship with the black students. They were suspicious of my meetings with them after classes. I knew that these students were excited to meet with me because I shared their culture and circumstance. I was a first-generation college student who modeled the success they saw for themselves. I was young and understood their rage. However, my colleagues read more into our meetings than was necessary. Where there should have been collegiality there were fear and suspicion. Because my colleagues had never had to think about mentoring a new black faculty member, they didn't. Not long after my first full semester, I really felt the disconnect with the department when one of my older students told me that he was surprised that I had accepted several thousands of dollars less than the department was prepared to pay me. Of course, that piece of information didn't help my attitude. In hindsight, I realized that my studies did not prepare me for the politics that are a part of the academy.

When I began teaching at Lincoln University in 1977, I realized how fierce academic politics could be, even on the bucolic campus of the oldest black college in the nation. In the opening faculty meeting, Gladys Willis, the first black woman to graduate in English from Princeton and the newly appointed head of the English department, and I, her newest faculty member, became scapegoats in a nasty battle between the faculty and the president, Herman Branson. In retaliation for his threatened faculty entrenchment, the majority of the integrated faculty called for our resignation, and we had not yet set foot in our classrooms. The tumultuous times that followed could have broken the strongest resolve, but I knew that if I faltered and allowed political wrangling to break me, then I would not be able to raise my head to teach these students who needed what I had to offer. I taught at Lincoln University in Pennsylvania for eight years, developing the first courses in black literature and journalism, organizing a lecture series that brought Gwendolyn Brooks, Margaret Walker, Larry Neal, Sonia Sanchez, and others to the campus, and founding the Langston Hughes Cultural Arts Festival in 1980. It turned out to be a good place to grow culturally. Nothing came easy but the mission became the reward. My husband, Alexander, and I began a long teaching career together and Jessea, our daughter, grew up in the halls where Langston Hughes, Melvin Tolson, Saunders Redding, and Kwame Nkrumah had studied and new eager students were dreaming of a promising education.

In 1985, fifteen years after I took my first teaching job, I was again the new black kid on the block. As an associate professor with a Ph.D. degree from the University of Chicago, a recently published book on Sterling Brown, and several years of teaching behind me, I joined the faculty of the English department at James Madison University. I should have been suspicious when all thirty-seven members of the faculty showed up for my interview. I learned later that some of them resented the fact that the provost of the university had actively sought to recruit me, an African American scholar, to the all-white department. At the first department meeting, I came early enough to get a seat on the next to the last row in the classroom. Not long after I had taken my seat, a faculty member who reeked of cigarette smoke and bourbon came into the classroom and said to his

colleagues trailing him, "Let's go to the Jim Crow section." I was not prepared for such outright rudeness, but I remained silent. I was outnum-
bered. However, just before the meeting began, this same man shouted to
the faculty members scurrying to find a seat, "Come on back here with us
niggers." Well, that was enough. I stood up and cornered him. With years
of rage that I had successfully contained, I lashed out at him, "If you ever
say anything like that again in my presence, you will not only need a lawyer,
you'll need a doctor." From that point on until he left the department, he
took a wide berth around me. And others in the department were put on
notice that this black woman would fight.

From a young girl, I knew the crashing sound of racism. However,
many years of studying and teaching in the university have given me armor
that protects me against a system that is still not fully open and egalitar-
ian. I continue to offer my students a welcome, a green-tree lined street
to discover literature. For the academy offers the best hope for a forum to
advance reason and intellect to heal a divided society and a tense and dangerous world. I am ever mindful of the many children, the students, and
the courageous adults who refused to stay in their places and thus made a
place for me in the academy. My teaching is a daily testament to them.

Obstacles or Opportunities

The Wisdom to Know the Difference

—ELIZABETH BROWN-GUILLORY

Somewhere along my journey I determined that I would do my very best to turn obstacles into opportunities, that I would strive always to move from chance to choice. I've come to view reading literature and writing as healing balms. I read to discover new worlds and cultures unfamiliar to me. I write largely to heal myself and others who might appreciate a laying-on-of-hands. Both processes are therapeutic, even salvific. Many of the realities that I bring to life in my creative writing—playwriting—are an outgrowth of a series of defining moments that forced me to turn obstacles into opportunities.

A defining moment in my life occurred in the late 1970s when my American literature professor asked if the class had any suggestions for texts as he fine-tuned his syllabus. I hesitated but then raised my hand and politely asked if he would consider including on the syllabus the works of women and writers of color. In an instant, he turned his back to the class, raised the flaps of his tweed jacket, and asked me to kick him because he didn't know any. I decided at that moment I would never be an arrogant, insensitive, ignorant teacher. I promised myself that I would study diverse cultures and do my best to transfer this knowledge to my students. After all, our very humanity necessitates that we know ourselves and other human beings from diverse cultures who people the earth. Back then, I was only one of two blacks in the Ph.D. program in English at Florida State University, and I earnestly was seeking literature that engaged me on many levels and served several functions. I longed to see other people of color and myself portrayed in literature, art, and the media without the heavy hand of bias. I often felt alienated, displaced, alone, fragmented—in need of something to help make me whole.

It seems to me that the mark of great poetry, or any other creative expression, is to delight, instruct, inspire, and heal. Artists who have made the greatest difference in my life are those who give us stories of healing experiences. So strong is my interest in healing, I decided to develop a course that both explores the pain of black people's lives and offers remedies for healing. I titled the course "Literature of Healing and Resistance," and the women writers included on the syllabus are Ntozake Shange, Tess Onwueme, Toni Cade Bambara, Gloria Naylor, Paule Marshall, Audre Lorde, and Tsitsi Dangarembga. In addition to the primary texts, I selected a number of seminal and recent publications by feminist/womanist theorists, including works by Trudier Harris, Deborah McDowell, Karla Holloway, Barbara Christian, Audre Lorde, and bell hooks, as well as a dozen or so essays exploring race and culture in African American literature. Additionally, I introduced students to postcolonialist theorists, such as Frantz Fanon, Homi Bhabha, Gayatri Chakravorty Spivak, and Stuart Hall. The critical and theoretical texts I selected contextualized the novels and plays, all of which deal with spiritual, physical, or psychological healing. The selected primary texts provided a wealth of examples of characters that turn obstacles into opportunities during their journey to wholeness.

As I worked my way through this new course on literature of healing and resistance, I suspected I would uncover big and small wounds of my own, all in varying stages of healing. As I prepared to teach Fanon, I found myself meditating on his argument in *Black Skin, White Masks* that blacks suffer from an inferiority complex foisted upon them by the hegemonic group. He argues that blacks spend their lives searching for validation from the very group that oppresses them. He claims blacks struggle to prove they are equal while their white counterparts look on with hostility or indifference. I was struck by Fanon's argument in *The Wretched of the Earth* that the colonized often replicate the violence bred within them by the colonizer. I reflected that the surrogate colonizer can be a member of one's own family, and a child can in one defining moment be transformed into Other.

It's painful to see this inferiority complex played out in black children, and it's especially painful to look back on my own feelings of inferiority. When I was a child, my mulatto grandmother had a powerful impact on me. I remember every facet of her physical appearance because she frequently called attention to her whiteness. She was cream colored with long, silky, salt and pepper hair, which hung down to her buttocks when it wasn't in a plait and twisted into a bun. She was of medium height and heavy set, weighing close to three hundred pounds. She was bowlegged, and when she walked, she wobbled back and forth like a chair that had one leg shorter than the others. My grandmother was a phenomenal cook and was known throughout the southwestern Louisiana area for her seafood gumbo, red bean and rice, biscuits, sweet potato and fig pies, cornbread, jambalaya, shrimp sauce picante, stuffed potatoes with shrimp, and other Creole dishes. She was caregiver to prominent white families during the week and to a dozen or more of her grandchildren on weekends in order for our parents to tend to chores or to enjoy outings. When she wasn't babysitting, she made her rounds throughout the community sampling other women's food and hunting news and gossip. She was an inordinate storyteller who could turn little half-truths into grand tales of love and adventure. She kept us in stitches with her funny would-be arguments with my blind, incorrigible, but lovable grandfather.

When I was twelve, my grandmother had come for a visit. My mother, her daughter-in-law, was busy cleaning and cooking, but my grandmother carried on a conversation with herself, as was her habit. She sat admiring her grandchildren's pictures layered on several shelves that circled the living-room walls. It was no surprise to me as she began praising the near-white qualities of my three sisters. I had grown up with her always reminding everyone that my sisters were beautiful because they had inherited so many of her features. In the past, when she'd set her gaze upon my picture, she'd note that I was smart and quickly move on to some other grandchild who was pleasing to her eyes. But on this one day, my grandmother didn't know I was in my room, hiding out to read Langston Hughes's and Margaret Walker's poetry. I could hear her from my bedroom, "Oh, chere, look at Lelia. She so pretty, with her high cheekbones and thin lips. Mais, chere, you know she look like our French ancestors, yeah. And look at Ann, my sweet bonbon; she got good hair, straight hair, just like white people.

And look at those precious bright eyes—just like white people, I tell you. And, look at Theresa. Just look at that yellow child . . . you know she got some white in her . . . ain't got much African in her, no child!" She almost sounded euphoric when she hit the high note on "yellow child." Then came the silence. I knew she was looking at my picture. I could feel her eyes scrutinizing my African features. When I was around, there were always those pregnant pauses before she commented on my photographs. I could hear her squirming in the plastic-covered chair. Then I heard her say those things that changed my life. "But look at Beth. Chere, that's a *ugly* child. Look like a little black buckwheat. She got that little nappy hair on her head. An', oh child, look at all that space between her teeth. Poor baby, she ain't got no flesh on those little skinny legs. She look just like a poor little starving child in Africa, big belly and all. Umph, umph, umph, c'est triste! I feel sorry for the poor little thing."

I must have gasped because my grandmother's cream-colored face turned beet red as she looked up and saw me standing in the hallway near my bedroom door. The ground underneath felt shaky at that very moment. I instantly understood my position as Other, as subaltern, as black and evil in the Fanonian sense. I wanted to run, but my feet were glued to the floor and my eyes pierced hers, the grandmother who cherished her white self and castigated her black self. If she could have ripped the mark of blackness from her body, she would have. In that one instant, something passed between us: her recognition that she had wounded me and my epiphany that someone I loved saw me as less than, as inferior. Maybe the whole world saw me as ugly and less than, I thought. She was my grandmother whom I looked up to and loved, almost worshipped. I trusted her; she would not lie to me. So there I stood seemingly locked in time. However, it couldn't have been more than a few seconds before my mother grasped what had happened and came running toward me. She scooped me up in her arms, though my eyes were in a deadlock with my grandmother's. My grandmother regrouped and called out, "But that's a smart child. She make four thousand points in school!" She was referring to my 4.0 grade point average. My grandmother continued without shame, "She gonna be a lawyer or a doctor. She might even be a healer, a treateur. She might help change the world. Yes, chere, she may be the chosen one."

Conflicting images swirled around me as I struggled to digest what had just happened. After what seemed like an eternity, I finally yanked my feet up from the floor and took flight back into my room and back into the healing poetry of Langston Hughes and Margaret Walker. I cried and cried that day and many times during my adolescence and well into my twenties about the day my grandmother introduced me to her version of blackness. Years later, I am still struck by her use of third person in her comments about my future potential. She didn't say, "You might become a lawyer or a doctor." She said, "She might . . ." Perhaps, even subconsciously, my grandmother was distancing herself from me, the Other.

She had transferred her own internalized hatred of her black self to me. She had grown up in a world that taught her to hate things black, and I had to forgive her in order to move on with my life. Her words, though she did not mean to hurt me, stung my soul and exacerbated my sense of alienation. There were times when I thought I would go insane, all because I had internalized my grandmother's self-hatred, which had begun to color my relationships with others in my community who also suffered from varying degrees of self-hatred. Back then, I could have benefited from knowing about W. E. B. Du Bois's explanation of double consciousness and his insights into the plight of black Americans who often internalize the hegemonic group's view of blackness as inferior.

While I continued to love my grandmother, I am not sure I liked her anymore, in the way that Sula in Toni Morrison's novel of the same title feels when she overhears Hannah, her mother, reveal that she loves Sula but she just doesn't like her. The sense of discomfort I felt with her manifested itself in subtle ways. For example, as my grandmother aged and became forgetful, she began mixing up her grandchildren's names. She lived several houses down the street from my parents, and so I had ample opportunities from the time I was twelve until I went off to college to walk past her house and refuse to respond to her call. She and I came to relish our ritual of her reaching out and my rejecting her. She'd sit in her rocker and call to me from the porch, "Lelia, come on over here." I'd ignore her and keep walking. "Ann, I'm calling you, child." I'd keep walking with my long, skinny legs, moving on down the street. "Theresa, chere, I know you hear me calling you." The Buckwheat in me was refusing to dignify her. Finally, she'd laugh and shout as I was almost out of ear's reach, "Beth, you black thing! You hear me calling you. Come over here and read my mail for me." Only when she named me correctly did I do her bidding. She'd laugh, holding her rotund body as it shimmied in the rocker. I'd laugh, too, because I recognized I was still paying her back. For years, my story of resistance was told and retold at holiday dinners.

It wasn't until many years after my grandmother died that I understood the full impact of her hurtful words. Though my self-esteem was lowered by her characterization of me, I managed to turn an obstacle into an opportunity. I became very focused on my studies to the exclusion of almost everything else. I think I decided at some point if I couldn't be pretty, I would certainly achieve in the intellectual realm. And so I did. I worked hard to earn not one but three degrees and became the first member of several generations of my family in the United States to earn a doctorate. I was squarely on my way to healing when I completed work for the Ph.D. at age twenty-five. I am keenly aware that if it were not for the support of my entire family I would likely not have achieved such a distinction. My whole family helped me through school, and we all take credit for the Ph.D., the symbolic banner of achievement for sharecroppers' children who grew up on a farm in southwest Louisiana without indoor plumbing. There was a tremendous amount of love in my family, and so abject poverty was a manageable foe.

My grandmother died when I was a freshman in college, but when I thank God for my many blessings, I often include her because she inadvertently motivated me to excel. While I internalized her view of me as ugly and pitiful, I also accepted her belief that I was the chosen one, that I would be the one to get a formal education and strike out into a world that had formerly been barred to our poor but industrious family. As I look back, I realize that my grandmother's words felt like a huge boulder had dropped on top of my head. By chance I had overheard her call me ugly, but by choice I could determine the course of my life. I had to make a choice. I could choose to let her negative words destroy me, or I could struggle to make sense of the chaos she initiated. With the help of my mother's deep love and nurturing, I was able to take small steps toward self-love. I chose not to have a breakdown but a breakthrough to the power of the possibilities. I set out to prove to my grandmother and to myself that all was not lost because I am chocolate-colored. I rejected her negativity about my physical appearance and embraced her validation of me as intelligent and earned a place in the academy. As I write this essay, I am thinking of my grandmother's haunting laughter from her rocking chair. Surely from where she sits in her rocker in Heaven she has seen me travel to Mexico, the Bahamas, France, China, England, Scotland, Wales, Canada, Brazil, Poland, Czechoslovakia, Germany, and Barbados—each time opening myself up to the cultures of others and ultimately transmitting that knowledge to my students. I smile as I envision her frown of disapproval as she learns I am planning a trip to West Africa. I am amazed at the ability of negative experiences to serve as a springboard to possibilities, opportunities.

My grandmother's view of me followed me into high school where I had another experience that shaped me, one involving a mentor, Bazile Miller. My previous teachers had been Catholic nuns, all white females who devoted their lives to black and American Indian students. I offer only praise for the nuns who did the best they could to instruct us, to see that we had an excellent foundation. I offer even more praise to my parents who struggled to pay for private school education for their eight children. I recall my mother saying repeatedly, "If I have to, I will sell popcorn balls to keep my children in a Catholic school." There was no Catholic high school in my little town, so public high school education was a new adventure. I was fortunate enough to find myself in a classroom taught by Mr. Miller, who found much joy and a sense of purpose in working with students. He was the school principal and was the first male and the first black person to serve as my teacher in a formal setting. He volunteered to teach one class of ninth-grade English in the 1968–69 school year. He was the most amazing man I had ever met, and straightaway I developed a huge crush that threatened spontaneous combustion. It is extremely hard to concentrate when you're fourteen and hiding a secret from a worldly man of words who walked around the class quoting such greats as St. Augustine, Langston Hughes, Emily Dickinson, Shakespeare, Countee Cullen, Milton, Ghandi, and Aime Cesaire. Mr. Miller, quite frankly, was an anomaly in my small community. He was a transplant from a town about sixty miles away. The men of my community were honest, hardworking farmers, and Mr. Miller was a gifted academic. He was the kind of professional my mother had hoped I would one day become. I can remember my mother rocking me to sleep as a child and singing, "My baby is going to be a teacher someday." Teaching was the most prestigious position one could aspire to in my small town. With the arrival of Mr. Miller into my life, I began to believe that it might be possible for me to become a teacher like this intellectual giant. He gave 120 percent to his students and taught us to work hard, think smart, speak persuasively, and claim the prosperous futures to which we were entitled.

I was terrified to go to Mr. Miller's English class because I didn't want him to find out I had a crush on him. I was shy and self-effacing because of my inferiority complex, and he seemed to know both of the above. He handled me expertly, though. He chose to initiate a conversation with me via written assignments. He once wrote a telling note on a composition: "Ugmo Brown, I see you have a gift for writing, a creative spirit is lurking within you." He addressed his favorite students by their last name with Ugmo attached. It was a term of endearment. I treasured his remarks on that and other papers throughout the year.

One day just before class started, he called me into the hall to tell me he was initiating Miller's Fattening Program. In addition to lunch, I was to go to the cafeteria for mid-morning and late afternoon snacks. Let me explain. I was an emaciated thing at age fourteen, weighing only about eighty pounds and standing at five feet nine. I suspected he might have heard students ridicule me, for some of the bullies called me "out of my name"— "Toothpick Annie" and "Stringbean Suzie." A good strong wind could and often did blow my frail body hither and yon. Back then, voluptuous was in and thin was not. I felt humiliated by classmates, and I prayed to gain weight to look like the other fourteen-year-old voluptuous girls who teased me mercilessly and who, because God is a good God, are now *voluptuous*. At any rate, Mr. Miller knew my parents were sharecroppers, and he feared I was not getting enough to eat at home. It was a magnanimous gesture on his part, one that still warms my heart. So I began this program the very next day. At 10:00 a.m. I went to the cafeteria where the cooks were expecting me and provided me with canned peaches, biscuits, sausages, milk, and juice. That very afternoon at around 2:30, after having had red beans, sausage, and rice at the lunch hour, I had a sausage sandwich, apple juice, raisins, and a Hershey bar. The daily routine remained the same the entire ninth-grade year with the food varying each day depending on the cooks' menu. I tried to tell Mr. Miller I was not starving at home. We were sharecroppers who had an abundance of food because we grew our own, but we didn't have two pennies to rub together. I didn't gain any weight that year. My metabolism rate wouldn't hear of it. In fact, three years later I went off to college weighing a grand total of eighty-nine pounds.

Mr. Miller's interest in my success motivated him to start singing to me in class. He developed a habit of serenading me as he walked around lecturing. He'd stop in front of my desk and sing lyrics from one of his favorite songs, "I'm gonna be a [big] wheel someday. I'm gonna be somebody." I'd blush and nearly swallow my tongue from excitement. He inspired confidence in me with that song. Here was a man who knew I was afraid of my own shadow, was almost inarticulate, and was paralyzed with fear of speaking up in class or in any public setting, all indicators of my inferiority complex. He especially provided opportunities in which I had to speak before groups of people. He insisted that I listen carefully to Walter Cronkite on national news and try to emulate his articulation of words. Mr. Miller was a phenomenal debater and had sharpened his skills in forensics at a historically black college. He worked with me and by degrees I made progress. One day, he called me out into the hall again and told me he wanted me to write, direct, and produce a play for the entire student body and community. The hallway began to darken and I felt like I was going to faint. Just as I was about to tell him I didn't know how to write a play and, in fact, had never seen a production of one, he pulled from behind his back a book, *How to Write a Play*. After some convincing on his part, I accepted the challenge. I could have viewed his challenge as an obstacle, but I chose to see it as an opportunity to tap into a self I barely understood and to show my gratitude to a mentor who believed in me. My classmates and I staged my first play, "Queen of the Alcoholics," in 1969, and I have been writing plays ever since. My plays have been produced in Los Angeles, Denver, New Orleans, New York, Houston, Chicago, and Washington, D.C., and all of my plays have the mark of Bazile Miller on them. I stayed in touch with my mentor until he died. One of his friends once told me that Mr. Miller designated an entire wall in his study to news clippings about my scholarly and creative work. He was proud of his protégé. His inspiration continues to motivate me to reach out to my students in creative ways. I make every effort to touch the lives of my students as he touched mine. To date, I have received four teaching excellence awards. I give Mr. Miller credit for a recent high honor. The University of Houston contacted 150,000 of its alumni and asked them to select phenomenal professors at the University of Houston. I was selected as one of four most beloved professors. This honor makes me work harder to deserve it and to inspire future teachers to embrace their students in such a way that their pupils will make a lasting difference in our world.

There have been other defining moments in my life, such as the day my mother died after a long battle with cancer, the day I realized I wanted to marry my husband, the birth of our daughter who survived while several pregnancies ended prematurely, the birth of several life-giving friendships. These stories I have published as short fiction or plays. For example, for two years after my mother's death, I worked painstakingly on writing "Beacon Hill," a short story that was published in *Louisiana Literature*. The pain and sense of loss were so deep after I lost my mother, I didn't know how to hold it together. So, every day I'd work on this story that seemed to be writing itself to heal me. I'm certain my mother's spirit guided me. Writing "Beacon Hill" allowed me to write about my mother and her ancestors. My mother loved unselfishly and taught her children how to love, how to survive, and how to laugh. She was one of the greatest joys of my life, always encouraging me to do better, to give more, to pray for guidance, and to thank God every day for another day of life. Telling my mother's story helped heal me as I struggled to live without her physical presence. I also wanted to write a story that my daughter might one day read, one which would connect her to me and to her foremothers who showed steady strength during rocky times.

Other painful occasions have prompted me to write. One case in point is the story of the public humiliation I experienced at one of the several universities I've worked over the past thirty years. I felt the strong sting of humiliation when a colleague secretly organized innocent students to demand that I be removed from an administrative position. I am not sure I was ever the real target; perhaps, I was merely the example of the havoc to come if he were not given an administrative appointment. The administrators caved in, made this bully/enemy their friend, and promoted him to a high-ranking administrative position as hush money and to ensure that they could keep their own administrative appointments. The former radical became an invisible conservative on campus. In hindsight, I never should have accepted an administrative position that was surrounded by political and racial tension. I was a young academic, without a mentor and untrained for a war zone. I was naive and eager to help students achieve their full potential. In time, I purged myself of this humiliation, but not before I began researching, developing scripts, and performing the lives of black women who conquered insurmountable odds, including Madam C. J. Walker, Josephine Baker, and Sissieretta Jones. The stories of these women's lives empowered me. In the interim, I continued to work and rework a play that helped me recover from the administrative debacle. I finally was able to turn that hurt, that obstacle, into an opportunity. I have performed excerpts from this play across the country. A version of the play has been performed in Danny Glover's theater in California, has won a first-place prize in a national competition, has been produced in several repertory and community theaters, has been published in a collection, and recently, with more revisions and a new title, *When the Ancestors Call*, ran seven weeks to capacity audiences in Chicago.

When I look back at these moments in my life, I realize that each was a growing experience. Though I grew up in abject poverty, I have been blessed on the journey to meet many loving people who have helped me to know my potential and myself. As I reach for tomorrow with all of its possibilities, I count my blessings, one of which is the wisdom to know the difference between the things I can and cannot change. Those things I can change become wonderful opportunities to help heal others and myself.

The Faith Walk of Writing

Connecting Head and Heart

—MARILYN SANDERS MOBLEY

And the Lord answereth me, and said, Write the vision, and make it
plain upon tables, that he may run that readeth it.

—HABAKKUK 2:2

I have loved putting pen to paper almost all of my life. Ever
since my mother taught me to read and write and gave me a
two-year head start on literacy in the breakfast nook of the
kitchen in our Akron, Ohio, home, I have loved what could happen when
the connection between head and heart flowed through my arm, down to
my fingers, and into whatever writing instrument I could get my hands
on. Writing was magic I could produce at any given moment and impress
adults, especially my parents. But it always impressed me too. That was
the joy of it all. Writing was a gift I could give myself. But that is not the
whole point of this story. The magic did not always come. Sometimes it
disappeared for weeks, months, and even years. It withheld itself from me
and tremendous self-doubt grew where the magic had been. Glimpses of
the magic would break through every now and then, but writing took on
dimensions—depth, texture, gravity—it never had when I was young, and
I have spent most of my life trying to get the magic back. I discovered in
the company of other women writers and sister scholars that I could do just
that: get the magic back and learn something new about the power of the

written word at the same time. I learned that writing had become a faith walk and it would never be the same.

Now at the age of a few years past fifty, as I reflect on the place that writing has had for me, I can see where and how writing at times has lost its magic. In retrospect, these losses and recoveries are defining moments that have shaped the writer I am now. In that sense, despite how trite it may seem, this is a story about the power of the word to heal.

Ironically, one of the first losses came in the seventh grade. My favorite class then, unsurprisingly, was English, where my teacher at West Junior High School, Mr. Harris, began each class with an expository essay. I don't recall exactly whether he gave us topics or the beginning of essays in the form of a first sentence only, but what I do recall is that for the first twenty to twenty-five minutes of each class period, we could write our thoughts, ideas, and feelings on paper. I looked forward to it, confident in my ability to express myself, proud of what my sixth-grade teacher had referred to as my "better-than-teacher handwriting," and almost giddy that every subject presented the opportunity for me to share that I had indeed, even at the age of thirteen, given some serious thought to some rather weighty matters of life and living. In other words, I thought I was deep. And given the very strict home in which I was raised, I had developed an inner life from reading that relished these opportunities to expound on what I thought I knew.

What slipped into the joy of expository writing, however, was an element of censorship that came, not from Mr. Harris, but from my mother. At the same time that school was a site of learning, it was also a safe haven, a refuge from home. My parents' pending divorce meant I could not count on my parents the way I once had. I was noticing big and small changes, nuances in their respective tone of voice, fluctuations in the attention they gave me and my brothers, and the unpredictability of their very presence, especially my father's. When my father finally left for good (there was a series of attempts at reconciliations that really amounted to constant disruptions in my prepubescent life), and my mother had difficulty, at least initially, at keeping the refrigerator and cupboards stocked to the level at which we were accustomed, I noticed. When, on more than one occasion, we had "breakfast food" for dinner, I noticed. More than noticing, I read it as a sign of poverty, as a fall from upper-middle-class grace, status, and comfort, so I wrote about it in an essay. I don't remember the specific focus of the essay, but I know I talked about that sign of poverty that had interrupted my life. I recall getting an A on the essay, the grade I received on most of my essays. When I showed the essay to my mother, however, the grade suddenly was insignificant. What she noticed was the reference to poverty. It created a wound in her that was visceral. She frowned, put the paper down, and said in that stern voice that said I should not even try to look away or forget what she was saying, that she better not ever read or hear me saying anything whatsoever up at that school about being poor. She assured me that I indeed was not poor, that I had never missed a meal, and that as long as there was breath in her body, I would not miss one, no matter what happened between her and my father. Well, that did it. No more references to poverty in my writing until my late forties. The vagaries of censorship had broken the magic. I began to self-censor, to check myself, to wonder whether there would be consequences for my writing that I would not like. Yet, that incident also told me that just as there was power in the written word to impress potential readers, I could just as easily insult them, hurt them, or alter their opinion of me or some reality we thought we shared. Although I had relished my ability to connect head and heart on paper, from that moment on I realized that sometimes that connection, if it showed up on paper, could create consequences for me that I might regret.

A later writing block—a rupture between head and heart—came during my undergraduate years. Again confident that I would be an English major, I took course after course at Barnard College in literature. I left the provincial life of Akron, for New York City, excited from the very beginning that the big city felt like home, contrary to what all my home folks thought. Arriving in New York as a devout Christian, raised in the Church of God, I was unprepared for how some of my reading would begin to raise questions about my faith I had never allowed myself to ask. Few of my classmates were getting up on Sunday morning to go to church, few were trying to live a "saved" life away from home, and even fewer were as interested in spiritual matters as I was. My interest in religion and philosophy took two different directions. On one hand, I began to learn about existentialism, which raised its own questions about the efficacy of religion and man's place in the universe. On the other hand, my courses with Rev. Dr.

James Cone on black liberation theology introduced me to an empowering perspective on the church that resonated with my understanding of black power, that recalled the language and teachings of my upbringing, and that raised important racial questions about religion as it was practiced in the United States.

All of this was heady stuff for a young college woman who was born and raised in a sanctified church that I once referred to as the "no-don't church"—so tired of the rules about makeup, dancing, music, theater, drinking, smoking, pants, card playing, and so on—that I often had no clue of what I indeed *could* do. I grew up thinking the church was the police of all pleasure. Though I clearly understood the church's stance on drinking, having seen what alcohol did to individuals, their families, and the goals and dreams of both, I didn't understand what was wrong with music and dance. I used to have to sneak to listen to James Brown as a high school student, but sneak I did, because even though the only cold sweat I really knew about was the one from dancing, discovering that I could be black and proud was the beginning of my own liberation theology. Having grown up with an understanding of the church's investment in matters of conduct, I was delighted to get another angle on spiritual matters that spoke to the black church's involvement in the very lives of black people and to see that that involvement took the form of resistance to enslavement, oppression, and racism. So the papers I wrote for Dr. Cone were a chance to begin to reconnect head and heart in the midst of the disconnect and skepticism that existentialism and even some black nationalist thought was stirring up in me.

Those papers on black liberation theology only began the connection, however. By the time I graduated from college, I was somewhere between a skeptic and an agnostic, feeling fairly comfortable that my black nationalist politics would suffice. Aside from undergraduate papers, I was not doing any meaningful writing. I had even stopped keeping a diary or journal.

But something else happened during the Barnard years that acted as a potent antidote to the dark poison of skepticism that started to infect me. While I fully understand that a healthy dose of skepticism is a good thing, the skepticism I ingested began to dilute the spiritual reservoir I had when I first arrived on campus. An intellectual curiosity for reading and research would shape my later life as a scholar and writer. I took a course with Professor Quandra Prettyman called "Minority Voices in Literature" that shifted my entire outlook on literature as something that people of European descent had a monopoly on to a cornucopia of expression that had enabled black people to survive and thrive through language. As W. E. B. Du Bois had proclaimed, I discovered that black people had been coworkers in the kingdom of culture. Reading the work of Phillis Wheatley, Harriet Jacobs, Toni Morrison, and others confirmed that my perspective on what matters and on what is meaningful was not odd, just different. In Morrison's *The Bluest Eye* I saw references to places my grandfather had taken me (Isaley's Ice Cream), attitudes toward life I recognized (such as Claudia's disregard for white dolls), and language that made me shudder with its accuracy of sound and nuance about black life. Moreover, when I began teaching Morrison's *Sula* as a teaching assistant to Deborah Billingsley, my Barnard classmate who encouraged me to seek an advanced degree, I saw just how powerful a connection between text and reader could be. My black women students in Columbia University's Educational Exchange Program (CEEP) feasted on Morrison's every word in *Sula* as if it were personally crafted to their vernacular tastes and experiential specificity. They constantly thanked Debbie and me for introducing them to her, for giving them an opportunity to discuss literature they could relate to, and for giving them a glimpse of what a Graduate Equivalency Degree (GED) could do for them. Through the power of the word, in Morrison's deft hands, the lives of these very women who had dropped out of school, had children, left men, worked two and three jobs, but read voraciously, were being transformed. I got to see up close and personal how good writing could do cultural work not being done anywhere else in quite as powerful a way in the 1970s.

The years after Barnard were marked by graduate coursework that was more a means to an end than anything else. In this respect, my dissertation was a fourth break in the magic of writing. While my own thirst for knowledge and access to what other people knew made me read and write voraciously to complete first my master's and then my doctorate, the title of my dissertation reflected my desire to connect head and heart in the academy. My committee knew my eclectic propensity to see connections where no one else had seen them before, so my dissertation director encouraged my cross-cultural study, an attempt to see correlations, informed by my reading of Morrison, between her use of myth, folklore, and narrative, and that of Sarah Orne Jewett, a nineteenth-century white woman writer from Maine. My original title, "Roots and Wings," however, is not a title that my publisher encouraged, so I selected a compromise—"Folk Roots and Mythic Wings: The Cultural Function of Narrative in Sarah Orne Jewett and Toni Morrison"—a title that was replete with academese but void of the sound that reflects my reverence for both my own roots and my desire to mediate between vernacular and standard English in my scholarship. At the point I wrote my dissertation, the desire to complete the task at hand overrode my desire to do battle with anyone who did not understand my linguistic proclivities. Thus, the dissertation was a defining moment in my academic life in the sense that I gained credibility to do scholarly writing, but it was also a manifestation of my stepping back from what I wanted writing to be. In essence, it reflected another moment of censorship, in which what I really wanted to communicate got lost in somebody else's shuffle of what my writing could say.

The turning point came with my divorce from my first husband, which devastated me and nearly shut down my writing life. At the same time, however, it created a space for me to explore neglected dimensions of my spiritual life as well as my connections with other black women that I had never fully allowed myself to experience. Then again, being a full-time wife, mother, and professor all at the same time can leave little time for the balance that sustained friendships with other women can bring. Aside from my journal, which had become my lifeline and repository for all the emotional debris that was piling up around me, I was producing primarily encyclopedic entries in various reference books. I had a few articles published here and there, but my writing life was virtually being held at bay by the weight of a disintegrated family. I managed to move from my huge fifteen-room house in Potomac, Maryland, to the nearby suburb of Gaithersburg, and finally to a garden apartment about a mile or so from campus in Fairfax, Virginia. Having very little of a social life in my postdivorce status, I concentrated on my baby son, Jamal, who was then a high school junior, and on trying to complete a book-length study on Morrison's narrative poetics and cultural politics. I had begun the book way back in 1989 on a Ford Foundation postdoctoral fellowship at George Washington University, with Claudia Tate as my host senior scholar. I was certain my inability to concentrate must have made me a nuisance for her to behold. Nevertheless, she invited me to join the First Draft Club, a group of scholars composed of her former colleagues at Howard University. Though none of us seemed to be as productive as Claudia, I appreciated the safe place to read my work in progress, get feedback, and receive encouragement to keep writing. When she moved on to Princeton University, I lost touch with her, but never forgot her stern admonitions to stay focused on my work. Later, even as I contemplated a trip to Princeton for a service in memory of her scholarship and short life, I knew that I would finally complete the Morrison book and dedicate it to her.

But this new resolve was due to the healing power of writing what was in my head and heart, even when I was not certain how to make the connection. Consequently, even though I wanted to focus on my scholarship as Claudia had advised me to do, a combination of administrative and service duties at my university were distractions I could not ignore. Moreover, these distractions were revealing some realities about academic life about which no one was writing, but about which many were lamenting, often behind closed doors. When I would go to conferences to help my department interview job candidates, I began to feel like an outsider in my own chosen profession when I would take breaks to attend a session or mingle in the hallways. I couldn't brag that my second book was published, and I didn't think anyone cared about my articles. At the same time, I was aware of how black women were doing more administrative work on their campuses, putting their scholarship at risk, and leaving themselves vulnerable to the politics of citation, in which white women scholars were citing one another for theoretical and critical ideas and referring to the scholarship of black women in ways that contained their presence in experiential, rather than critical ways. I began to chafe under the reality that I was not the only one noticing this, and though I had white women scholars whose work I respected, I could not help but notice how this trend was changing the academy in what I thought were some problematic ways. How could our graduate students come to respect us as scholars if they didn't see our work? What if, as the late Barbara Christian suggested at one MLA meeting, the academy had taken our texts and left our bodies behind, citing the trend of letting changes in the curriculum suffice for an earlier commitment to affirmative action? What if, as Claudia Tate said, we were being

forced by our race and gender, especially on predominantly white campuses, to "present and represent the race"? What did this pressure do to
our writing?

I had no real answer for all these questions. In fact, I tucked them away
and continued to feel bogged down with everything. What I did know,
however, is that my research project was not going to go anywhere until
I addressed it, no matter how many distractions I let get in the way. One
Friday evening during the fall of 1995, I decided to clean my closet, my
bedroom, and my office as a prelude to my work on my Morrison project.
As a divorced woman, I had tried dating, but having been married for over
twenty-one years, I had few skills in that area, so the weekend became an
excellent time to do some work. To my surprise, however, about twenty
minutes into my cleaning, I grabbed a Post-It note and wrote three sentences. Where they came from, why they came then, why I felt a need to
write them down are still a mystery to me, but all I know is like divine
intervention, the magic had returned. Smiling with delightful self-satisfac-
tion, I returned to my cleaning. Then almost as suddenly as I had stopped
my cleaning before, I stopped again, went to the drawer where I kept my
journal, and sat on the bed to record the three sentences in a safe place,
realizing that if I did not record them, I might lose my Post-It note and
have no record of the inspiration that that pale yellow square piece of paper
contained. In that moment, my novel, "The Strawberry Room," was born,
and though it is not completed as I write this essay, it is well on its way.

For the first time in that moment, I confirmed what others had always
suspected about me: that I did indeed have a novel inside, that I did not
just teach literature, but that I too had a fantasy—no, a hidden desire that
I couldn't deny—to produce literature, and that I would eventually admit
it. Yet at that time, I was content that I had at least produced the seeds of
a novel. I was content to have a title and three sentences that had become
three pages. Where I would go from there I had no clue, but the fact that
it was safely tucked away in my journal reminded me that at the right time
I would return to it and give it more substance. The good news is that this
humble beginning was a moment of sheer magic. Referring to a moment
out of my own private life, I had wrapped it in language that gave it new
significance, that might communicate to a reader, especially if she were
a woman, some hint of the pain of marital trauma. But I knew the book

would do more than that whenever I got to it. Through the connection between the personal and the political, the private and the public, it would bear witness to a story of survival, not just of pain. Part of my survival strategy was marrying again and nurturing the seeds of creativity that I knew were in me.

But the recovery process would take another unexpected turn. Perhaps it was a new way of avoiding my research agenda, just as I sometimes thought was true of my "novel," but all I know is I began to view the crisis in my scholarship as an opportunity to look at the context in which I and other black women in the academy were doing our work. I received an invitation from Sharon Harley to join a Ford Foundation Grant project to study the meanings and representations of black women and work with a group of scholars at the University of Maryland and from other institutions in the Washington, DC, metropolitan area consortium. I finally had a place to explore, in collaboration with some other women scholars, the very complex set of issues that had my own writing on hold. For nearly three years we came together, presented our own draft essays, and listened to one another, recorded our sessions on tape, revised, revised, and revised some more. We found a publisher and produced our work in a volume published under the title *Sister Circle: Black Women and Work* (2002). One of the most significant rewards of my participation in that collective, however, was that it enabled me to give myself permission to write about what I needed to write about when I needed to write it, and to regard the process itself as empowering.

The most recent defining moment in my writing life has been the most significant moment in my life as a whole. Two days after the terrorist attacks on the World Trade Center and the Pentagon in 2001, I had an experience that rocked my world. Having shifted from signing e-mails with the words "peace and blessings," to "in a prayerful mood," I received a phone call from my mother to pray for my brother, Ben, who had had a serious eye injury. When he and I finally talked, I was relieved to learn that the seriousness of his injuries had been arrested in emergency hospital care, but I still believed prayer was in order. After I finished praying for him on the phone, he exclaimed, "goodness, Maril, you prayed like an evangelist." I blew off this comment with the words, "Aw, come on, get serious." He responded, "Okay just kidding," and we said our final greetings and ended the phone call. When I hung up the phone, however, I could not move. I felt as if I weighed a ton. Suddenly, I started weeping, silent, slow-flowing tears. I had no clue why I was crying. After about five minutes, I went next door to my husband's office and said, "Honey, something is happening to me. I can't say how or why, but the Lord is speaking to me and I'm afraid." His response was "You're getting the call." What made him say that, I'll never know, but I whispered, "David, you can't say that." He said, "Honey, why are you whispering?" I whispered my response, "Honey, I don't know." My husband then turned and wrote the words "Call to the Ministry" on his calendar. Suddenly I was angry, not whispering at all, when I said, "David, you can't write that on the calendar. I didn't say I was called to the ministry. Okay, so I think it's in the neighborhood, but I don't know what is happening to me."

Well, for a month I wrestled with what I now know is the call to the ministry. In October 2001, at the women's retreat for the women of my church, I attended the earliest prayer service, at which time one of the evangelists, Rev. Doris Crews, prayed me over the threshold from denial to acceptance. I keep the words to her prayer tucked away in my heart, but since that moment in October, I have fully embraced my calling. Having preached my initial sermon in February 2002 on the subject of putting first things first, I have now discovered what my work is for the rest of this journey we call life. The good news, however, is that my calling has empowered me to embrace the magic of writing, not give it up. When Joanne Gabbin invited me to return to my second visit with the Wintergreen Women Writers, I originally wasn't sure that I would read. I hadn't been able to work on "The Strawberry Room," thanks to a busy year of administration, the emotional turmoil of trying to understand what a call to the ministry would mean for my work, my marriage, and my life. But when the invitation to Wintergreen came, I pulled it out just to see where I was in the narrative. Having vacillated at one point as to whether it would be a collection of creative nonfiction essays, fiction, or scholarship on black women and divorce, I came to the understanding on that occasion that I could tell more of the truth with fiction. I began editing, revising, and writing, and before I knew it, the magic was there, moving my fingers on the keyboard, assuring me it would be safe to share my progress with my Wintergreen sisters. My novel would tell the truth of my life lessons through fiction.

In truth, it would be my testimony. Informed by the connection between head and heart, I was doing writing that was giving me sheer joy. As I prepared to go to Wintergreen, I remembered the day I went to get new tires put on my car, only to learn that an hour wait would be a three-hour wait. Undaunted, I went across the street, ordered a salad, and found a window full of sunlight. I took out my notepad and wrote for almost three hours, basking in the warmth of the sun and in the joy of writing through the lens of memory, experience, and imagination. When I finally got up to go across the street, I thought, I am finally a fiction writer, not just a scholar.

The beauty of my second trip to Wintergreen is that my sisters there confirmed my thoughts about myself as a writer. Warning me in language I could hear and learn from that it would be in my best interests to make a firm decision as to whether I was writing fiction or nonfiction, they helped me let go of the facts of my experience. As they encouraged me to continue to let my creative eye and intuitive ear lead me for the rest of the novel, I found myself open to their advice. Moreover, when they congratulated me on my calling to the ministry, I was relieved to be among sister writers who created a safe space for all the parts of me that needed expression, all the parts of me that I am. Ever since my graduate school days at New York University, my friend Linda Williamson Nelson had been that safe space where I could call any time of day and night, smack in the middle of a sentence, and ask absolutely anything about my writing. For my writing life, she has often been my best illustration of Jesus' reminder that "where two or three are gathered together in my name, there am I in the midst of them" (Matthew 18:20). Between us, we had always salvaged writing projects through the power of prayer, the oral tradition, and the ability to laugh at ourselves as we gave constructive critique. Wintergreen offered me a roomful of inspired readers and listeners, who understood my struggles with language and who offered themselves up as midwives. I left Wintergreen knowing I could finish "The Strawberry Room" and that there would be at least one group of women beyond me and Linda, an expanded circle of readers I could trust who would understand the head and heart connection my novel represented. The magic of writing came back at Wintergreen and I am grateful.

My writing days are now full of magic. I move easily between my scholarship and my novel, which has become a mosaic of fiction and nonfiction writing, working on both simultaneously one day, on one alone the next. I write notes on sermons no one has asked me to preach, and I see connections everywhere. Writing is a faith walk because, on any given day, I do not know where language will take me. The destiny, however, is not my concern when I pick up my pen and use the time between meditation and prayer to write in my journal. What I do know is I no longer have to avoid my writing. I no longer have to wonder whether I have anything to say or how I will make the shift between my life as an academic and my life as a fiction writer, or my life as a fiction writer and my life as a minister who writes. Thanks to the communities of women to which I have been welcomed and to my willingness to trust the voice of God within me that was urging me to connect head and heart, the magic is back. In my daily morning meditation, I have discovered new paths to faith, new connections to the sacred, and the power of writing, not only to heal, but also to sustain both my intellectual and my spiritual life. While the magic lasts, I plan to write my truth as plainly and as clearly as I know how, grateful for the power of the word to change hearts and minds, and to offer my own words of faith as a ray of hope.

Silence . . . A Dangerous Luxury

On My Return from Exile

—LINDA WILLIAMSON NELSON

In retrospect, it is easy to say that my identity as a writer was present in some embryonic form from very early on, during the teen years, at least, and likely in the making long before that. Although the trajectory of my writing life resists submission to discrete benchmarks, my written voice increased in volume from what felt like an imposition of silence to an increasingly amplified resistance. The early silence was the debt I believed I owed for not measuring up, based upon the sedimented shame that is foisted upon the social other. I really did not know this during those years when my words were constrained by homogeneity, purified for public consumption. However, I sensed that censure or silence was best, even though I felt fractured, separated from whom I knew myself to be. I believed I was safer in silence than in the telling of familial legacies that marked my marginality. Better silence than words that threatened to tell of angry people, courageous, but also prone to a narrow meanness which erupted periodically when the polite smiles and the tempered voices gave way to underlying rage or despair. I believed I had to leave them alone, words that is, or at least rein them in, until I fully recognized how such a choice could only encourage the continual erasure of the lives we knew.

My acquiescence to silence had little to do with any objective doubt of my ability to write; more likely, it reflected my latent recognition of the fundamental potential of words to challenge and inscribe an unauthorized and unruly truth. However, before I could work the craft in this singular and personal rebellion, I lived as if on foreign soil, as if exiled from my true home in words. But, I am really getting far ahead too soon. There is a beginning to all of this when I was still a child in the South Bronx.

It was the 1950s, and once the days grew shorter and colder, the afternoons were still and colorless. We lived one flight down in the basement apartment on Bathgate Avenue. Aside from homework, which, except for book reports, never seemed worth the trouble, the hours between three in the afternoon and bedtime seemed interminable. The television, once it came into the house, was no more than ten inches square, someone else's cast away, fixed and fumbled into semi-working order by my father. Although I could not have been more than eight years old, I can remember only two channels that delivered a discernible form. Watching took much more concentration than I was willing to spend for such a meager return. Books, paper, and pencil, on the other hand, could always deliver. With the former, I could try out new identities, prance around with seven dwarfs, an easy choice over waiting for some prince in white tights and a blouson. Alice, too, had considerable appeal, particularly since she chatted with a Cheshire cat who smoked a pipe like my father's. Not long after, once I found them, Huck Finn and Jim were just my style; they, too, appeared to float outside the world they were taught to accept without question. Moreover, they were no better able than I to articulate an alternate view. Like Huck and Jim, I could envision no freedom upriver. However, I could navigate the hills of Crotona Park and imagine real monkeys inhabited the trees of Monkey Island adjacent to the Bronx Zoo. I have no idea how this expanse of trees and brush became known as Monkey Island since the closest uncaged monkeys were hundreds of miles across the southern latitudes. That did not prevent me, however, from seeing the primates swing from tree to tree high above my head as I crossed a small waterfall by foot, risking limbs or worse.

The paper and pencil offered another route altogether. My mother mostly had that shiny onionskin, on which she wrote lengthy letters, numbered meticulously one through sometimes eight or nine pages, to her mother and siblings in Jamaica. It had to be airmail paper, she told us, lightweight, so it could be carried easily on the planes which took it "home" to Meadsfield, Jamaica, which was then BWI. Therefore, when she ripped off one or even two sheets, I appreciated the sacrifice and had to use them slowly and well. Mother encouraged me to write letters myself, or if

I couldn't be convinced, word lists and stories appeased her and prompted her encouragement for me to "keep it up, keep it up." Within our "narrow financial straits," as my mother elegantly put it, I knew she could never offer a material reward for anything I produced on those pages, no matter how unanticipated or clever. Nonetheless, the enthusiasm in her voice and her patience in deciphering my childlike meanings told me that my words mattered. Her admonition to "keep it up" carried a vague promise that something good would come of this.

For a long while, I was satisfied with her breathy "oohs and aahs" that settled over my words as she read them aloud. However, by the time I was finishing grade school, she would interrupt her hyperbolic praise to resume the role she abandoned on a red clay hill in Meadsfield. The pupil teacher of long ago would surface again, as she would gently push me to fix the spelling and say more of this or that. "Build it up some," she chided. It was decades later that I would hear her again in my own voice as I coached my writing students to "tell me more." Mother seemed to intuit that our kitchen table tutorials would lift me out of that basement apartment, past the boiler room, the dumbwaiter, and the coal bin, and let me down in a gentler place. It was in this way, under the sound of her relentless urging to "keep it up," that I began to form a relationship with words on the page that promised to resist the containment of my blackness and femaleness.

My family stood between two distinct worlds of material scarcity and literate abundance. While meaningful work eluded my father, a former Mississippi sharecropper with only a third-grade education, my mother, a Jamaican woman with a penchant for writing poetry and reading British novels, hoped to find in America the means to earn money enough to build a home in Jamaica. Instead she and my father grew a family of five children while their earning capacity never approached the needs of seven people. Although the icebox was nearly empty, Mother sought to nourish our appetites for words. She dared not send her children to school without first teaching them to read, write, and sign legibly for our own library cards. By five years old, we all passed her muster.

In these early memories, I was never without books. Mother must have known that if I worked at it my words could tell a larger truth. However, as a child, I had no idea that there was a larger truth to tell.

The world that both fascinated and frightened me was awhirl in contradictions, forming an ironic kaleidoscope of have and have-nots, joined inevitably but unwillingly by their inescapable need for each other. In the eyes of my innocence, I simplistically saw two kinds of people, divided by color and status, which marked a series of high and low correspondences. We were the super's family, living in subterranean rooms of the tenement building that my father tended. Our nearest neighbors were the coal bin and the roaring furnace, which was fed with the glistening black rocks, pushed in a wheelbarrow by Father to its gaping mouth twice or more a day. If he drank one quart too many of his favored Schlitz, sleep would overtake him and he'd fail to stoke the furnace. Upon feeling the cold seep in, the upstairs tenants would take to marking their complaints with incessant banging on the pipes—a routine mechanism of alerting the super to his dereliction. Having endured this expression of their anger for so many years, for us, the word "tenant" became the mark of the enemy. When tenants weren't ranting through the pipes, Father was busy unloading the garbage they packed carelessly, or so it seemed, onto the dumbwaiter. Potato peels and grimy beef fat clung to floor sweepings, the medley having escaped from the brown paper bags intended to contain it. This was Father's employment and proof of the consequence of limited schooling. Behind the peep-holed apartment doors, which opened into the marbled hallways, the tenants sat on soft, paisley sofas, (at least in my mind's eye), safe from the threatening roar of the furnace, which Mother feared would "one day blow us all to Kingdom come!" Each Saturday morning, finished before ten o'clock, my father would mop the marble floors before the landlord came to collect his rent and to make sure the ledger balanced out.

When at P.S. 58 we were called upon to write about the profession of our fathers, as some elementary school teachers required of us, I would embellish my father's routine responsibility to touch up apartment paint jobs to Painting Contractor, in spite of the fact that my mother assured me that being a superintendent was honest work. While I never doubted the fundamental truth of her words, I also knew it would not be the subject of my fifth-grade composition. It would be many years before I could reconcile my understanding of words as valuable commodities with the imperative of naming my everyday truth.

It was still permissible for teachers in the nineteen fifties and sixties to require students to write about personal family matters. "What did your mother make for dinner?" "What kind of work does your father do?" Although likely not the case, these seemed directed at me, with a rising into-nation on the word "your" in the phrase "your father." The teacher suspected my secret and wanted to expose me for what I was, another poor black kid on home relief. My shame about the world I intimately knew led me away from that world to inhabit, in words, safe and sanitary spaces far from home. Ironically, words would carry me home again, but only after I learned that boiler rooms and coal bins held stories that wanted telling, too.

I moved into adolescence listening to mother's lyrical verse, as she called it, while she stretched the cornmeal porridge and rice and beans "as far as they could go." All the while, language in all its mysterious and pliable potential, Jamaican Standard and Mississippi Black Vernacular, filled the basement, the rooming house, and the eventual housing project apartment we called home. In my early teens, as the youngest of five, I was in the center of a nearly continuous stream of impassioned words. Between vitriolic complaints, we tried to feed each other with explanations of our condition as Negroes and later, Afro-Americans. We tied strategies for survival to success in practical studies, like secretarial work and my sisters' choices of the co-op course—work a week, go to classes a week. It seemed as if the spoken and then the written word became, for me, a way to ease the sting of lack that defined our lives.

By the high school years, English teachers praised my prose, and in my tenth-grade language arts class, Miss Greshen publicly announced that I would write short stories one day. Though she reached this conclusion without my knowledge or approval, I accepted the pronouncement as one of the first public validations of my written work. By this time, I was con-vinced of the potential cooperation and resiliency of words. I discovered that I could rebound and stand upright in the written word. There was a place for me in language even as I mostly evaded the unpleasant realities of my life. This was specifically true of poetry, for it wrestled me away from verbal drama and emotive expansion, insisting as it does on words, sparse and clean. Not that I could say in truth that I achieved this. In retrospect, the verses I wrote at fourteen or fifteen were far more committed to effusive sentiment than to form, but they were, nonetheless, patient and receptive to the rapid rise and fall of a young girl's search for a witness to her truth. These were the earliest days when I began to speak aloud of my plan to teach English and to define myself as a writer.

Of course, all defining moments are not equal. Most that choose to write soon discover that few paths if any are congenial and even. For quite some time, mine was largely an uncertain passageway, meandering around foothills large enough to block my view. I eventually learned the importance of the listening stillness, when to stop and when to push ahead, to choose one path over another as I moved over landscapes, guided by my peculiar vision.

Though I began to admit a correspondence between the writing need and lived experience, early recognition came to me for my ability to manipulate the public language of power to write and speak forcefully of the world that seemed to hold merit. By the time I entered the university, it was the mid-sixties and I was less reluctant to write from what I knew experientially. The teachers enthusiastically guided me through my rites of passage, teaching me the rules of the cabal of letters. They guided me to the elegance of Faulkner, Dickinson, and the Playwright of Stratford on Avon.

However steeped in the canons of European culture, we were by now at the crest of the Black Nationalist movement and civil rights activists incited my interest in more than the master narratives. Seeming too insignificant now to warrant merit, my very first published piece, a small poem, "Black Mother," in an obscure magazine of the arts, was public confirmation at the time of my status as a writer. Those days, when I left the university classroom in downtown Brooklyn, I found myself in the bookstores in Harlem and Bedford Stuyvesant, hungrily combing the stacks for the paperback editions of Sonia Sanchez, Nikki Giovanni, and LeRoi Jones. I had already read some Baldwin, and one of the two or three additional African American students majoring in English at my university passed me his copy of Toomer's *Cane* and Du Bois's *Souls of Black Folk*. Under the tutelage of these writers, I began to envision vaguely another landscape, one upon which I could write about people who knew my father's blues. I recall those being perhaps the most painful years, the years when the poetry that came to me was filled with tears and mourning, for our collective losses as well as our resilience.

My need to write was incessant though fraught with so much anguish at times that I would only write when the discomfort of not writing would threaten to cut off my breath. Words on the page would provide the only available relief. I crafted each line over and again until I could satisfy the urgency to *see* what I meant. Yet I was still the only audience, for the most part, except for one or two pieces, in the hands of a friend, which slipped out of hiding and found their way to the public eye.

Then and for a long time after, I was still fighting an amorphous, visceral discomfort that all but restrained my writing hand each time I approached the desk. I now recognize the large and lingering fear as an outgrowth of the long-ago coal cellar womb that spawned my social consciousness. I was still restrained by a fear of telling, for I must have sensed then what I know now. Writers, honest and worthy ones, do not allow their pens to tell a lie except to clarify their truth. However, for me this was not entirely possible; I could not forget that many years before we were sworn to secrecy. "It's nobody's business," Mother's warning reiterated. No one need know what we ate or that we lined our see-through shoe bottoms with linoleum, cut to resemble Dr. Scholl's inserts. No one needs to know what we knew. At the bottom of the strata, in a land of profit, plenty, and purported mobility, those who failed to thrive were simply unworthy. No one ever said this, but all the signs were there.

It was only decades later that I would come to understand the irony underlying my resistance to writing for an audience beyond myself. Although I was blocked by inhibitions born out of my sense of shame, my written voice would have to legitimate the very experiences that I learned not to tell. It would only be in telling that we could disrupt the hegemonies that counted us out. My fear, however, was not a fear of self-expression in any all-encompassing sense. My fear was hardly recognizable as such, as I easily fulfilled the assignments of graduate school and enjoyed the facility I gained in explicating the words of the masters in literary, and later, anthropological studies. It was more a deeply embedded and nameless apprehension that grew in direct proportion to the degree to which my writing approached the subject of America's ethnic minorities, women, and the economic underclass. In this way the silence in not writing sustained my personal exile, for I was divorced in my own written, public language from what I knew as home.

With the publication of an essay on dialectal code switching in writing, "On Writing My Way Home: Finding My Authentic Voice in the Academy," I located my own linguistic history in the British tinctured Jamaican Standard English of my mother and the Mississippi Delta, creolized Black Vernacular of my father which still sings of the African past. In the former, I saw the way others listened; in the latter, there was no public currency, but value and poetic beauty, nonetheless. In that essay, I named my multifaceted, diasporic inheritance and left the place of exile and silence. I was on my way home. I began to accept that I could write creatively and analytically about my culture and class of origin. Moreover, I believed I would do nothing I could deeply value if I could not write of these things. The conceit of my metaphor of exile suggests the solemnity and drama of this alienation from what I believed to be my truest word. I wanted to situate my work on a native landscape where my inquiries could contribute to a more complex interrogation of social relations in America than my early education had granted me. Others who lived as I did should not believe their own silence was the unavoidable price of the degradation they suffered, that they were taught to regard as their own doing.

In time, I came to know more and more about the systematic ways in which women, people of color, and the poor are taught to collude in their own silence. The social hierarchies in our homes and schools, reflected in the iconography of most media, seemed to conspire to maintain our silence. Fortunately, my growing awareness and discomfort was quickly taking on significance much larger than myself. I was only one small voice in many vast, global communities, linked by the common experience of political and economic disenfranchisement and fundamental outsider status in relation to the centers of power and cultural domination. Further, there were by now so many on my side that I could recognize, though they had been there all along, those who had resisted fear and isolation by staying home in their words. They had successfully described the various forms of outsider status and their particularized struggles, in order to overcome them in labor markets, in educational systems, and elsewhere. Accepting my exile was a luxury I could no longer afford. I needed to send out my words so that they might not only construct a narrative but also elicit a response crafted from the organic rudiments of the same cultural knowledge out of which others had written.

From the late eighties to the mid-nineties, as I researched and wrote my doctoral dissertation on the thematic content and cultural codes in life narratives of African American women, I had fully emerged as a scholar and writer. I had crossed the threshold and had begun to focus on the political economy of language choices in general, and culturally constructed cues in Black Vernacular, in particular. The positive reception to my essays on dialectal code switching, and to my discussion of indigenous anthropology in the essay titled "Hands in the Chit'lins: Notes of Native Anthropological Research among African American Women," solidified my shift from timidity to courage. Having returned from exile, I could challenge the knowledge that passes for the only truth. Because I am one of many thousands who read the same signs, and know them for having been reared in them as well, my self-knowledge is inextricably bound to my association with others. Acquiescing to this knowledge, I came out of silence and accepted the significance of my stories and my representation of others like me.

The very circumstances that compel me to write have been the ones that separated me from my most meaningful work. In retrospect the exile, as I am calling it, was useful, for it forced me to recognize that silence is a dangerous luxury. While I felt safely clothed outside my stories, in that place I was restless and agitated. I was choosing exile over the fear of sanctions, for it must have been that just below the surface of consciousness lay the old uncertainty of the legitimacy of our lived knowledge as African Americans and as women. I chose a form of silence over writing, and the silence was as mournful as any forced separation from home. But exile was too painful and far too dear. I had to choose disorder. I had to come home. I had to write.

Of History and Healing

—JANUS ADAMS

The first time I ventured onto the civil rights battlefield, I was eight years old. In the wake of the Supreme Court's 1954 *Brown v. Board of Education* school desegregation decision, I was one of the four test children selected to break New York City's *de facto* segregated "neighborhood school plan." One morning, just outside my new school, an adult raged at my trespassing on what I saw as school and she claimed as turf. She spat at me and tore my dress. I spent the entire school day like that—ripped apart, outside and within.

"What happened to you was mean and wrong," my parents consoled that night. Taking extra care to soothe the day's wounds, my mother and father drew me close, lathered me in bubble bath, softly brushed my hair, smoothed my tiny furrowed brow, and laid me to sleep in their tourniquet of love. "We are a people of struggle," they said, in the language of generations. The four of us—a battalion of eight- and nine-year-olds that included my cousin, Ted, and me—were courageous children, they said. "We're so proud of you. What you're doing is good for our people, 'good for the race.'"

"Just like Mrs. Tubman?" I asked. African American history and the Diaspora were mainstays of our home even then.

"Yes."

"Just like Frederick Douglass?"

"Yes, baby. Like Marcus Garvey. Like Granny Nanny of the Maroons. And, just like Rosa Parks, too."

Mrs. Parks was our newest hero. Her refusal to give over her seat to racism launched the Montgomery bus boycott that brought a young Dr. Martin Luther King Jr. world acclaim. Transferring schools two months into the boycott, I didn't yet know if it would succeed. But, I knew that Black folk united had dared say "no!" and that was a victory in itself. Sitting down like Mrs. Parks meant standing up to those who were "mean and wrong." That was something I wanted to do. The next day I went back to school armored. I walked a gauntlet of White hate shielded by my bunker.

Painful as those civil rights movement years were, it was a hopeful time. It filled us with possibility—a sense of power over our destiny. A new day was dawning, we dared believe, super-patriots that we were. Who else would risk their lives and the lives of their children for a promise and a dream?

As an undergraduate attending college in upstate New York, I realized that my campus had more African foreign students than African Americans. A top math student, I was a real blow to my calculus professor's comfort-level. He publicly accused me of cheating off my classmates, then posted himself at my elbow for the next few exams until my anxiety soared and my grades plummeted from a disturbing A+ to a satisfying C.

Who could I turn to for redress back then? That's what it meant to be a First, Second, Third, even Twenty-Third. It meant isolation and alienation. I changed my major from math to theater and moved on. Years later, the thought hit me: "He must have thought me pretty good to know which answer to cheat from which lesser student." As grateful as I was to achieve that insight (even though I didn't realize I was still seeking it), it was like putting a Band-Aid on a sore left twenty years to fester. By then the wound was too deep for a mere Band-Aid.

It's amazing how naive I was back then—how I thought to brandish excellence as a shield—convinced that once others knew how good I was they'd accept me. I didn't know the name of the game was power, or that this was by any means necessary. My parents only wanted the best for me—a best that brought risk. But, considering the times, what other options did they have? They didn't know to tell me that the problem wasn't being Black; it was racism and the Doctrine of White Supremacy. And what they didn't know, they weren't able to apply to the racial wounds their child suffered.

Along with the progress made over time, that legacy of hurt is one I, like most African Americans, still struggle to heal.

Still in college, having changed my major, I was racing rain-slick side streets from a late-night rehearsal to my off-campus housing when a state car pulled up next to me. Why was I out past curfew? Didn't I know the danger? Get in; he'd take me home. We were there in minutes. As I angled myself out the car door, thanking him, he grabbed me between my legs, pulled me back into the car and sped off with the car door flapping. He cuffed my neck with one hand, driving with the other. When he slowed for a turn, I stabbed him with my umbrella and escaped.

Running back to the house, I arrived hysterical. My house mother called the state police. They were supportive until I gave a description of my assailant: a White man in a gray suit with a slight sheen to it; his dark, wavy hair brushed back; brown/black attaché case in the backseat.

"Why, you whore!" they glared. They weren't going to ruin a good man's life for "some little whore" like me.

That weekend, my mother and my aunt drove up to school. My aunt's first words: "What did you do to attract that man?" My mother sent her outside.

"What happened to you was terrible," Mom began, in those tones cultivated over decades of striving. But, there was nothing she could do. If she challenged the police, she feared I'd be a target and would really get hurt. I could transfer out, but that would mean credits lost, an extra year of school—and an extra year's tuition that we could ill-afford since my father's untimely death.

I took to my bunker and survived.

Degree in hand, I entered the world of work as the first African American in Saks Fifth Avenue's elite executive training program. I was at Saks the night Dr. King was assassinated. I arrived at work the next day dressed in mourning—winter white wool dress, shoes, white rabbit fur coat. Naive, I was a walking target. Steps from the employee entrance, police dragged me toward the gutter, accusing me of looting my own coat in the riots that gripped the nation the night before. An officer seized my purse. "Match my license to the monogram in my coat," I told him. "Smart one, huh." When he found a car registration with a different name, he had me. "The car is registered to my mother," I struggled as his partner handcuffed me.

Totally unaware, a White colleague whisked by with a casual, "Hi, Janus!" and disappeared inside. "You see, they know me here," I pleaded. "I work here." I'd wanted to say "I belong here," but I knew better—so did they. Arms pinned behind me, I was a criminal for all to see. They shoved me up to the personnel office for official identification where I was set loose, but hardly set free. In this New York, I was a Black girl in fashion, but not in vogue.

My family commiserated with the injustice. "You've had opportunities and used them well. Now, you get to show the world who we are as a people," they said. It was the duty-honor-country speech given every warrior. "When you have the ability, you have the response-ability," Mom prodded, quoting her Garveyite dad. "That's why we're put in these situations. A less fortunate Black person in the same predicament would be rotting in jail. But, a passerby waved, 'Hi Janus!' They'll think twice the next time," said Mom. "The police learned something today."

So did I, I thought, freshening up my bunker.

On vacation that August, I was strolling the eucalyptus walk at Mills College in Oakland, California, with a cousin when the Dean of Students ran up to ask if I'd like to attend Mills. Making me an offer I couldn't refuse, I enrolled two weeks later. As Mills's first Black graduate student, I had a full tuition-free assistantship, but my tenure was hardly without cost.

The phone would ring. It would be the dean. "You know that lovely little green Donald Brooks you have [a couturier suit from my Saks wardrobe], wear that today, would you? Mrs. So-and-So is coming to tea." With such command performances, I later learned I was the whipping post to which the few Black undergrads were being tethered. "Why don't you dress like, speak like, act like Janus?" No wonder they wouldn't talk to me. When I found out, I asked the dean why she'd invited me if we were all to be treated like that. "I knew you were the one," said she. "I'd never before seen a Black girl in white kid gloves."

That semester, across the bay at San Francisco State University, the cry went out: Black Studies! Relevance! The dean who'd brought me to campus ran the walk hysterical, "The Panthers are on campus! The Panthers are on campus!" By December, I exchanged my designer chic for dress-down slacks; my straightened hair for a natural. Encouraged by courageous faculty members, I changed my concentration from music to Pan-African culture, eventually earning what is considered the nation's first graduate degree in Black studies.

Flying home to New York for the Christmas vacation, still just twenty-one, I desperately needed my mom's laughing embrace. In the airport terminal, face to face, she looked directly at me and moved away, still searching for her daughter. So dramatically had my look and outlook changed that year that my own mother didn't recognize me.

A spiritual message from the ancestors recounts the price paid by those who escape from slavery to freedom:

> *I told Jesus, be all right*
> *If He changed my name . . .*
> *He said your mother won't know you child*
> *If I change your name . . .*

In 1968, my name got changed, and my mother didn't know her only child.

Considering these incidents, these race and gender "firsts," I now realize how formative they were. But, you don't know these things at eight or eighteen, or even twenty-eight. While they're happening, you don't notice how such experiences contort your sense of self. Somewhere along the way, I began to confuse acknowledging abuse as the price paid by generations in the struggle with accepting abuse as the price paid for life's basics: going to school, taking classes, entering the workplace and even, eventually, starting a family.

By 1975, having worked in television news and been honored with a special Emmy as a writer, I was hosting my own radio show heard daily throughout the Northeast. Named National Public Radio's first Arts Correspondent, I found my sojourn at NPR was not without its racial land mines. But, unknown to my colleagues, the real battle I faced was at home.

Married, I was the mother of twin daughters and a stepson. My husband was a celebrated musician; we were guests of the White House, feted in foreign capitols. Our marriage seemed the All-American Dream. It was a nightmare. I was pregnant the first time he hit me. Over the next twelve years, his battering only escalated.

With all I appeared to have going for me, professionally, why did I stay in that abusive marriage so long? Because I didn't know how to leave; because—crazy as it sounds—I still felt bound by the mission. "If a 'successful' Black family can't make it . . . ," I heard myself stumble at a particularly vulnerable spot, "what will White folks think?" This from a woman who certainly knew better than that.

Forged in childhood, borne out in adulthood, this was my history; the values staked in youth that trailed me into womanhood.

A turning point came in that stifling summer of 1994 when however hot the day, the last thing you wanted was more O.J. The O. J. Simpson case was in-your-face, in-your-head terror, violence, threat, 24/7. Tellingly, the coverage wasn't about saving women from battering or deterring men from being batterers, it was about race and sex in America. And because it was more titillation than salvation, quiet as it's kept, many women experienced severe trauma that summer; sleeplessness and other more revealing symptoms. I know. I was one of them.

A routine visit to my doctor one July day erupted into molten lava of long-suppressed memories. A nurse had made flippant mention of my being "silly" and "oversensitive" about my privacy. I was sensitive; she was rude. Within moments, a cauldron of images, more throwback than flashback, sent me reeling. The terror was so palpable I felt my inner self sliding away. Day's end found me crouched into a fetal ball inside my bedroom closet. How had I come to this emotional state?

Ironically, though, I was a historian. My history was dragging me under. I would soon proudly write the *Glory Days* of our African Diaspora; the herstory of our *Sister Days*. But, my own little link on that eternal chain was weighing me down.

For years I'd been able to resist being sucked under by the quicksand of painful memories that seized me from time to time. I had children to raise, work to do, places to go, worlds to conquer. Now, in this O.J. summer, my daughters were grown, conquering worlds of their own; my defenses were gone. Hours passed before I found my way out of that closet. Days passed before I could leave the house. For months I walked in a haze.

"When you lose your way," a friend told me, "sometimes it's best to go back to the beginning." We were talking music, writing, creativity. It seemed good counsel for life. It was a concept to which the historian in me—the African in us both—could relate. *Sankofa:* an Akan word meaning "to go forward, one must go back."

When, at last, I ventured out, I went back—mentally, emotionally— retracing the years that had brought me to that day I'd sunk so low that I crawled into a closet and almost died inside. With time, I understood that my closet—my bunker—had been planned and secured long before that summer. The first time I crawled in I was eight years old entering my elementary school—Mrs. Parks in the lead, Marcus Garvey and Granny Nanny alongside, Frederick Douglass and Harriet Tubman watching my back. But now the time had come to turn from history to healing.

Call it my personal epiphany.

When storm damage forced me to take stock of the surrounding woods, I studied the paths around me, seeking to uncover the mysteries of replenishing my soil. In working the soil, I began to understand the passion of trees to come back from the dead of winter to start each spring anew. As I reconfigured the view, I refreshed my point of view. Nature tells us what to do—if we're ready to listen.

It was while writing my book, *Freedom Days,* that I discovered Dr. W. E. B. Du Bois's essay "Separation and Self Respect." In 1934, twenty years before the *Brown* school desegregation decision that forged my life, Du Bois wrote:

> *A Black man born in Boston has a right to oppose any separation of schools by color, race or class. But this Black man in Boston has no right . . . to send his own helpless immature children into school where White children kick, cuff or abuse him, or where teachers openly and persistently neglect or hurt or dwarf his soul.*

Oh, the circles we make—the moving forward and sliding back.

More than a half century later, in that life-changing summer, *mi Sankofa,* my mind went back, retracing my roots—and routes; to the mission my elders had nurtured in me. I was a First: a member of the Integration Generation; a foot soldier enlisted to break barriers of race and gender bias on every front. From *Brown* to that summer day, I had built my bunker high and wide—the better to survive each onslaught.

Wounded by the struggle, a beneficiary of the struggle, I do not regret my life of "firsts" or the price paid. I feel gratified by the opportunity and its sense of empowerment. Yet, as important as it is to forge our history, it is as vital to honor the personal.

The breakdown I suffered that summer may have been my healthiest moment in years. It was the moment my "me" rebelled against its continued suppression. For the first time since I was eight, I said *No* to abuse, *No* to violence and humiliation, and I would not be talked out of it.

In that recovery of self I learned that healing, too, is "good for the race."

ALAMEDA FREE LIBRARY

The Conscientious Outsider

—CAMILLE DUNGY

I had only been back from Ghana for about a week. I was try-ing to relax. We were supposed to be playing ping-pong, but I found myself explaining to a well-intentioned questioner (whose mother was of Irish decent and who was hoping to be able to enjoy with me the experience of being Irish American) that I was probably a little bit Irish, but that there wasn't much of a record of when or how that ancestry made its way into my blood. Yes, Dungy is an Irish name. My middle name, Thornton, is Scotch. In fact, all the surnames on both sides of my family are Scotch or Irish. But the surnames in my family, I explained across the ping-pong table, are a legacy of the fact of the sheer number of men who emigrated from the United Kingdom to the slave-holding South. I reminded my ping-pong buddy that my ancestors were likely owned by, and perhaps fathered by, the men who gave them names like Dungy, Thornton, Mickens, and Meadors.

We were only playing ping-pong. He was just trying to make conver-sation. I think the sudden history lesson came as something of a surprise. But, for the conscientious outsider (which is how I am thinking of myself these days), life is a perpetual lecture hall.

I was on leave from my regular teaching position, just back from an extended trip to Africa, and staying for a month on a New York estate that served as an artists' retreat. The idea is that a person goes to such a retreat or colony, as they are often called, to get away from the things that typically pester her in life: insistent phone calls, cooking, dusting, preparing for class.

Within the grounds there is a carefully constructed atmosphere of tranquility under the influence of which an artist is free to create. I was there to focus solely on writing some poems. That was the idea anyway, but in my experience as a conscientious outsider, teaching moments are nearly impossible to avoid. A few days before the ping-pong conversation there was the dinner conversation my lesbian friend refers to as "the one where I was backed into a corner like a hissing, feral beast." Talk about a lecture hall.

When two of my fellow colony guests began to talk over dinner about *The Hours*, I stayed mum. For one thing, they were talking to each other, not to me. Furthermore, I was on a retreat, and I didn't feel like putting any energy into explaining why I didn't see the film or read the book. I'll tell you now, from everything I'd seen, heard, and read, the story struck me as slightly overwrought and, well, white, and I hadn't mustered the mood or time to care about it. But it's hard to explain to a table full of white folks that sometimes I'm just not interested in spending time or money on films and books that focus on the melancholy of the white experience.

Let's not call her "my lesbian friend." The other is always identified by that which sets her outside the norm. I don't want to follow that convention. Let's give her a name. Let's call her Seattle.

Seattle hadn't seen the film either. Her reasons for not having done so were more carefully reasoned than mine, a fact I learned because she was pressed to justify her position to all six of her fellow colony guests. This despite the fact that her initial proclamation of disinterest in the film had been made in the context of a dialogue with one other person. We'll call him DuPont Circle.

Opening her conversation to the table, Seattle laid out the basic reasons she had not seen the film, several of which had to do with the film's representations of lesbians. In a point related to her argument, Seattle asked us to name ten publicly lesbian actors working prominently in Hollywood today. We came up with Ellen DeGeneres and Rosie O'Donnell. Seattle said, "I'd like to point out that neither one of those women was comfortable coming out publicly until she had solidified her career. Still, that's two. I asked for ten names." No one had anyone else to add. "I'll make it easy on you, just give me three more." People mentioned Jody Foster but, of course, she's not out.

"But Los Angeles is totally progressive! Are you trying to suggest that Hollywood is closed to gays and lesbians?" asked a writer from Long Island.

"I'm just looking at the numbers," said Seattle. "Tell you what. You're a writer. Name some lesbian writers whose work gets talked about these days."

There were six actively publishing writers at the table. The poet from the North of England knew no one, DuPont Circle named two authors, and I nodded to second Pacific Palisades's nominee. That brought us to a total of three names.

"I haven't heard of any of those people," said our girl from Long Island.

"My point exactly!" Seattle pounded her fist on the table, thinking she had confirmed something.

I felt vindicated in my disinterest in a film about three middle (to upper middle) class white women. My indifference to other people's anxieties was not, apparently, unique. The general lack of knowledge the table betrayed about lesbian literature and film confirmed my suspicion that Americans often don't care much about the things that concern people who aren't like them. The difference, as Seattle's situation made clear, is that, whereas the conscientious outsider will likely expend some thought and care justifying her reasons for not seeing a film that (mainstream) critics and audiences agree is the film of the season, the mainstream masses don't bother with realities that don't concern them. They needn't waste their time.

Consider a friend of mine who, three weeks into the fall semester of his second year in a creative writing graduate program, found himself so dejected he felt compelled to interrupt my leave and call me at the artists' retreat. "Half my poetry craft class has dropped. Half! Today, I overheard one guy repeat three times that he *would have* dropped except the class was 'stupid and easy' and so he was going to stick around."

The course was being taught by a young-appearing African American woman who boasted, among her many qualifications, several books, a Guggenheim, a faculty post at an Ivy League institution, numerous teaching awards, and a position on the Board of Governors of the American Poetry Society. Her syllabus consisted primarily of books by black women writers. My friend was relatively certain that most of the people, all white and mostly male, who had dropped the class had done so because they just couldn't stand to be, as he termed it, "decentered." A Sister was teaching a class about writing by Black women. Clearly, the content would be "stupid and easy," if not downright unworthy of the time it would require to even sit through the lecture. What could Black women possibly teach about the craft of poetry?

Back in the colony's dining room, our friend from Long Island adds perspective. "Maybe no one's talking about these writers because they're not any good." She was certain this explained her (give it a name) ignorance. If a thing hadn't crossed her threshold of experience, it must not be worth noticing. She took a large bite of pie and smiled through pink lipstick.

I uttered my first words of the evening, which were something like, "Christ Almighty!" and left the table under the guise of returning my plates to the kitchen.

When I came back, the seventh member of our company, a composer from Brooklyn Heights, was beginning to understand Seattle's point. "This is sort of like Blacks in Hollywood. For so long there were so few and the only roles they could play were maids."

"No black woman has played a maid in a movie for, like, twenty years," said Mrs. Long Island.

In my normal life as a professor I give lectures on the representation of Black women in American film. I had numbers and films to dispute her claim. But I was at an artists' retreat, not in the classroom. I was supposed to be able to get away from my normal life. Why should I have to be the expert tonight?

"Maybe not maids exactly," said Brooklyn Heights, "but the point is that there was a limited opportunity for many years and that limited opportunity meant that there was a limited scope of representation for blacks. Isn't that right?" He turned to me.

Brooklyn Heights was on the path Seattle had tried to pave, but things could turn against her again at any moment.

"Help me out here," Seattle pleaded.

There's no way around it. When you are the only one at the table, eventually they will always turn to you. "Right," I said.

It had been barely five days since I'd completed the twenty-eight hours of travel that returned me from Ghana. I was still jet lagged. I was feeling a little queasy even before the conversation began. I wanted to make as short work of my involvement as possible. "Sure," I continued.

"What are you talking about?" Long Island was incredulous. "There is a load of opportunity available to Black people in Hollywood today! Didn't Halle Berry just win an Oscar?"

In my course on the representation of Black women in America, I give a whole lecture investigating the fact that the only three Oscars to be awarded to Black women in the history of the prize had been for roles in which the women were conduits for the love lives and redemption of white people. (This was before Jennifer Hudson, who had the opportunity to serve as a conduit for the love life and redemption of light and lovely Beyoncé Knowles.) I gave a mini-version of this lecture that night.

"But Black people are the mainstay of popular American culture. The movies, hip-hop, everything. Everybody wants to be a part of Black culture. Everybody loves it. Both my sons are dying to be black."

There was too much in Long Island's statement for me to tackle at once. Defeated, I sat with what I thought was a blank face.

"Why are you blinking your eyes at me that way?" She was a mother after all. I'm sure she was well used to identifying faces like mine: contempt in the guise of indifference.

"Give them two days as a black person," I suggested. "See what they think after that."

I was full of fear for these boys from Long Island. They had no idea what they were hoping to get into. And how could they? When did they first start noticing black people, and when they noticed us, what was it they thought they discovered? When and how and why did they embrace black as something they wanted to be? Where do you see Black people in the US media these days?

After my first three weeks in Ghana, I found myself in a house with a satellite television system tuned to CNN. After watching the US news for over an hour, I flipped to a local station and caught the end of a Ghanaian commercial wherein a big-boned black woman walked into a room and every man whistled in admiration. At this point, I realized what had been odd about watching the US network after several weeks away from Western

TV. Hitherto, the only television I had watched in Ghana had been either the news broadcast each evening by Ghana TV or Big Brother Africa (there were eight contestants left when I started watching, only one of whom was white). The images I saw in television programs, commercials, billboards, and magazines were almost exclusively black, and I could wander around the city for several days without seeing a European face. Outside of the historical context that can't be ignored in a former Portuguese, Dutch, and British colony, it got so I hardly thought about white people. I loved it when people spoke to me in Twi, assuming I would understand the local language. What a relief it was to see people like me at every turn, not to be the obvious outsider for a change. What had been odd about watching the US network after several weeks away from Western TV. There was nothing but white people on CNN.

When you belong, you forget the totality of otherness, the way that being other pervades every aspect of a person's life. My name, for instance, my taste in films, the things I choose to write about, all are influenced by the particular position (or number of positions) I occupy in American culture. My otherness manifests itself in what I eat, what I watch, what I read, what lipstick I can wear.

"Look," I said. I was in the conversation now. I might as well try to help Seattle prove her point. "I am the only Black person at this table, which means that I become the representative of Blackness here."

"I don't see you as *a black woman*. You're just who you are," Long Island's nod of support suggested that Pacific Palisades had taken the words from between her pink-glossed lips.

I've made the readjustment almost completely now, I wrote a friend after I'd been back from Africa awhile. *I am feeling very American again.* Being home means being able to predict the direction an argument will take.

I am certainly who I am (an ornery individual at the moment), though I take umbrage at the idea of limiting my scope with a word like "just" when it is used to suggest I am a simple person. If I may borrow a phrase from the great poet of our early democracy, "I am large. I contain multitudes." "Just" in that context erases various complexities and dimensions of my being. There is a certain danger in refusing to, or tacitly agreeing not to, recognize my black womanness. Black womanness is part of what makes me the unique individual I am. To claim you do not see that aspect of my personhood and insist, instead, that you see me as a "regular person" suggests that in order to see me as "regular" some parts of my individual identity must be nullified. Namely, the parts that aren't like you. I'd made this argument before. I made it again.

"The fact of the matter is that I am the only person of color at this table. The fewer people there are to represent a particular segment of a population, the less likely it is that accurate, or diverse, perceptions will be drawn about that population." And the more likely, I thought but did not say, that one individual will be asked to speak for the lot. I was in this odd position of both defending and shaking my claim as spokeswoman for the race, after all, because someone singled me out. This happened, in turn, because another outsider felt compelled to justify her (hitherto private) decision not to see a film at which she took offense. Seattle was lesbian spokeswoman for the night, and as resident black girl, mouthpiece for the disenchanted masses, I was called upon to back her up.

Life is like this when you are a conscientious outsider. Dinner can be a dangerous and tiring affair.

When I first got back from Ghana, I was ready to turn around and go right back. I had felt a sense of comfort and freedom there that surpassed any happiness I've known before. There is something undeniably relaxing about being phenotypically one of many (or most) rather than one of few (if any). Perhaps it would be a more stable world if everyone could experience both the sensation of oneness and that of otherness a few times in life. A person who isn't reminded several times a day about the implications of the color of her skin has time to consider the implications of other things. Having lived a life where my outsider status is called to my attention on a regular basis, it was a noted pleasure to blend into the crowd. In Ghana I was left free to discover the possibilities of so much unmolested psychic space.

The artists' colony is constructed to serve a similar goal: the creation of a space in which the creative mind can roam unfettered. But considering the conversations that implicated me at dinner, over ping-pong, while walking up the stairs to my bedroom, or while waiting for my breakfast egg, it was difficult to let my mind feel at ease.

There were two sources of experience for the poems I found myself writing at the colony. One set of poems was based on slave or runaway narratives. The rest of the poems were about visiting the giant fortresses on the coast of Ghana, often called slave dungeons, or conversely, slave castles, from whence the Portuguese and English slave ships left for the Americas. After my time in Ghana and the great relief at the experience of *not* being the other, this work, coupled with the sheer amount of energy I expended in explanation as the only woman of color at the colony, was a startling reminder of the many implications and tolls of otherness.

At breakfast one morning, several of the guests waxed delighted about how their rooms were cleaned regularly, "as if by fairies." We were living in a mansion. So as to allow us time to create, our meals were cooked for us, our bedrooms cleaned. We were invited, for the duration of our stay, to behave as if the mansion and its amenities were our own. There is something about privilege that can place one in a position to erase the realities of others. Those weren't fairies pushing the vacuum cleaner and cleaning my tub. They were women with lives and flesh and history, and my life and flesh and history demand I remember that and remind people (lecture if I have to) where I can. That is what it means to be a conscientious outsider. A life of reminders.

The Mother's Board

—OPAL MOORE

We are all Eve, we girls.
Betrayers at birth. Eaters of apples.
Bibles and Boys are not safe.
I am nine. I have been given my fate.
I feel the poison in me, sweet and tart
as apple sugar illegally melting
in my Sunday mouth.
My sister is seven.
A black hole is growing on her baby teeth.
We are Eve, new generation.
—*FROM "THE GARDEN"*

My sister tells the story of how, as a child, she had interpreted our denominational anthem as a document of birthright and exclusion:

This is the Church of God in Christ . . .
You can't join in
You've got to be born in it
This is the Church of God in Christ.

You can't join in / You've got to be born in . . . was to her child's mind an endorsement of her own unearned specialness. She was a part of something that had been bestowed at birth, something unearned and wonderful because of its limited access—like a country club for full-blooded royalty. Those so unfortunate to have been born incorrectly could not get in, no way no how. She does not know how she came to realize that this "birth" was a metaphor for conversion. She tells a related story of how, as an adult, she had hoped to amuse the brethren by revealing her mistake at a church program where she was the speaker. They were not amused. She had stood before the tight-lipped congregation chuckling at her early naiveté alone. Why didn't they see the humor in it? she says. She did not bother to tell them about the "bomb in Gilead."

Another of my sisters has a story—one day the pastor asked everyone to stand and testify to their aspirations for service to the church. One by one the congregants stood to take credit for their aspirations—they would be ministers or soloists in the choir or deacons or drummers/pianists/usher board leader . . . . The church liberally affirmed these dreams with enthusiastic shouts of "amen" and "praise God." When my sister's turn came she stood, thought for a moment, then declared: I want to be, uh . . . *a member*. Her declaration inspired an awkward silence, then hilarity. The pastor, wiping his mirth-filled eyes, endorsed my sister's simple wish. "Everybody can't be a chief," he admonished the laughers. "A church has got to have Indians! A*men!*" My sister, of course, was already a member. I believe what she meant was, she wanted to *feel* the embrace of The Church. She wanted, I believe, to know the completeness of feeling as if she belonged to and was accepted by something profound and unifying of the body, mind, and soul. Both of my sisters were expressing in different ways a natural longing to belong in a deep and irrevocable way to one's group, to one's kin, to something larger than themselves.

Let the church say amen!
The sun is too warm,
and why have the church mothers
who belong at the Pastor's left hand
forgot. They sit this Sunday on his right . . .

My mother keeps a clear glass bowl of flowers,
at the bottom are marbles

cool black to hold cut flowers upright.
I'm not allowed to touch the bowl
Am I dreaming of the bowl breaking,
of bright slivers of heavy glass and marbles
chasing water across the floor?
I dream of broken glass, scattering marbles
and water water water.
Pastor of the dry throat in the parching pulpit
preaches to make the mothers relent,
relinquish their silence, obey, bow down
in Paradise as it has been written,
    say amen!
From *"The Garden"*

I was born into the church, literally—both my parents had been converted in their youth and were faithful servants. My father's father had been the pastor of this same church; therefore, I was "born in it." I had watched the church sisters, mostly, dancing up the aisles filled with the Spirit, crying out and weeping with joy. I had watched the pastor's grandchildren entertain themselves practicing "shouting" and "getting happy" in the back of the church under the supervising eye of their grandmother—they would sit down as soon as the music stopped. I had already learned that women could not be ministers in our church and were not permitted to walk across or stand in the pulpit—this was why women who had something to say to the church would stand on the main floor and not step up to the microphone affixed to the pulpit. If necessary, a man would hand the microphone down to her so that she could say whatever it was she had to say.

One Sunday morning I watched two of the church's elder Mothers be harangued and dragged from the church, for no reason that I could know then, and none that I have been able to learn since. Later, at the end of service, I stood over the Mother who had been left lying in the vestibule. I remember looking into her face but she did not look at me. She was talking up to the walkers, she was preaching and singing. I remember my mother shaking me roughly and saying, *don't look at her!* Something was wrong. Women did not lie on floors, anywhere, ever, that I knew about. I had been told that it was bad to step over a person, yet people stepped over the Mother to exit the church.

In the poem "The Garden," I try to create, through the eyes of a girl, that Sunday morning when one woman defied the voice from the pulpit. The Mothers who have a dispute (of an unrevealed nature) with the pastor are at fault because they have chosen to "put themselves forward" during the Sunday service. The poem celebrates the manner by which the Mothers covertly disrupt. Understanding the subtleties of what may be called a "vocalized silence," that is, the black woman's role as a scripted Greek chorus to the "master narrative," the women defy the absolute authority of heaven's translator. They are Joanne Braxton's Outraged Mothers. They are Toni Morrison's pariah whore/mothers who make their homes at the margins of black respectability. They are Sapphire—aggressively prodding The Community of men toward respectability. They are taking themselves way too seriously. They are "put out" and fixing to be put out of doors.

A Pentecostal church service is a ritual in search of predictable chaos. The only disorder to be tolerated is the prayed-for Visitation of the Holy Ghost. The Spirit may come fiercely or decline to attend. The Mothers suggest to me a different kind of Visitation. Some women scholars have speculated that the Holy Ghost, the third and most mysterious aspect of the Trinity, is a vestige of the ancient Goddesses of earlier Africanist religions. Perhaps the ancient spirit of Oshun got into those women to disrupt the Black patriarchal Christian narrative and speak to Her daughters of their buried powers and forgotten obligations; perhaps it was the Furies, the ancient Mothers pounding the sky of their nether exile with their grain paddles demanding justice. Perhaps it was just two women old enough to know better who had heard enough of the mono-vocal performance from the pulpit and decided to put in a call, direct to the On High, singing *Jesus on the mainline / Tell Him what you want!*

The Mothers are an instruction in civil disobedience. In the poem, they choose silence as their tool of dissent. Understanding the delicate balance of power built into the Call and Response, the women decline to respond, they do not "bear up" the words of the pastor. Their deliberate silence is loud. It is a disruption, an imbalance, an absence. In a second layer of disturbance, the women have usurped for themselves the seats traditionally reserved for the Deacon's Board, which are located at the pastor's right hand and a step below the pulpit. The men have been displaced to the area designated for the elder women of the church—the Mother's Board—at the pastor's left hand and a step below the pulpit. The reversed seating sets the room off-kilter. Later, when one Mother begins to hum softly as a counterpoint to the minister's sermon, the room begins to quake. The pastor is so incensed by these two women, he directs the church ushers to "remove these demons from my church." The deacons are forced to lay hands on the Mothers. This laying-on-of-hands is not a healing

close your eyes
this is not for your eyes
say the whisperers
but i can see her eyes
heavy heavy full and open.
and were these god's hands
that heaved her up god's sweat
of creation: get her up there!
get her up! just pull here. get her up
underneath the arms. grab. there. there pull
pull her up—
they tugged dumped her to the floor
she. sprawled. fleshily mobile.
spraddled now. open.
the men pull.
the whisperers say keep your dress
down cover your knees.
her knees are for everyone now.
the men pull
and her sacred clothing that covered her
70 years—they drag her. they roll her.
dress caught
in the flesh somehow
and caught rides up and pulls
there. see. the tumbling fleshiness.
the womanness. the lump and fold.

the forbidden.
i keep my eyes open
i do not want to see
the tops of things strings knots
her private body. my future.
the way they drag her
dress hoved up and her underneath.
slips and sounds. skin screeching
across linoleum. slide! pull!
to the vestibule where i cannot see.
they just I guess dump her and leave her
to lie there.
and from where they dump her down
she cries out no weak crying
and weeping but raging. so
the deacons shut the doors.
From "The Garden"

The girl in my poem is both character and self. I could not have been more than ten, perhaps younger than that because I was still of an age that I could be forced to serve in the "Home and Foreign Mission Band," a group of children conscripted weekly and costumed in frumpy homemade capes to collect a separate offering (presumably for the heathens who had not been alert enough to be "born in").

From my place of invisibility, I watched as two women were dragged before their brethren. I heard The Church say "Amen." But what I saw had no meaning. What I saw offered questions that no one was willing to answer. I saw the deacons moving deliberately up the aisle, one left hand folded, white gloved, behind their backs. I saw that they could not drag the Mother with one hand and had to bring that reserve arm forward and put it into service. I saw what was to have been kept hidden.

The Mother who refused to leave the church, who made the men drag her, did not change my life. She changed my position in the universe, my angle of vision. She changed what I was able to see. I had not yet read Thoreau's *Civil Disobedience*. I had not heard of Ghandi. I did not know about the Montgomery bus boycott or the freedom riders or the civil rights struggle that was brewing in the South—yet the Mother who made them drag her was some part of all of these even as she was ahead of her own time and discourse. She was fighting for something that had not yet been defined as a struggle or a need. She was fighting for the right of a woman, a Black, to be heard *in her own voice in her own community*. She was fighting for the possibility of a woman's dignity *among her own Black people*.

The disobedient Mothers did not change my life—it went on as usual. They left me a *tableaux vivant* to interpret at my earliest convenience.

The year we broke from the Prayer Garden Church, my family did a period of wandering during which we walked "in the wilderness" of churches seeking a new church home. Each Sunday my father unveiled a new church possibility, and each Sunday seemed, to me, to leave us one brick lower in the Chicago pyramid of churches. At each successive church, the women's dresses were plainer and longer, until they finally began to resemble roughly stitched hospital bed sheets with matching nurse shoes. The churches descended from padded seats with armrests to wooden folding chairs. (Note: It is impossible to sleep in a wooden folding chair without landing on your head.) These churches inspired stories from my mother about how, as a girl, she had attended revivals in a tent. I interpreted these stories as "be-glad-you-have-a-chair-to-sit-on" speeches, artfully camouflaged equivalents of the "be-grateful-you-have-grits" and the "one-day-you'll-wish-you-had-beans" speeches so familiar to saucy black children who thought money grew on trees and who ought to have been more like the starving Africans who were *never* so ungrateful.

In our wandering I touched the two edges of freedom—to be self-defining and a pariah. I could not sustain my childhood: I was forced to view my world from this newly revealed outside, forced to form questions in the absence of answers—Why had I never seen a woman minister? Why could women and girls not step upon the raised platform called a pulpit? Were we unable to hear the voice of God? If so, how could we be saved? What was the destiny of a woman's prayer? Had Eve's daughters been excluded from the grace of God? How reliable were men in negotiating for the souls of women?

Story: My mother decided one night to visit the church of our excommunication. My brother and I tried to dissuade her from it. But my mother is a singer, a solo soprano, and the state choir was to be there in rehearsal. She wanted to hear it, to be swept out of herself, I believe, in the music. And besides, it had been years since our split from the church. Surely it would not be a problem, she said. My brother and his childhood friend, Kenny, and I thought we knew better and insisted upon riding with her into the city. We entered the church and took three seats that lined the rear wall. Within moments a woman at the front of the church noticed us and walked briskly back to where we sat. My mother stood to greet her.

As the woman approached us, I recalled a stranger had once entered the church at the beginning of the midnight service and settled in a seat on the back wall. The usher, one arm folded across his back, had immediately taken the man by his upper arm and walked him out of the church. My mother had later explained that the man was a drunk, probably.

The woman spoke to my mother in hushed tones, and though she did not dare take my mother by the upper arm, moments later we were standing on the sidewalk in the balmy night air.

Kenny and my brother were always natural clowns, so my mother was soon laughing and we could all pretend that our tears were the product of laughter.

The Mother, lying on the floor of the vestibule, did not change my life. She changed my point of view. Changed the way I looked at the women around me. Changed my eyes. Because of her, I was destined to inquire into the conditionality of my femaleness in the church. Because of her, I would never hope for full membership in the institution. Because of her, I trust questions more than I trust answers. I trust myself more than I trust preachers. I trust creativity more than tradition. Because of her, I have never doubted the possibility of human justice or questioned its desirability. Unlike my sister's revelation that there was no bomb in Gilead, my epiphany's source is not elusive. My enlightenment was women.

The Church my grandfather made
still stands at the corner of State
and 58th, at the corner of childhood.
He left this to me: Garden of Eden—
finite Paradise between innocence

and birth, Garden of Gethsemane—
sweet hour of prayer, of betrayal,
of inevitability. At the Garden gate
twines the secret of Love:
how Eve must be routinely driven out
of Paradise bearing the gift of pain.

Eve's daughters are blessed and cursed with the gift of pain, the price of seeking a knowledge that would make us full participants in the life of the Garden. So far, the curse may seem to exceed the blessing, yet it is written that Eve is irrepressible.

Pharaoh Saunders sings: all we need is imagination. Imagination lets us try on possibility like a garment. In my imagination I see three women, the trinity of my hope for salvation through women's spirit and questing. In a companion poem, "The Creation Sisters," I imagine three exiled Mothers building a new point of departure for our spiritual awakening by force of their collective imagination. Their "upper room" is a damp basement; however, unlike the Invisible Man's blinding underground, this new beginning is lit by a single dim bulb. All of the burning is in them.

their souls can compress
the gray ash of living
into one live lump of coal
dull black for heat.
this heat is life.
. . .
in their upper room
the mothers moan
they burn on desire unspecified,
ragged as loose coals lit
and striving they burn for newness
for revelation
for original intention
for something they
thought they knew
and never knew

From *"The Creation Sisters"*

The Mothers in my poem search their souls for the voice of Creation, for imagination, for new songs that will be revealed to them one word at a time. They believe that the souls of women are not disconnected from the Source. They sweep. They pry open a window. They make a place. They sing forward. The single word singing in their hearts is *"yes."*

Spirit Houses

My Father's Passage

— MARI EVANS

*I cannot imagine a writer who is not continually reaching, who contains
no discontent that what he or she is producing is not more than it is.*

Who I am is central to how I write and what I write;
and I am the continuation of my father's passage.
I have written for as long as I have been aware of
writing as a way of setting down feelings and the stuff of imaginings.

No single living entity really influenced my life as did my father, who
died two Septembers ago. An oak of a man, his five-foot-eight frame loomed
taller than Kilimanjaro. He lived as if he were poured from iron, and loved
his family with a vulnerability that was touching. He was indomitable to the
point that one could not spend a lifetime in his presence without absorbing
something beautiful and strong and special.

He saved my first printed story, a fourth-grade effort accepted by the
school paper, and carefully noted on it the date, our home address, and his
own proud comment. By this action he inscribed on an impressionable
Black youngster both the importance of the printed word and the accessi-
bility of "reward" for even a slight effort given the right circumstances. For
I knew from what ease and caprice the story had come.

Years later, I moved from university journalism to a bylined column
in a Black-owned weekly and, in time, worked variously as an industrial
editor, as a research associate with responsibility for preparing curriculum

materials, and as director of publications for the corporate management of a Job Corps installation.

I have always written, it seems. I have not, however, always been organized in my approach. Now I find I am much more productive when I set aside a specific time and uncompromisingly accept that as a commitment. The ideal, for me, is to be able to write for long periods of time on an eight-hour-a-day basis. That is, to begin to write (not to prepare to write), around eight thirty, stop for lunch, resume writing around twelve thirty, and stop for the day around four thirty when I begin to feel both fulfilled and exhausted by the effort. For most Black writers that kind of leisure is an unaccustomed luxury. I enjoyed it exactly once, for a two-week period. In those two weeks I came face to face with myself as a writer and liked what I saw of my productive potential.

When I began to write I concentrated on short stories, but I was soon overwhelmed by the persistency of the rejection slips. Everything I sent out came back, and although many of the comments, when there were comments, were encouraging, the bottom line was that none were accepted.

I drifted into poetry thought by thought; it was never intentional. I had no "dreams of being a poet." I began to write about my environment, a housing project, and to set down my reactions to it—to the physical, the visual aspects of it; to the people I touched in passing; to what I understood of their lives—the "intuited" drama and poignancy a brown paper bag away. It was not from wisdom that I followed that path; it was Langston Hughes who spoke to me.

When I was about ten I took a copy of his *Weary Blues* from a shelf and, eyes bright with discovery, mouth shaped in astonishment, rhapsodized, "Why, he's writing about me!" He was my introduction to a Black literary tradition that began with the inception in the area of Meroe on the African continent many millennia ago.

He was the most generous professional I have ever known. What he gave me was not advice, but his concern, his interest, and, more importantly, he inspired in me a belief in myself and my ability to produce. With the confidence he instilled, what had been mere exercise, almost caprice—however compulsive—became commitment, and I accepted writing as my *direction.* I defined it as craft, and inherent in that definition was the understanding that as craft, it was a rigorous, demanding occupation, to be treated as such. I felt that I should be able to write on demand, that I could not reasonably be worthy of the designation "writer" if my craft depended on dispensations from something uncontrollable, elusive, and unpredictable called "inspiration." I set about learning the profession I had chosen.

A state employment agency referred me to an assistant editor's vacancy at a local chain-manufacturing plant. Watts was already in the air, minority employment quotas were threatening in the background, and the company opted to hire me. In their ninety years of operation, I would be the first Black to cross their sacred office threshold for any purpose except to clean. The salary would be almost 50 percent less than what I had previously earned, but I took the job. Writing, as a profession, would start here.

The director of the plant's information system was far from flattered at having as an assistant editor the first Black employee to work anywhere in the company other than the foundry or delivery. There was much crude humor at his expense, with me as the butt, and a good deal of it within my hearing. Almost his first act was to call maintenance and have my desk turned away from him so that I faced the wall. An auspicious beginning.

I am cautious, Cancerian, rarely leaping without the long look. But having looked I am inclined to be absolutely without fear or trepidation. It was a gamble, undertaken in the heart of Klan territory; it paid off.

He knew how to write. His first draft was as clean as my final copy. I resented that so much that even his hassling became a minor annoyance. I revised and revised and revised, and only part of it was voluntary. In time, he began to allow me a certain creative freedom; and I became enthralled with industrial editing.

Time softened the hostility, but nothing ever changed the fact that I was a Black woman in a white job.

Those three years, however, underscored for me the principle that writing is a craft, a profession one learns by doing. One must be able to produce on demand, and that requires great personal discipline. I believe that one seldom really perfects. I cannot imagine a writer who is not continually reaching, who contains no discontent that what he or she is producing is not more than it is. So primarily, I suppose, discipline is the foundation of the profession, and that holds regardless of anything else.

To address specifics: I insist that Black poetry, Black literature if you will, be evaluated stylistically for its imagery, its metaphor, its description, its onomatopoeia, its polyrhythms, its rhetoric. What is fascinating, however, is that despite the easy application of all these traditional criteria, no allegation of "universality" can be imposed for the simple reason that Black becomes catalyst, and whether one sees it as color, substance, an ancestral bloodstream, or lifestyle, historically, when Black is introduced, things change.

And when traditional criteria are refracted by the Black experience they return changed in ways that are unique and specific. Diction becomes unwaveringly precise, arrogantly evocative, knowingly subtle—replete with what one creative Black literary analyst, the late Stephen Henderson, has called "mascon words,"[1] words that reconstitute on paper, "*saturation*"[2] occurs. Idiom is larger than geography; it is the hot breath of a people— singing, slashing, explorative. Imagery becomes the magic denominator, the language of a passage, saying the ancient unchanging particulars, the connective currents that nod Black heads from Maine to Mississippi to Montana. No, there ain't nothin' universal about it.

So when I write, I write reaching for all that. Reaching for what will nod Black heads over common denominators. The stones thrown that say how it has been/is/must be, for us. If there are those outside the Black experience who hear the music and can catch the beat, that is serendipity; I have no objections. But when I write, I write according to the title of poet Margaret Walker's classic: "For My People."

I originally wrote poems because certain things occurred to me in phrases that I didn't want to lose. The captured phrase is a joyous way to approach the molding and shaping of a poem. More often now, however, because there is a more constant commitment to my conscious direction, I choose the subject first, then set about the task of crafting a work that will please me aesthetically and that will treat the subject with integrity; a work that is imbued with the urgency, the tenderness, the pathos, needed to transmit to readers my sense of why they should involve themselves with what it is I have to say.

I have no favorite themes nor concepts except the overall concern that Black life be experienced throughout the diaspora on the highest, most rewarding, most productive levels. This concern is hardly chauvinistic, for when that life experience is possible for our Black family/nation, it will be true and possible for all people.

My primary goal is to command the reader's attention. I understand I have to make the most of the first few seconds his or her eye touches my material. Therefore, for me, the poem is structure and style as well as theme and content; I require something of my poems visually as well as rhetorically. I work as hard at how the poem "looks" as at crafting; indeed, for me the two are synonymous.

I revise endlessly, and am not reluctant to consider a poem "in process" even after it has appeared in print. I am not often completely pleased with any single piece; therefore, I remember with great pleasure those rare "given" poems. "If There Be Sorrow" was such a piece, and there were others, but I remember "Sorrow" because that was the first time I experienced the exquisite joy of having a poem emerge complete, without my conscious intervention.

The title poem for my second volume, *I Am a Black Woman*, on the other hand, required nearly twenty revisions before I felt comfortable that it could stand alone.

My attempt is to be as explicit as possible while maintaining the integrity of the aesthetic; consequently, I work so hard for clarity that I suspect I sometimes run the risk of being, as Ray Durem put it, "not sufficiently obscure." Since the Black creative artist is not required to wait on inspiration nor to rely on imagination—for Black life *is* drama, brutal and compelling—one inescapable reality is that the more explicitly Black writers speak their truths, the more difficult it is for them to publish. My writing is pulsed by my understanding of contemporary realities: I am Afrikan first, then woman, then writer, but I have never had a manuscript rejected because I am a woman. I have been rejected more times than I can number because the content of a manuscript was, to the industry-oriented staff person, more "Black" ergo "discomforting" than could be accommodated.

Nevertheless, given the crisis nature of the Black position at a time of escalating state-imposed repression and containment—in a country that has a history of blatantly genocidal acts committed against three nonwhite nations (Native Americans, the Japanese of Hiroshima/Nagasaki, the inhabitants of Vietnam), a country that has perfected the systematic destruction of a people, their land, foliage, and food supply; a country that at the stroke of a presidential pen not only revoked the rights and privileges of citizenship for 110,000 American citizens *identifiable, since they were nonwhite,* for what they "could" do, summarily remanding those citizens to American internment camps—I understand that Black writers have a responsibility to use the language in the manner it is and always has been used by non-Black writers and by the state itself; as a political weapon, a political force.

I think of myself as a political writer inasmuch as I am deliberately attempting the delivery of political concepts and premises through the medium of the Black aesthetic, seeing the various art forms—music, theater, dance, poetry, essays, the novel—as vehicles. I am a continuation of my father's passage because it is to him I attribute my political fortitude and my understanding of the power of the written word.

As a Black writer embracing that responsibility, approaching my Black family/nation from within a commonality of experience, I try for a poetic language that says, "This is *who* we are, *where* we have been, and *where* we are. This, is *where* we must go. And *this*, is what we must do."

[1970]

Notes

1. Stephen Henderson, *Understanding the New Black Poetry* (New York: William Morrow, 1973), 44.
2. Ibid., 10.

From: Evans, Mari. *Clarity as Concept: A Poet's Perspective.* Chicago: Third World Press, 2006. 15–20.

A Blessed Life

—MARYEMMA GRAHAM

To welcome the birth of my last child, Margaret Walker sent me a bouquet of flowers and a fuzzy blue and white stuffed animal, a lamb. The note hidden inside said, "May you be as blessed as I have been in my life. My children are my greatest treasure." It was just the kind of affirmation I needed. I was past thirty and well into my professional teaching career and here I was, having a fourth child! The other three were still young, and the oldest had barely started school. Even my own family thought I was crazy. I was beginning to think I was too, but Walker's note saved me. I knew who she was, an established writer who was still in her prime in the 1980s and a literary legend. I had gone to Jackson, Mississippi, to visit her when I first arrived at the state's flagship institution in Oxford. It was my gesture as a young, admiring scholar who wanted to let her know that I had moved to *her* state and intended to honor her legacy by teaching her work.

The visit was after the birth of my third child, now a very capable toddler. I felt it important that all the children get to see a living "legend," regardless of what they understood at that juncture in their young lives. Standing there in her living room with three children, two of whom were rather unruly, I looked as unlike a college professor as anyone could, and I couldn't decide whether what I saw in her face was bemused contempt or wonder and amazement. I was so taken by her presence that I missed the moment when my oldest child let go of her grip on my hand. Always an adventurer, she was drawn to a colorful poster on the door that led to Walker's office. I bounded out of the room, and in a very uncivil voice, heard myself squealing "Malika!!!" I was horrified when I found her putting the finishing touches on the carefully crafted cursive letters of her first name, spread across the bottom of a rare poster advertising *For My People*. No words would come; my cheeks burned.

"Don't worry about it," Walker said. "Nothing my grandson hasn't done." With a coy smile, she turned to me as I tried to gather the three children and scurry them out the front door fearing further damage. "Are you thinking of having any more children?"

I felt an implicit criticism but decided to offer my pat answer. "I've always said I wanted six and I'm halfway there."

"No wonder you moved to Mississippi," she laughed, her voice cracking. I left that day not knowing whether I was being congratulated or being sent away into permanent exile. It was certainly not the impression I wanted to leave, and I knew I never expected to hear from her again.

I was naturally curious about the note. It could have been that Walker— a notorious gossip—had been hearing things in Jackson—only three hours south of Oxford—about my husband and me as the rather odd couple who had left Chicago to return South when most younger black scholars were trying to get as far away from there as possible. Mississippi's reputation as the last bastion of racism made it a most unattractive place to live or work even in the 1980s.

When I read her note, all I could see were those letters of my daughter's name on the poster of her office door. I felt a shot of adrenaline go through my body. I had never told my mother about the incident, so she asked if the flowers were from the English department where I was teaching. When I told her they had come from Margaret Walker, the poet and novelist, she recalled hearing her speak once a few years earlier. "This is a sign that you are supposed to do something important," my mother offered. Though I was loathed to admit it then, Mom is never wrong. We were still using land lines, and I called the operator to see if there was a listing for Margaret Walker, whose married name I knew to be *Alexander*. Nothing there. Then I remembered to ask her to look up any Alexander on *Margaret Walker Alexander Drive*. I had heard that the naming of the street after her was a big thing. "There's a Fir—how do you say it, "Fir-nist?" she asked, dragging the last syllable out in an uncertain manner. I recognized the name from a biographical entry I had read, and I knew it was the right one.

Walker answered the phone in a slow deliberate manner. I hadn't expected to encounter her voice first, so I stumbled. It became easier as we talked briefly. In response to my "Yes, it was a very short labor, and the baby is fine," she told me how lucky I was and recounted her four painful deliveries and one miscarriage that nearly cost her her life. It was more sharing than I'd expected, and I felt as if I were already becoming the guardian of her record. I said my thanks and before I could hang up, she'd invited me down to visit her again. "Let's talk," she said. "I want to know how things are going up there."

"Okay, but if you don't mind, I won't bring the children this time," I announced confidently.

That was the beginning of a journey that would take nearly twenty-five years to complete. At times I didn't know I was on the road, for nothing ever seemed to be moving in any direction at all. I made myself one promise that day, however, to read everything by and about Walker that I could. In 2004, six years after she had died, I was still reading what she left behind. There is no writer, I have concluded, who wrote more over the course of her life than Margaret Walker.

I cannot recall how it was, or when it was that I first discovered the name of Margaret Walker. Hers may well have been one of the required poems we had to memorize and perform for the poetry reading contests in Augusta, Georgia, where I grew up. It was an event that was still central to the life of a child whose parents believed that conquering the fear of speaking in public would ensure one's success as an adult. But I knew by the time I got to graduate school at Northwestern that Walker was a prominent graduate of the university, returned to teach there on occasion, and that she was an award-winning writer. Because of the poetry revolution in the 1960s, we were loving poetry again, especially poetry written by a new generation of black writers. Both she and Gwendolyn Brooks, whose reputation has surpassed Walker's, had been the senior women writers in an era that had grown accustomed to the strident voices of its youth who were calling for revolution by any means necessary. Walker had been reborn during those years through her novel *Jubilee*, as much as through the Black Arts Movement; the result was to keep her from falling into literary oblivion. *Jubilee*, which appeared in 1966, came out just as the battle lines were being drawn between those who wanted to continue to call themselves "Negro" and those who insisted upon "Black," and between integration and black nationalism. In fact, the tension between these ideologies lies at the very core of her novel that traces the path from slavery through the life and times of Vyry, born on an Alabama plantation and fathered by the plantation owner/slave master himself. Walker based the historical novel on her great-great-grandmother.

By the late sixties, the covers had finally been pulled off of white racism, the more subtle and prevalent white privilege, and black identity—the claiming and the visible pronouncement of it—had become a weapon in the arsenal of an exciting new movement. These were also the beginnings of the canon wars, and Walker felt fully prepared to take her rightful place in the dialogues and debates that were raging. Her own personal battles had come much earlier in life: growing up in the Jim Crow South, then going to Northwestern where she had to sit in the back row and endure taunts from fellow classmates, and braving the years following the Great Depression when she lived jobless in Chicago. She knew what it meant to stand in soup lines, her only relief coming after she got a job with the Federal Writers Project making the handsome sum of thirty-four dollars per month. She could have gone back home to New Orleans, but felt that Chicago was the place for a black writer in the thirties, especially since all glamour and appeal of New York was now gone. Her hunch had been right; she had developed her craft, had published in leading magazines, and had become known as a poet.

I had heard her name linked with Richard Wright, not knowing what all the fuss was about. It was hard to imagine that the woman I was beginning to know, matronly and fiercely conventional, had any risqué encounters or bohemian tendencies, which I knew to be the case with many writers in the 1930s. Years later, when I read her journal entries confessing her undying love for a man who in the end paid her no mind, I began to understand how important words were for Walker. She had been changed by the emotionally charged relationship, both politically and personally, if not romantically, during one of the most critical periods in the twentieth century. She began to write furiously then as she always would in order for those moments and the many others in her life to become enshrined in her memory.

My entry into Mississippi in the mid-eighties paralleled another critical period in the twentieth century. The Black Arts Movement was officially over, or at least had receded to the background, and higher education was slowly acknowledging its mandate to transform the society, even if begrudgingly. It was the age of the Equal Rights Amendment and Pro-Choice. Black liberation and women's liberation wore equal hats, which underscored the importance of equality for all people of color within the US borders. A visible sign of this was the explosion of literary and artistic talent not only within the African American community, but also within the Hispanic community, the Native American community, and among those with Asian and the Pacific Island backgrounds. It was not uncommon to have any and all exclusionary practices regularly challenged. The calls for greater inclusion, the ongoing liberation struggles, and the decolonization of subject peoples worldwide created a seismic shift. Walker supported and agreed with all she saw taking place. But she railed against the new kinds of exclusion that she saw occurring within the academy that separated the "scholar" from the community. She found some of the new language and those who spouted it pretentious. Ironically, those who found new points of access closed to them included Walker herself. It caused her to feel isolated and unappreciated.

Fortunately, Walker's attention was never diverted away from the concerns that made her a writer. Even when there was a vulgar curiosity about her relationship with Richard Wright, she took the bold step of writing a biography of him, encountering even more criticism. She had no place for insensitivity and voyeurism. Moreover, because her commitment to a people's art was reaffirmed during the Black Arts Movement, she became one of its earliest advocates.

Our regular meetings during those years brought several revelations. Walker grew up in a male-dominated world, and she learned to conduct her struggle for recognition by the rules established in that world. It was for this reason that the affirmation of her identity as a wife and mother were extremely important. I soon learned to view my own growing family differently, as far more complementary and less conflictual in terms of my own life and work. Walker was absolutely clear that what fostered her creativity also affirmed her identity. While she believed that every writer needed a "quiet place to work," she understood that the responsibilities of womanhood nurtured one's art. She could not write if she had not experienced the fulfillment that came from being "wholly and completely" a woman, she was fond of saying. Teaching provided her with connection to a primary community and the interrelationships she could not do without. These were crucial lessons I would need for myself, not just to understand her life.

I rediscovered that note Walker had sent me when I was packing up my office to go on sabbatical several years ago. The proposal to write the biography had earned me a paid fellowship. When she died in 1998, I had laminated it to make it my focal point for writing, but it got stuck between two books. I needed it to help me tell her story, so it made its reappearance at precisely the right moment. I knew that Walker's joy was not in publishing all the books she wanted, which was why she took far too much time to finish her projects. I could understand how she recovered from the rejections in her personal life, and also from the public humiliation in her professional one, and overcame costly court battles that left her angry, bitter, dismayed, and penniless. But did she feel truly blessed, I asked myself? Her works are known by a relatively small group of mostly black teachers and readers, and of all her work, she is recognized for her early poem "For My People," even though it is one of the most widely anthologized poems in American literature. I wondered then and I still do.

One day when we were talking she said to me, "Nobody is interested in the story of my life; there's nothing sexy about it, no drama or mystery. I'm planning to write my memoirs so that my children will have them for posterity." I took it to mean that she was not comfortable with a biography being written. Nothing else to be said, or so I thought. When she died, the words that Nikki Giovanni had used to describe Walker kept haunting me: "The most famous person nobody knows," Nikki declared. When I learned that Walker had left her papers and journals to Jackson State University, I was interested in seeing what was there. By this time, my own children were in college or nearly so, I was divorced, and Walker's voice was still in my head. It was the voice that wanted me to tell her story. I had no choice.

Looking for the arc of Walker's life, I found a first clue in one of the quotes in the unpublished memoir: "Since I was eight, I have lived with three dreams, a deep and abiding faith in God to lead me into a good and useful life, to marry and have a family, and most of all, the dream I thought was impossible, to write books." As I continued reading, it became clear that Walker had operated with a sense of her own place in the world. She dreamed of that place, agonized over it, and worked diligently to make it happen. By the end of her life, she believed she had been at least moderately successful in meeting her expectations. In the preface to her final volume of poetry, *This Is My Century: New and Collected Poems*, she said as much:

> If I could write my epitaph it would read:
> Here lies Margaret Walker
> Poet and Dreamer
> She tried to make her life
>   a Poem.

Walker looked to no one as a judge or to set her standards. More often, she waited for the world to catch up with her, as she did when winning the Yale Series of Younger Poets Award in 1942. She submitted the manuscript that became *For My People* to Stephen Vincent Benet three times, then moved on with her life. Then one spring Benet tracked her down in New Orleans, to tell her that he wanted to award her the top honor because he had seen no work as good as hers the entire year. Her work hadn't changed; the world apparently had. Examples of deferred gratification came often in her life; but it never worried her. With an intuitive sense of what she could and would do, she mapped—in her journals—and tried to control her life from the time she was aware of the world. At the same time, she was intensely driven by forces that she struggled to comprehend through ongoing self-analysis and therapy. Because she was so driven, she was very good at reinventing herself, adjusting to one life change and social movement after another, always finding a new purpose that was more fulfilling than her original one.

The metaphor of a "house," which she had used often in her journals, is appropriate for understanding how Walker's world was both contained and expansive. As I completed my reading of more than 135 journals, her unpublished manuscripts, papers, and letters, and reread all of her published work over a period of six years, I realized that Walker had extended that metaphor and given me the title she wanted. If I expected to do justice to her life, it would have to provide the reader and me with an understanding of what she called the "house where my soul lived."

Walker left an extraordinary archive, including an early unfinished draft of her memoirs. As a result, the narrative is more than an accurate and detailed account of the facts and events in an extraordinary woman's life. Rather, I know that I can bring the reader into her life as Walker might have lived it. I can pay attention, for example, to the visual images, sounds, and smells that intrigued her, so many of them stored away for the poetry and prose that she would later write. The sensory perceptions that were so keenly and early developed paralleled her curiosity about the world as a whole. Had she been a child with less educated parents, who could not have provided her with the necessary access to books, a superior education, and the freedom to develop her innate abilities, hers might well have been a wasted and very tragic life. Moreover, had she not the grounding in an African American culture where the rituals associated with family, church, and service to one's community were so powerful, she might not have lived a life characterized by such intentionality and purpose.

The biography that I would write would have to be the revelation of Margaret Walker's soul journey. Because any life is both intellectual and spiritual, inner and outer directed, I know that Walker's was characterized by recurring periods of intense self-critique and self-loathing, where she retreated into her dream worlds. But these were always paralleled by equally intense periods of publicly meaningful work. In other words, what was private for Walker was also public. Well aware as she was of the difficulties of a woman writer, she struggled to find balance that made everything worthwhile.

I would agree that Walker's life does not provide that drama or sensationalism that we sometimes look for in popular biography. But it was indeed a blessed life. I am further convinced that she wanted her life not only to be part of the public record, but also to have it contribute significantly to an understanding of the history of the South and of the lives of African Americans in the twentieth century. I can think of no other reason she would leave her most private possessions—the journals that she kept from age twelve until her death at eighty-three—to Jackson State University, a historically black institution in Jackson, Mississippi, rather than to Northwestern University, her alma mater, or to Yale, whose university press launched her career, and where so many of the papers of her close friends—Richard Wright and Langston Hughes among them—are housed. The deliberateness of this act is telling in many ways, suffice it to say. Margaret Walker lived by her own dreams, fulfilled her own prophecies, and thrived on complexity. But she always managed to keep all the pieces of that life together in the house where her soul lived.

A Birth and a Death,
or Everything Important
Happens on Monday

—DARYL CUMBER DANCE

I was going to be a grandmother. It had taken all too long. I gave birth to my first child, Warren Dance Jr., when I was only twenty-one, but Warren Jr. was going to be almost thirty-six when his first child was born. As excited as I was, I decided to wait until a week after the July 4, 1995, appearance of my new grand to visit him in Houston, Texas. Other members of the family were going to be there for the birth, and I wanted time to enjoy this baby *all by myself*, so I planned to arrive after everyone else had left. I convinced myself and announced to my children that my tardiness was dictated by a concern about Taddy having someone there to help her with Yosie after the other visitors had left.

For seven glorious days, I enjoyed this beautiful baby boy, sharing him only with his mother and his father. I held him, rocked him, fed him occasionally (he usually nursed), changed him, sang to him, just looked at him and floated off in dreams of this new life. I called for the family progenitor, Abraham Brown, and all the other ancestors to witness and look over this newest branch on our family tree. I felt younger, renewed, and more optimistic about life than I had in eons. I sang, I danced; when I glimpsed my face in a passing mirror, I caught myself smiling rather than frowning, as was more often the case in recent years. I vowed to improve the quality of my own life—eat better, exercise more, focus on positive thoughts. Life was beautiful, and I had a lot more living to do.

On the evening of the seventh day of my arrival, my daughter, Daryl Lynn, called from my mother's home in Charles City, Virginia. Joyfully I grabbed the phone to share with her the excitement of my day—Yosie's smile, the way he followed me with his eyes, the tight clasp of his little hand on my finger. She didn't seem very eager to hear my gleeful accounts, and I paused, sensing that my mood was about to end.

Change swoops in without ceremony, warning, or explanation, suddenly and abruptly altering everything in a moment. Death was competing with life for my attention. My mother required immediate surgery for colon cancer, the dreaded disease that had claimed the lives of my grandmother and aunt. Surgery was scheduled for Monday, the day on which Mother always declared everything important in her life happened: "I was born on Monday, I got married on Monday, you [meaning me] were born on Monday, Allen [my father] died on Monday, my first grandson [Warren Jr.] was born on Monday . . . I know I will die on Monday."

Not only had all the joie de vivre that I had recently experienced vanished, but hope never showed her face. Already I knew it was time not only to add a new line to my genealogy chart from Abraham, but also to prepare to fill in the closing dates to another entry in the generation before my own.

Though Mother's surgery proceeded well, the doctor informed me that because of the spread of the cancer, she would live only a month or two.

Should she be told?

I talked to my children. We agreed that we could not conceal this knowledge from her—she had always taken charge and charted the course of her own life; she would certainly insist upon controlling, or at least dictating, her final days. I arranged for the doctor to meet with Mother, Daryl Lynn, and me to discuss the prognosis, though we agreed not to speculate on any precise time.

Mother was neither visibly surprised nor overwhelmed. After inquiring about possible treatments and learning that they would be futile, she began planning for what time she had, calmly observing, "Mama lived exactly three months after *her* surgery."

That was longer than her doctor gave Mother, but I didn't tell her that.

She, of course, wanted to see her new great-grandson, and his parents quickly arranged to bring him for frequent visits. Each visit was a booster for her. She held him, cuddled him, posed with him, played the piano for him, found joy in the new life that she experienced through him.

She surprised everyone, lingering to enjoy all the familiar rituals of another full year with us, including (through pictures) her great-grandson's first birthday. Considering the ominous prognosis, it was something of a surprise to have her with us to celebrate Thanksgiving and then Christmas and then Easter, going to church as she had every Easter of my life. We knew it would be her farewell to Elam Baptist Church (founded in 1810 by her great-great-great-grandfather Abraham), but it was appropriate that she would have us deck her out in her beautiful Easter outfit on the day of the resurrection. I pinned a lavender orchid on her lapel, and she basked in the attention lavished on her by her church family, who crowded around to express their delight to see her out. This grand appearance took its toll; her only trips after this would be to the hospital, where we observed Mother's Day *and* one trip to see the water.

When Daryl Lynn and I had left the hospital to take her home after surgery, she had declared that she wanted to see the water, but then when I offered to drive her to the shores of the James River, she decided instead to go directly home. She had left over a month before, clearly recognizing the possibility that she might never return, and she was eager to see if her lilac trees were still blooming, to sleep in her bedroom decorated by her in shades of purple, to eat at her table, even to piddle around in her own kitchen—and to get her business affairs in order. So a trip to the river was forgotten until the leaves of one last fall had turned all orange and golden, the snows of one last winter had melted, and the buds of one last spring had blossomed. Nearly ten months after she returned home following her surgery, on one bright June day, I remembered her expressed desire to see the water and suggested we drive down to the James River. She eagerly assented. With much difficulty, Daryl Lynn and I got her into the car, and we drove off for the James. I turned onto the wrong road, but Mother took charge and directed me to the proper one. I drove up to the water and parked. She smiled as she gazed out over the James, sat there, contentedly perusing the deep, calm, inscrutable source of life, and finally announced that she was ready to go home. As I prepared to turn into the driveway to her house, she pointed in the opposite direction and announced, "Next time we'll go that way." She never left her house again. Sure enough, her next journey was "that way"—when we left the church and passed her house, heading to the old church burial grounds. How quickly a year passes! How brief is the journey from the waters of life to the dust of eternity!

But I'm getting ahead of my story. Within a few days of that trip to the James River, Mother glanced up at me from her bed and said, "I'm ready."

"Ready?" I asked. "What do you mean?"

"Ready. R-e-a-d-y," she impatiently spelled it out to me.

"What are you talking about, Mother?" I insisted.

"I'm so tired," she declared.

"Tired? What are you tired of, Mother?"

"I'm tired of this pain."

"Well, let me get some of your medication for you," I readily offered.

"I'm tired of the medicine. I'm tired of this bed. I'm tired of everything," she exhaled as she turned her head away, as if she had said everything she ever had to say to me in this lifetime.

I called her grands.

They came to say their good-byes, first the younger grandson, Allen, from Maryland, and then the older grandson, Warren Jr., and the just-turned-one-year-old great-grandbaby from Texas. I feared they would not make it on time, and I kept telling Mother that Yosie was on the way. Her tired body painfully continued to breathe laboriously, awaiting Yosie's arrival.

Yosie sat on his father's lap by her bed and reached out to her hand— that hand that was already so cold and clammy that I avoiding holding it, choosing instead to pat and massage it through the sheet. He sat quietly and patiently, looking at her as if seeking some explanation. She lay peacefully, eyes focused on something we could not see. The old folks would have said that she was looking at the angels. One child of Abraham was going to join that long line that had gone on before and another child of Abraham was watching over this journey and giving her permission to go. I . . . I was a medium, interpreting a ritual to which neither of the main participants could give expression.

Yosie left to return to Houston on Sunday night. Mother died on Monday. Both of the lavender lilac trees in her front yard burst forth in their most radiant blooms ever to bid her adieu.

Ambrosia

—NIKKY FINNEY

*‡ In classical mythology, Ambrosia was the food and drink of the gods;
mortals who ate it became immortal. ‡*

I t was Mama and Daddy who pushed me into the world, but it
was Grandmother Beulah who gave me the hands and heart
to be a poet. Beulah Butler Davenport was born in 1900 in
a small rural township in South Carolina. She lived out her ninety-nine
years all within a twenty-five-mile radius of her sacred birth spot. A self-
sufficient farming woman most of her life, she could in one moment wring
the life out of a chicken, by way of its neck, and in the next, with a great
and delicate care, peel the white, spidery, bitter membrane off the bellies
of twelve well-chosen oranges for her Christmas ambrosia. I was always
amazed at what her hands could do, all in the name of a day's work. In
1975, at the age of seventeen, I left home to make my way out in the world,
first and foremost by attending Talladega College in Talladega, Alabama. I
was guided out into that brand new world by the spirit and power of my
grandmother's hands and by what, with a dedicated touch, could be made
in this world.

By the end of the summer of 1979, I had arrived in Atlanta, Georgia,
enrolled in graduate school at Atlanta University in a master's program in
African American literature. I hadn't really wanted to go to graduate school.
I had no desire to get married or return home like so many others in my
class. I wanted to choose something different for my life. The majority of

the things I was being told I should do, I had no interest in doing. Very few of my fellow English majors (there were six of us) were going on to graduate school. I wanted to be a writer, but there was no handbook available on just how to do this. I only knew I had to remain sharp-eyed out in the world. I knew I had to pay attention, keep moving, and take advantage of any opportunity, and I knew I had to keep my grandmother's smart hands close by my side.

During my undergraduate years at Talladega College, Dr. Gloria Gayles had been my most passionate teacher. Dr. Gayles had introduced me to the world of Black women writers. Before taking her African American literature classes, I had no idea of the history or the names that lived under that powerful twin awning of Black Woman and Writer. I certainly had heard nothing about these women back home in my newly integrated, high school honors English classes. In Dr. Gayles's classes, as well as in the pages of those stunning writers, whole skies began to open up to me. Under her brilliant unwavering tutelage, I came to know intimately Zora Neale Hurston, Toni Morrison, Alice Walker, Toni Cade Bambara, Mary Helen Washington, Carolyn Rodgers, and others who would quickly lay out the map of my future. There were no creative writing classes at Talladega. There were no writing workshops at Talladega. I didn't know it then but there were very few writing workshops being taught at any of the historically Black colleges.

Creative writing as a discipline was seen as something special but nothing integral. To the administrators in those institutions, "Creative Writing" carried the thin air of something to only do on the side, a hobby, a club, certainly not an area to focus one's life. Dr. Gayles, who had been essential to every aspect of my undergraduate training, had also guided me toward the golden idea of graduate work. Frequently, during my senior year, she would stop me and soon launch into many a finely tuned, extra-long soliloquy about how important it was that I continue my academic studies. I applied to and was accepted into several schools. I decided on Atlanta University because of its historical relationship with Dr. W. E. B. Du Bois, one of the world's greatest writers and intellectuals. At graduation Dr. Gayles handed me a three-by-five-inch index card with Toni Cade Bambara's name, address, and phone number. I knew as soon as she handed it to me that I would probably never use it. I was far too shy to even consider the possibility. What would I possibly say after ringing this great writer's door-bell? *Hi. I'm Nikky Finney and I was wondering if you could help me become a poet?* There had to be a less intrusive way to reach that esteemed literary landing.

In 1979 I began attending classes at Atlanta University and becom-ing familiar with Atlanta's many neighborhoods. One weekend I noticed a bright purple poster on an information board at a neighborhood health food store. It advertised a writer's conference, the first of its kind, organized by a newly formed group, the Southern Collective of African American Writers. The conference was to be held at a place that would later become central to my life and time in Atlanta, the Neighborhood Arts Center. I decided to head over that Saturday to see if they needed any help organiz-ing the conference that was less than a month away. When I walked in that early weekend morning, there were several people already in the room stuffing and stamping envelopes. I simply fell in line where I was needed. A woman arrived an hour or so later. I remember her bright purple shawl and big silver hooped earrings. She was so visually memorable. I remember how the room seemed to open up when she walked in as if it suddenly had much more to accommodate.

She said her big Hello to all, dropped her large Guatemalan bag, and started in on a pile of envelopes. I immediately recognized her from the back of all her books that I had positioned high up on my favorite shelf. Toni Cade Bambara had walked in and made a place for herself at the table across from me. The great American writer who had edited *The Black Woman*, who had written *Gorilla, My Love* and *The Seabirds Are Still Alive*, whom I had also written my senior thesis on, was sitting across from me telling stories, chewing gum, and pressing bright flyers and their stiff edges down into envelopes. I could hardly look up. The room had changed. The boring work had changed. And soon, very soon, my life would change.

My neophyte understanding of writers and artists: Writers and art-ists avoided quotidian tasks and saved themselves for the real work that was always done back at their desks or in their studios. And yet there she was up early with the rest of the worker bees, inches away from me, fully engaged in the mundane but necessary work of organizing a conference. Before the night ended, I gathered the courage to introduce myself and brought her greetings from Dr. Gayles. "Gloria sent you and you have not yet been by the house!" She was appalled. Stupefied. She could not stop mumbling under her breath for the rest of the morning. I was not going to be easily forgiven. I would, in fact, spend the next two years working off that ridiculously modest miscalculation. But the very next words out of her mouth were about the serious business of writing. Her face changed quickly, and she focused in on the writing workshop that she called forth every first Sunday of the month at her home. I would later learn from someone else gossiping at the worktable, Spelman College had refused to accept the syllabus that Bambara had turned in to the department heads that year. She refused to miss a beat; instead the story unfolded that Bambara simply decided to host the same workshop at her home. She named it the Pamoja Writing Workshop. Pamoja was Kiswahili for "unity." Lucky me. Lucky us all. She invited me by that Sunday and she told me not to come empty-handed. I thought she meant that I should bring something to eat. A potluck of sorts? It was indeed a potluck. But the smorgasbord was not a table of cornbread and greens but rather a feast of delicious words.

I didn't know what a writing workshop was. I had never had the opportunity to be a part of one, to sit inside a fully operating one before. I had always come bearing the work of others under my arm. My own work had remained stuffed inside file folders, cardboard boxes, and trunks. All my life I had closely and studiously read the beautiful work of others. Everything I thought I knew about writing had come from the minds, hearts, and hands of others. Even the move to my new Atlanta life and the enrollment in graduate school had continued my steps in that tradition. I was studying the sterling poetic voices of African writers Ama Ata Aidoo and Wole Soyinka with the great teacher, Dr. David Dorsey. I was discussing Richard Wright and Langston Hughes with the eminent African American scholar, Dr. Richard Long. Dr. Margaret Rowley was bearing down on me brilliantly about African American history. No one around me was concerned if my metaphors and similes were strong and clear. My graduate professors cared only about whether I could synthesize original research and intellectually interpret the work of others. I could do that work just fine, but I was quickly learning that the work of others was not what I had been put on earth to do.

I kept a calendar on the wall of my tiny apartment in Atlanta. The first Sunday of every month, straight through to the end of the year, was soon circled in bright red. Sundays had long been special to me as a girl. It wasn't only that my family looked beatific and trotted off to church together. For me Sundays represented the quietest day of the week. It was surely a day of early meditation. It was a day when the world did not seem to move so fast. It was a day when I could walk more slowly and dream more deeply. It was a day of both wonder and wandering. This feeling I had for Sundays made the walk up the hill to Toni Cade Bambara's house on Simpson Avenue, on the first Sunday of every month, that much more special. On that one day, every month, writers from every corner of the community sat together and experienced the sacred: taking our precious turns listening to something original, something one of us had seen, felt, or imagined and then written down, only to return the most honest of feedback and commentary directly to each other. I didn't know it then but those twenty-four or so Sundays, spread out over those two years, would end up prescribing the rest of the days of my life as a working poet in America in this twenty-first century. There was something in them that reminded me of home.

My grandmother loved Christmas more than any other time of the year. If you were privileged to sit down at her Christmas table, then you were privy also to discover how much she thought of you, and maybe of the preciousness of life itself. I have never seen anyone, before or since, spend so much time—intimate, loving time—with bowls and baskets of fruit. To Beulah Davenport it wasn't just fruit. It was delicately sliced oranges, peaches, pears, grapes, apples, strawberries, and one whole precious coconut that somewhere near the end was grated, like some crown jewel, on top of the mound of sweet fruit. It was just pretty food to me. But to my grandmother it seemed to be much more. You could tell by the way she handled it, from the big bowl to all the little bowls, her eyes saying, *One cup of this and you will live forever.* The way she watched all of us take in each spoonful, it was as if to say, *One sip of this and you are protected even when you step away from my sight.* She loved how pretty it was, but more importantly, there was something about her ambrosia that maybe back then none of us could understand.

In her mind there was something sacred about her fruit. My grandparents were hardworking farmers who lived very close to the land. Everything they had and everything they respected came from the bounty of the earth and the hand and eye of God. Their world did not include excess or frivolity. The everyday task of surviving another season was what woke them up every morning. Their only priority was to make sure the children had warm clothes, and the animals that worked the farm stayed alive and lively as long as possible. They made their living from farm animals and from whatever the fields yielded that surrounded them on all sides. Whatever grew was what they ate and also what they made a living with. They sold most of what they grew and put away a little for their neighbors, for their family, and for themselves. There was little excess. There was no extravagance. I didn't know it then, but now I believe my grandmother's ambrosia was the family's once-a-year extravagance. It was the most extraordinary thing she could make and do for us. In her mind the green beans, potatoes, cabbage, and corn was basic everyday love. Her Christmas ambrosia was the year's bounty. It was as beautiful as holiday lights in a bowl. It was striking to the eye, exquisite to the tongue, and it fed the body and mind things that the body and mind needed to fully bloom. She made her apple pie fritters throughout the year. Small, tiny pies that were gone in two bites. Her fritters often sat cooling on the edge of the stove every weekend of summer. And when she came from the garden there were always tiny strawberries staining her hand. Her children and grandchildren had all pulled down pears and peaches while wandering through the piney woods. But it was the assemblage, the gathering together of every bud of fruit on her land, at this one special time of year that seemed to absolutely govern her joy. All but the oranges and the coconut had been grown there on the land that she and my grandfather had spent their lives working.

Land meant freedom to my grandparents. Complete freedom. It was "land," my grandfather routinely reminded, "that was the very reason we, as a family, no longer had to work for the white people." The white people, who at one point in history had erroneously believed that they had owned Black people. "When you own your own land," he would say at the dinner table, "you don't have to ask permission from anybody else what you should grow or be. You work your land. You pay your taxes. That is what being free is." He was adamant. He was unapologetic. In his mind this was the way he had been able to stay a free man. This was the way he had been able to send his children to college when others around him had not. This was the way the ugly past could and would never repeat itself. One hundred and twenty acres of pine trees, open fields, and starlit sky, that he could, and did, walk beneath any time of day or night. Cows, mules, chickens, fruit trees, four barns, a clear spring stream that ran through the middle of the woods, that we hungrily leaned over and drank readily from, a smokehouse, and a home house where the family lived, that he had first sketched out on a piece of newsprint and raised up from the red dirt with his own two hands. My grandfather's brother lived across the road to the right. Their mother and sisters lived across the road to the left. Foxes roamed. Wolves. Raccoons. Possum. A whole village of family and creatures lived in a bittersweet coexistence. Freedom. It meant what you could grow, raise, keep, and call whatever was your own, "your own."

I wouldn't say that Toni Cade Bambara and I were friends. Not friends in any let's-get-together-and-socialize kind of way. I was eighteen years her junior and too young and in awe, too grateful, with too much bubbling respect, to ever call her a friend, though there was nothing I would not have done for her. She was a generation ahead of me. She was brash and urban and unsympathetic to any status quo. She had the most brilliant serious mind and the sharpest, funniest wit I ever met or heard. She hated excuses and ranted about "bullshit." She saw through both veils efficiently, with a brusque wave of her hand and a stiff exhale of her cigarette. "Friends" is too slippery a word for what we were, but I would say "family" in a heartbeat. She took so many of us in who were out in the world looking for our writer maps. She taught us how to fight in subversive powerful ways. She taught us to not relinquish the arena to the foolish. If she ever saw something that we needed and she could give it to us, she gave it. I didn't see a lot of her in my lifetime. But whenever I saw her, she opened any door she could for me—if I was ready—and urged me to walk through it. If I wasn't ready to walk through then she kept going. She would move on to another who was. Mostly the doors she opened for me were in my own mind. There I was, a quiet college girl, a quiet southern girl, pursuing another degree in higher education, wanting poetry to swoop me up somehow, walking up her house-hill every Sunday, to sit with secretaries and mothers and bus drivers. All of us had writing up our sleeves, in our socks, and tucked inside hats and berets and belt loops, too. If I thought for a minute that writing was about doing something "pretty," Toni Cade didn't. The moment when the truth about pretty hit the floor was in one of my last Pamoja workshops.

I had written something I was very proud of. I couldn't wait to read it in the next workshop. I remember thinking that it was certainly one of the prettiest things I had ever written. It was one beautiful metaphor after the other. I read the poem to the circle and was feeling pretty full of myself. The rest of the room seemed equally impressed. And then Toni Cade spoke up: "So you can write pretty, so what? What does all that pretty stand for? In the end, what difference does it make that it's so pretty? What risk have you taken?" Sometimes workshops can become a stage for the ego and not a toolshed for the writing itself. I had crossed this line in error. I was very young. I was also speechless. The room fell into an unusual quiet. She was tough. She was really tough on me because I could write pretty, and she wanted me to give the world more than that. She wanted me to give myself more. She taught me that there had to be more than a pretty moment to what I was doing. She taught me strategy and mindfulness long before I knew what to call it. She taught me so much more—so many life lessons—I will never, could never, forget.

I had to leave Atlanta. I was running out of patience and interest for graduate school. I had to get a job somewhere, and one had been offered back at Talladega College, my undergraduate institution. I had been offered a good job. A quirky job. A job as a photographer. I had loved photography for years. My uncle had given me a 35 mm camera in high school. He had bought it overseas while serving in the Vietnam War. The camera had helped me learn how to see the world in much closer, clearer ways. In my new job as Campus Photographer, I would have full use of the antiquated darkroom and the school's ancient photography equipment. Even if the bulk of my time would be spent taking snapshots of the Talladega College president accepting oversized checks, as well as working around the clock with stoic yearbook designers, still I would have the camera close and I would be out in the world creating. I decided that graduate school and literature courses had run their course. It was very risky, but I decided to move back to the deeper South and finish my first books of poems. I decided to walk away from graduate school, with a 4.0 and an unwritten thesis. But I had twenty poems pushing up at the cover of a black notebook and more new ideas coming every day. I decided that I didn't want to spend the rest of my life interpreting the brilliant work of others. I decided I wanted to create unknown literary worlds of my own. I knew the choice would not be popular with my family, but I believed it would make me a woman who owned her own mind and her own creative self.

Toni Cade Bambara had a very unreliable car and a very young daughter, Karma, when I knew her in the early 1980s. She called me sometimes, out of the blue, to ask for rides all over town. I loved it whenever she did. I always dropped whatever I was doing and drove over to Simpson Avenue and picked her and Karma up. When I did, I knew a lesson or an adventure or both were coming. The last time I saw Toni Cade in Atlanta the two of us drove out to Greenbriar Mall to see a movie. Toni Cade had a special affinity for film; the narrative and the visual world spilling all at once, there in the sparkling dark, was something she was more than passionate about. She would spend the entire day, if she had the time, going from one screen to the next, in the same theater.

On one of those days I told her that I was leaving graduate school and returning to Talladega, where I had rented an old farmhouse and was planning to learn everything I could about photography and finish my first book of poems. She didn't seem impressed and didn't say very much. "Sounds pretty romantic to me," she offered as a response in her most flat-footed voice. It was classic Toni Cade. After the movies we were walking back to the car. A man approached. He was holding on to a handful of papers. He wore mechanics' overalls. His name "Eugene" was stitched over the left pocket. "Excuse me," he said. Toni stopped and turned to him. "Are you that writer lady?" I smiled and took a step back to give them room. I expected him to ask her about her latest book or maybe a story from one of the older books. Wasn't that what people stopped world-class writers to talk with them about? "Yeah," Toni said, "that's me." She pushed back her big wild head of hair and cupped her hand up to keep the sun out her eyes. She was already reading the top sheet of paper in his hands. The man dropped his large black glasses back down to his nose. "Well, I need your help because I'm trying to buy a house next week, for me and my family, you see, and I don't really know what all these papers are saying. I'm supposed to sign something somewhere, but . . . " He tried to brush off his need and his embarrassment. I blinked my eyes a few times. Toni Cade took the papers in her hand and shook her head a little up and down. "Yea, hmm huh, I got 'cha." Then she looked back up at him. "What you doing tomorrow, around four o'clock?" She seemed to already know he wouldn't be at work then. She seemed to already know that this was the hour that he wouldn't have to figure out the hard choice between his two necessities. "I can do that," he answered. Toni handed him the papers back. "Come by the house tomorrow, around four, we'll work all this out." She waved her hands in front of the wrinkled stack of paper like a black wand full of some kind of Toni Cade Bambara magic.

Except it wasn't magic at all. She gave him what she gave all of us, without a drop of fear, the address of her Simpson Avenue house. It was the same house where, once a month, she tried her best to teach a circle of old and young writers that pretty is as pretty does, and what was really needed in the world, then, and 'til the end of time, was more ambrosia, that immortal food that black grandmothers made, year after year, for their precious circle of family that fed more than a belly, that fed the future.

What Roots Us

Cotton Pickin' Authority

—TRUDIER HARRIS

Authenticity. That's the issue. How did black southerners manage to claim it in a society that devalued their
very work as human beings, a society that certainly
did not hear their voices on practically anything? How did they claim
voice, authority, and authenticity? There was little opportunity for them
to acquire it through the larger, white society, so they usually resorted to
claiming it in the realm and within the earshot of relatives. Some of them
acquired it through the cotton picking in which they had actually engaged
as well as through the mythical history associated with cotton planting,
chopping, and picking. A history in cotton measured the distance between
working class and middle class, elementary and high school dropouts versus folks holding advanced degrees, and mother wit versus the pollution of
book learning. Having worked in cotton is comparable to having worked in
God's vineyard; it is the preparation ground upon which all *true* southern
black experience, from this group's perspective, is founded.

Anyone who is the daughter or son of black parents and grandparents born in the South in the first five decades of the twentieth century is
subjected to endless tales about the plight those parents and grandparents
suffered in comparison to what their offspring have had to endure, which
the parents generally view as a less physically difficult life. Validating their
experiences usually boils down to an essential phrase that might have slight
variations in its delivery: "You ain't never picked no cotton" or "You never
had to pick cotton, so . . . " If that phrase does not emerge in the conversation, general references to the hardship of working in cotton will serve to

illustrate the relatively "easy" life descendants of such parents have in comparison to the lives of their parents.

Cotton pickin' authority posits, first of all, that physical labor is preferable to brain work, or at least brain work should occupy a comfortable second place in the hierarchy. There is a certain romance surrounding the people who, in the spring of the year, would get out of bed at four o'clock in the morning, hitch up their horses and mules, and be in the fields by early light to begin the process of breaking new ground for seeds. They worked all day—literally from can't see to can't see—and were still able to appreciate their families for a short while before they retired to bed to begin the process all over again the next day. The process continued with weeding and chopping the cotton during the summer, thereby nurturing it into the produce it would yield in the fall. And of course there was the physical labor associated with picking x-number of pounds of cotton in a day. When I was picking cotton in the 1960s, my mother and brothers routinely aimed for two hundred or more pounds per day. On one glorious day when I was eighteen, I managed the grand sum of one hundred fifty-eight pounds.

On those brief occasions we children picked cotton, we were aberrations to the usual cotton picking system. Older folks could pick cotton six days a week, if necessary, for as long as was necessary to finish up the yield from a particular crop. When they asserted, therefore, that "you ain't picked no cotton," it did not deny the fact that you might literally have been in the fields picking. What it denied was the consistency with which you were able to really pick cotton, day in and day out, as a way of life. We nitpickers were just passing through. These old heads really knew what it meant to labor physically. They therefore knew how to diminish any upstart efforts we might have made to unseat their authority by referring to our puny inability to survive in a blazing hot southern sun for more than a day or two at a time.

Implicit in the references to physical labor were notions of strength and weakness. You were strong if you could last in the fields all day. You were weak if you had to go home at dinnertime (the noon hour) and rest or if you could not return to the fields at all. When cotton picking was no longer the primary arena of work, the standard of measurement implied by cotton picking was still there. You were strong if you could accept the challenges the society constantly put before you instead of wimping out and asserting that you couldn't do anything. If we complained about how long school lasted or about being tired of doing homework when we were in elementary or high school, Momma might say, "You oughta be glad you can go to school. Why, when I lived on the farm, we could only go to school for a few weeks a year. We had to pick cotton." Or they had to plant it, or weed it, or whatever else the season required. There was no sympathy to be had for anyone in the 1960s who complained about having to sit around on their butts and read books, work math problems, learn to spell new words, or write essays. To anyone who had picked cotton in the 1930s and 1940s, that was luxury indeed.

We elicited a similar response if we dared to complain about food. "Black-eyed peas and cornbread again? We had black-eyed peas yesterday. Why can't we have fried chicken sometime during the week instead of only on Sunday?" "You better get in there and eat that food. Starving folks around the world would be happy to get what you eating. And I woulda been too when I was growing up. When we had to go to the fields to pick cotton, many times we only had a bucket with fat meat and cornbread in it. And when I went to school, we had only a baked sweet potato to carry to eat at lunch. You don't work in the fields and you get a nice hot lunch at school, so don't sit there complaining about them black-eyed peas and cornbread." This was the voice of reason, always putting into perspective and relativity the circumstances of our lives. Momma was the authority, and we might complain, but with that cotton pickin' authority, the complaints got nowhere.

The same was true if we dared to be less than grateful about the clothes or shoes we wore. It also brought us back to cotton and to the general deprivation that my mother experienced as a country girl isolated on a farm in Green County, Alabama. She would tell the story of the two dresses that she owned during her school years and how she wore one and washed the other one *every day;* the dresses lasted because the school year was so short. She would also relate to us the path that she had to take to school and how rain, slush, mud, and occasionally snow made her efforts to acquire an education even more difficult. But she kept going. She suffered nearly frozen hands and being wet for entire mornings at school because the lone wood stove in the one-room schoolhouse did not give off sufficient heat for her

and the other rain- or snow-soaked children to get dry. She ate her baked
sweet potato for lunch. And she prized all those inconveniences, which she
didn't even recognize as such at the time, because they were a step up from
picking cotton. We, by comparison, had nothing for which a complaint was
justified.

Authority derived from mastering the difficult task of cotton picking
also came in handy at other times. If we wanted to go to the movies (yes,
there was one black theater in Tuscaloosa when I was growing up), and
Momma didn't want us to go, she would emphasize that we had our yard
and the fields behind us in which to play, and all that freedom was a con-
trast to picking cotton, so we should be thankful for it. Why should we
need further diversion when we had this?

Trying to go up against cotton pickin' authority was comparable to a
staccato call and response in which you were destined to lose. In cotton
pickin' tradition, some of the scenes might go like this:

"Momma, I don't like this government milk."

"Drink it, 'cause you didn't have to pick cotton to get it."

"This gabardine material Miss Daisy gave us to make dresses is ugly."

"You gon wear'em anyway, 'cause you didn't have to pick cotton to pay
for'em."

"All we got to do is sit around on the porch."

"It's better than picking cotton."

"Cleaning Mr. Bland's store is too hard. I have to scrub and scrub that
floor."

"It's better than picking cotton."

"This blue gym suit is too big and baggy."

"And how many pounds of cotton did you pick for it?"

It took a l-o-n-g time, but we finally learned that we could *not* win
against cotton pickin' authority. We learned that we might as well embrace
it as *the* standard of measurement for work and a host of other things. It
always put us in our place, and it always put perspective on poverty, eco-
nomics, and personal preferences. The continuum between "then" and
"now" was always designed to encourage us to see "now" as preferable, as
a progression that made our lives easier, though it consistently gave the
power to name that ease to the "then" generation.

No matter the ages of her children, Momma would still evoke cotton pickin' authority when it came to giving permission. She had raised us so strictly that I had not had an alcoholic beverage by the time I was a freshman at Stillman College. Rosa, my best friend during that year (who is still one of my best friends), was from LaGrange, Georgia. She was as uninitiated in the ways of alcohol as I was, so we made a deal. I would go with her to visit her grandmother for Christmas in 1966. We would go out to a club where I would proceed to have a few drinks and she would watch over me. We would then return to Tuscaloosa, go out to a club there, and I would watch out for her. Her end of the bargain went (mostly) according to plan. We went to a nightclub where I proceeded to down a few rums and Cokes. I knew I was in trouble when the stairs leading down to the lower club level where the restrooms were located started to look like train tracks receding in the distance. That was the beginning of an ordeal that ended with her shushing me—and not really succeeding because she was giggling so much—as we tried to sneak into her grandmother's house. The next day, I walked around at a ninety-degree angle for the first three or four hours.

Back in Tuscaloosa, the next night, we selected our club and were getting ready to spend New Year's Eve there when my mother announced, "Y'all ain't going out tonight." Oh, the embarrassment. How could she do this to me? Rosa had held up her part of the bargain, and now Momma wouldn't budge. "This girl's folks trusted her to be at my house," she went on to say, "and y'all ain't going nowhere. Ain't no telling what might happen. Things have changed too much since those days when we lived on the farm. If you were going to the cotton fields, that would be different, but you ain't going to no nightclub." And she went on to elaborate on the responsibility we had for this visiting nineteen-year-old female. She knew, because of her experiences as a farmer, that the other world out there was too much for two neophytes who thought they could handle themselves against those seasoned, foreign forces.

So, Rosa and I had to stay home. Neither one of us has become a big drinker. I went from rum and coke to scotch in graduate school and to bourbon, martinis, and mai tais in my first few years after graduate school, but it was mainly occasional, social drinking. These days, I seldom have any alcohol beyond a glass of wine if I'm eating out or have houseguests.

Rosa simply can't drink. All she has to do is look at a glass of anything with alcohol in it, and she gets giggly. To this day, I have never seen Rosa drunk. And to this day, I have never been as drunk as I was on that fateful holiday evening in 1966. While I won't say that my mother's farming background prevented us from becoming lushes, it was nonetheless the stone that water could not wash away.

Cotton pickin' authority could also be used to control familial/social behavior. One of my brothers tended toward delinquency in high school, and my mother was at times in conversation with the principal or his teachers about it. After one of those conversations, or when any of us had misbehaved, Momma would make one of those self-sacrificing speeches designed to make any miscreant feel lower than a snake's belly: "I work hard for you children. I try to raise you the best I can. I take you to Sunday school and church. I have worked my fingers to the bone for you. I picked cotton so long and hard sometimes that my fingers would be bloody from where the cotton stalks scratched them. And this is all the thanks I get. You go to school and act out. Lord, have mercy, what am I going to do with you children?" Anyone who caused a speech like that to be recited was supposed to feel miserable—and probably did. Here was this widow woman raising all these little knuckleheaded children by herself, and one of them had had the audacity to act out in public. What was the purpose of picking all that cotton and trying to improve their lots if they still acted like fools? None of us wanted to contemplate Momma's bloody fingers against the backdrop of those pounds of white cotton that she picked and then dropped into the long heavy croaker sack that she dragged behind her. The image of the hardworking, self-sacrificing mother who injured herself for the sake of her children was not a burden that any of us wanted to ponder for long.

It was even worse if Uncle Waddell, my mother's brother who lived down the street, or Uncle Dexter, another of my mother's brothers who dropped in unexpectedly at times and distinguished himself by eating black-eyed peas and cold biscuits for breakfast, got wind of some childish misdoing. Their lectures were like aches in the ears. "You children ought to be ashamed of yourself. Here yo Momma trying to do the best she can for you. I remember the time she worked from morning to night in the fields, always thinking of y'all and trying to do the best she could for y'all.

She picked cotton so y'all wouldn't have to—at least not for all yo lives. And now you up here acting up. What good did it do to take y'all off the farm? If y'all gon act like this, you might as well be pickin' cotton."

On the lighter side, when those same uncles gathered with my mother and other persons who *knew* the cotton picking life, there could be easy conversation about this shared experience. Stories would be told about old so-and-so who had picked an excessive number of pounds of cotton. There were also the stories of how to cheat the "weigh-in" at mid-morning or at the end of the day if you happened to be working in the cotton fields of some stingy white man in Alabama. "Dell," my Uncle Dexter might relate in reference to Uncle Waddell, "didn't like to pick cotton for Mister Jimmy. So he would put big rocks at the bottom of the cotton sack to make it heavier at weigh-in. Now that worked as long as Dell could pour his sack of cotton into the truck bed after weigh-in and toss the rocks aside. He never got caught. But member how stupid Bud was. Instead of puttin' just a couple of big rocks in his sack, he put in seven or eight. Them rocks wuz clanking so loud against them scales that everybody heard'em. Mr. Jimmy made him take 'em out and still docked five pounds from his total weight. You really had to be slick to get past Mister Jimmy." While I certainly was not present during that generation's cotton picking, I do remember that one of my brothers poured a couple of buckets of water onto the cotton in his sack to make it weigh more. Most cotton pickers depended on nature to supply the water, which means that folks got to the cotton fields as early as they could to begin picking while the dew was still on the cotton. Early morning cotton naturally weighed more, so pickers had to do whatever they could in such a limiting economic environment to make the most of their labor. Even when I picked cotton in the 1960s, the price was a mere three cents per pound. In the days during which my mother and her brothers picked cotton every day, all day, it was obviously much less. Perhaps the intensity of their remarks about these experiences was designed to punctuate the fact that so much labor was given for so little economic reward. The imaginative rewards, however, were far more expansive, for references to cotton picking were the creative ground on which stood human interaction and behavior, the measurement of a mother's love for her children, and entertainment among relatives.

And so it went. It might reasonably be argued that our existence in Tuscaloosa in the 1950s and 1960s was merely the foreground to the background of the cotton farming life that we had left to move to the city. It was a touchstone, an ever-ready reference point to delineate the distinctions between then and now, between mind-numbing labor and the possibility of moving to a different level of existence. It was the measure of the difference between doing what one *had* to do in order to survive and learning what one *could* do if one simply studied long and hard enough. It was the distinction between having lived and gathered a wealth of knowledge from those living experiences and merely speculating on what living could be. In other words, it was the difference between experience and innocence, knowledge and initiation. For those of us not properly initiated in the cotton fields of Alabama, the voices of authority derived from cotton picking served to guide our development into creative, resourceful, hardworking human beings.

From: Harris, Trudier. *Summer Snow: Reflections from a Black Daughter of the South.* Boston: Beacon Press, 2003.

The First Time I Saw
Big Daddy Grinning

—LOVALERIE KING

Every now and then, when I am supposed to be reading or doing research for the next chapter in my book or the next scholarly essay, a memory of some event from my distant past will surface suddenly in very vivid detail. Such intercessions have resulted in a drawer full of unfinished poems and short stories that I keep telling myself will one day form the fragmented narrative of my life. For example, in an ongoing letter to my dad (who died in 1987), I've tried to capture the culture shock I experienced upon entering an elite graduate school in my early forties. There's the poem about caring for my mother when she was dying of cancer, and another poem about the mother of a childhood friend—a medium-complexioned patient, a gentle woman who was married to a very dark-skinned man. She did housework for a woman whose husband had a certain reputation, and one year she gave birth to a child that was almost white. I wanted to capture the community's empathetic stance toward her and her family. Then there was the time in my early thirties when I struggled with an early morning witch straddling my body and was moved to write a short story about a young woman who needed to break away from the family she loved in order to become the person she could be. Right after that came the poem about the taboo lover. I blush just thinking about that one. Another poem tries to articulate what it feels like sitting in a community college classroom across from a South

African woman whose face so resembles my own, and yet another recalls the experience of encountering a homeless old woman.

Earlier this year, in those moments between awakening and arising, the memory of a long-forgotten experience invaded my conscious mind and interrupted thoughts of autonomous subjects, identity, critical race theory, and African American literature. The memory concerned something that must have happened around 1963 because that was the first time I had ever been to the field—the cotton field. Big Daddy, my grandfather, hauled field hands for Mr. Ronny Mann's farms scattered throughout Arkansas, Missouri, and Tennessee. He used a big old yellow school bus, and since I had always lived close enough to school to walk every day, I had never really ridden on a school bus or any kind of bus other than Big Daddy's field bus.

My first day in the field now reminds me of that book title about the grass always being greener over the septic tank because that's the gist of what I learned. For me there had always been a mystique about the field-workers coming home in the evening. I never got to see them in the morning. They left too early. But I had watched for years in the evenings as my brothers and, before that, my parents—until my dad got a job as a factory gofer and my mom got hired to clean house for the Kohl family, who owned a restaurant where we couldn't eat—carefully prepared their lunches for the next day. Salami sandwiches, bologna sandwiches, pressed ham sandwiches. Pressed ham? Anyway, sometimes, but not often, there were leftover pieces of chicken or pork chops to be made into sandwiches on Wonder Bread, with sandwich spread (the kind with the pickles) or Miracle Whip. We didn't really like the taste of mayonnaise.

By the time folk usually got to eat those sandwiches around noon the next day, they would have been sitting for anywhere from five to seven hours in their brown paper bags on that hot bus. I know this because eventually I would become a regular fieldworker (even if I didn't quite survive that first day). On the hottest days in the cotton fields, the temperature reached more than a hundred degrees. Totally exposed (and *sans* sunscreen), you could see the heat waves coming toward you across the fields. Seriously! I remember one of my brothers showing me the heat waves for the first time. (That would be the brother who later died in a hospital emergency room after waiting four hours for a doctor.) Maybe that's why some people packed only canned meats—sardines, potted meat, Vienna sausages—and crackers, or Bush's pork n' beans and crackers. Before I was old enough to go out with the workers, we younger children used to raid Big Daddy's bus in the evenings after he had dropped off all the field hands, to see what treats had been—deliberately or inadvertently— left behind. Sometimes there'd be a whole package of Hostess chocolate cupcakes, but even we scavengers passed over the Hostess snowballs. I wondered how anyone who had been routinely exposed to homemade pound cake and sweet potato pie could then turn around and eat a Hostess snowball! Maybe it was because it was exotic.

Big Daddy kept a big red metal container for pops and ice at the back of the bus. In addition to whatever Mr. Ronny Mann paid him per head for the field hands, and whatever percentage of the haul he might have received during picking or pulling season, he made money selling pops to his thirsty workers. Sometimes, if he had pops left over at the end of the day, he would let us have them—not often, but once in a while. Big Daddy could be stingy, or so we thought in those days. Now, I know he was just thrifty and resourceful. Pop was such a treat, such a luxury for us. Water was, of course, free and provided at regular intervals throughout the field-worker's day by the water boy—usually someone too young to be effective at chopping, picking, or pulling cotton—trekking up and down the rows, regardless of whether it was chopping, picking, or pulling season.

For those of you who might be wondering what the hell the difference was between chopping, picking, and pulling cotton, let me explain it the way I learned it. Chopping cotton was not really chopping cotton. Well, it was and it wasn't. You were actually weeding the cotton, but—especially during the early days of growing season—you also had to make sure the cotton plants were not growing so thick that they choked one another off. You had to thin them out by chopping away every other small section so that what was left behind had room to breathe and survive. The chopping was done with a long-handled hoe, and I can remember that some people brought their own hoes (even though the person hauling them to work usually carried a supply of sharpened hoes). Later on in the chopping season, thinning was no longer necessary, and all you had to do was search for weeds, like cockleburs, which we pronounced cukkabugs (which reminds me of a hair joke).

After the chopping comes the picking. Summer was cotton picking time, once the cotton was high and still deep green, and the bolls had opened to reveal the fluffy white stuff inside. We were supposed to remove the fluffy white stuff delicately so as not to contaminate it with anything other than the fluffy white stuff (optic white, you say?), and place it in the cotton sack that would be hooked over your neck and shoulder. Those sacks used to come in small, medium, and large sizes to accommodate the novice, intermediate, and well-heeled pickers. By late summer and early autumn, the cotton stalks were turning brown and crackly, yielding less and less of the fluffy white stuff.

Pulling season was the last ditch effort to get whatever cotton remained on the dry fall plants. By the time this last season was over, it could be downright cold in the early mornings of mid-autumn. I remember my older brothers making small, well-contained fires at the edge of the field to warm us. Gloves were highly recommended because the tough, crackly, sharp-edged boll could be taken right along with the cotton in one strong tug and tossed into the cotton sack. It goes without saying that you were paid less per pound for pulled cotton than you were for picked cotton, since it was not cool for the owner to find bolls or sticks or dirt or anything other than fluffy white cotton during his random checks of picked cotton. He nevertheless tolerated a certain percentage of non-cotton objects amidst pulled cotton. Big Daddy hauled laborers during all these seasons, and my four older brothers and five male cousins made up a large part of his haul.

We were part of a pretty insular community. My mom and her sister had married two brothers, so that made their offspring double cousins. We thought this was a little strange, but someone explained that in rural southern communities, especially back in the 1930s, it was really a matter of logistics, a matter of who lived within walking distance—walking distance being measured in miles, of course. Whatever the case, even in our town, we all lived near one another. In 1963, I had lived around my grandparents all my life. We were all afraid of Big Mama, because she hated the idea of sparing the rod, and, unfortunately for us and the neighborhood children, she was the person designated to babysit us all while our parents worked.

Big Daddy instilled another kind of fear in us altogether. First of all, he was a giant—standing something like six feet three or six feet four, weighing well over two hundred pounds, but I don't recall that he was fat.

He looked like twisted steel to me. He was hard all over, and I know this because once in a while he would take it upon himself to whip one of us children, and he did this by holding us to him and laying it on our behinds. That was the most frightening thought of all—a Big Daddy whipping. He had the hardest arms, the hardest chest, the hardest legs, the hardest jaw. Everybody respected him—or feared him. He didn't frown at you when you did something counterproductive, he sneered—as if only a damned fool would consider doing anything other than what was appropriate, expected, and productive. Big Mama referred to children who stepped out of line as half-raised, but Big Daddy had a way of looking at you like you were the biggest fool and the most ungrateful idiot alive. "Trifling shitasses" is how he described sorry people. I often wonder what he would think of Generation X or the Me Generation. Having been born at the turn of the century, and having grown up under Jim Crow, Big Daddy made very efficient use of his time and resources. Still, he managed to run his own business, such as it was. He owned a decent home on a nice piece of property that's still in the family, and he even had a car, which he kept up immaculately. Few people owned automobiles in our community, so this was no mean accomplishment. Big Daddy couldn't read or write, but the man could drive anywhere in these United States he wanted to go. I guess he knew which highways went where, and he was good with numbers. Big Mama called him B'love. He loved her cooking, and one of my favorite memories is of him sitting at the kitchen table eating her leftover biscuits with *butter*, not margarine, smiling over at his granddaughter (me), who desperately needed a hero. The other thing about Big Daddy is that I don't remember ever hearing him complain about how difficult his life must have been—not that he would have talked to me about it, anyway. Yet, he always seemed to be thinking, contemplating some deep and abiding issue. I would learn more about the kinds of everyday problems men like my grandfather and my father faced from books than they ever told me about themselves. Perhaps this helps to explain how my personal past and my professional present keep getting mixed up together. Imagine the difficulty of trying to attempt a sustained (objective) critical analysis of *The Third Life of Grange Copeland*, for example.

For my maiden visit to the cotton fields, I probably braided my hair and put on a straw hat that Mama would have provided—not knowing how essential that hat would be. Like everyone else, I packed a lunch, and Mama probably gave me some money for pop. Somehow getting up early to go for a long ride on Big Daddy's bus to work alongside my older brothers, my cousins, my parents' friends, and even people I didn't know that well, to eat sun-warmed pressed ham sandwiches with ice cold pop from Big Daddy's cooler seemed a great, romantic adventure. I remember waking up that first day even before my alarm clock went off at 4:00 a.m. I dressed in my layers of clothing—usually an old dress or skirt with at least one pair of pants (though most wore two) underneath, a couple of shirts, and at least two pairs of old socks. I learned later (or figured out), after so many people I knew had died of cancer, that the multiple layers of clothing was as much in defense against the early morning dew (that mixed with some very harsh pesticides) as it was against the midday and afternoon southern summer sun. I don't even want to think about the mosquitoes. What kind of shoes did we wear? Old ones, of course, but I can't remember how comfortable they were. Maybe it didn't matter so much, or maybe comfort was just in the fact that one had shoes. I don't remember how far we had to ride that first day, after the bus meandered through the community picking folk up, but I do know that the idea was to work ten hours a day, and the earlier we began, the earlier came quittin' time. We needed to begin work as soon as we could see what we were doing. Though I couldn't believe they actually expected me to work in the semidarkness, I did well enough after a quick tutorial from a cousin—identifying the weeds, chopping them away, and then carefully thinning out the cotton—not too thin, maybe six inches or so between clumps. Somebody told me that I was going to make a good fieldworker.

By eleven o'clock I had vowed never to set foot in a cotton field again! It was a vow that I would not be able to keep, though by noon I was suffering from something. Exhaustion? Heatstroke? The longest sustained amount of physical labor I'd ever performed? I was eleven, and Mama had begged me to wait another year or so for my first day, but I couldn't wait. I wanted to be one of those tired, but strong-looking comrades who exited the bus in the evenings. I was eleven—okay—and it was the closest (and safest) thing to a romantic fantasy I had going. I spent most of the afternoon of my first day in the bus, sleeping, and waiting for the real workers to finish for the day. No one was going to take the time to drive my sorry behind back to town.

The following morning I awoke to find that the dew (and whatever poisons might have been mixed with it) had turned my fresh mosquito bites into pus-filled sores, which left me feeling disgusted. As demonstrative and vocal as my grandfather was reserved, Mama said I told you so (or rather "wouldn't nothin' do you but to go!"), which, knowing Mama, I expected.

The fact that I eventually failed at my first day of fieldwork is not the point of this story, however. After that first day, I stayed away from the cotton field as long as I could—until fieldwork became as mandatory for me as it was for my brothers. It was toward the end of my first day that I heard Mr. Mann's pickup drive up—though I would learn later that most of the workers believed that, like Douglass's Covey, he was always hovering nearby. He had arrived to settle up with Big Daddy. When I gathered with the returning workers near the back of the bus to collect my partial day's wages, I saw Big Daddy grinning, really grinning for the first time in my life. I imagine that over the years that they dealt with one another, the two men developed certain routines. My Big Daddy's eyes were cast slightly downward and off to the side. What was this stance, and why was he so jovial (not a word that would have come to mind at the time)? I could only remember having seen him smile slightly on a couple of occasions, but here he was transformed into . . . what? Whatever it was, it was something I had not previously seen—not with Big Daddy, and I instinctively didn't like Ronny Mann for bringing it out. I was not innocent of race and racism. I had been called "nigger" plenty of times by the few white people poor enough to live among us, but this thing between my Big Daddy and the white landowner was something I had not observed before. I forgot the image, or so I thought. Then, one morning this year, almost forty years later, the whole scene flooded my memory and I raced to my souped-up computer with the Pentium processor to commit it to paper.

At least a year transpired before I ventured again into a cotton field, but by that time I had started bleaching my skin. My grandfather died not long after—when I was fourteen—of a stroke while trying to intervene in a fight between my parents. By the time I turned fifteen, I had found a way to spend my summers in places where no one was growing cotton and expecting me to cultivate it. By the time I finished high school, I had stopped bleaching my skin. And though faint shadows remain, the calluses I developed working cotton fields for a couple of years during my adolescence have almost completely disappeared, as have the scars from the leg sores that appeared the morning after that first day. I have fresher scars now that I will shed as the years go by. Looking back, Big Daddy's grinning was to me as incongruous as my naive confidence upon entering an elite graduate school in my early forties. Big Daddy was there with me in spirit, however. This time he was a woman, still tall, strong, and purposeful, and never, ever grinning unless she was seriously amused. I made it through, and now I write the books, articles, poems, stories, and letters that circumstances precluded Big Daddy from writing.

On Gardening, or A Love Supreme

—JOYCE PETTIS

My houseplants are being caressed and nourished by soft rain today, a rare treat for them. They are seldom outside. Instead, they lived massed on a small screened-in porch from mid-spring until fall when the first frost threatens them. So this late August day as fall begins to make its presence felt and excessive sunlight is not a threat, I have put my plants on the adjoining deck so that they may exult in the sprinkle of rain and have a leaf bath, too. My plants are not exotic varieties but the average ones that any family might have: angel-wing begonia, schefflera, snake plant, Christmas cactus, philodendron, Chinese bamboo, dieffenbachia, and several others. The split-leaf philodendron is too heavy and unwieldy for me to drag onto the deck for the rain. Like the other plants, it is quite happy to live on the porch for a few months and to enjoy the humidity of the North Carolina summer. Not all of my plants enjoy this luxury, however. The leaves of some of them, African violets for example, do not welcome the strong light of summer. Even if they did, I have to keep some of them inside for my eyes to feast upon anytime I look about the house. Plants live in every room in my home.

My collection is neither large nor extravagant; that is, I have not sought out unusual or expensive plants. I do not constantly add to the collection. In fact, many of my plants are very old and very large. The dieffenbachia and the split-leaf philodendron are at least twenty-five years old. The dieffenbachia, commonly called dumb cane (though I never call it that) loses its lower leaves, a malady that results in a tall, bare cane stem. I cut (and root) these stems, thus keeping the plant reasonably compact in its container. The size of the split-leaf philodendron, however, betrays its age. Its top leaves are taller than my five feet three inches, and its woody gray/brown stem where its leaves have dropped off over the years is six inches in diameter. It lives in the largest container that I have, a circular ceramic pot fifty inches around.

"I never thought you'd be interested in plants and gardening," my mother said when she first noted them in my home and listened to my complaints about the poor soil in the first yard that my husband and I had. "I couldn't get you into the garden when you were growing up," she added. I had no quick response for her. I had not analyzed what, in hindsight, appears to be a correlation between creating a home and the role plants would play in that creation.

My mother's garden, like that of other families on our street, had collards, green beans, mustard greens, beets, corn, onions, cabbages, tomatoes, and sage. A fig bush and an aged pear tree occupied a span of land between the garden and the house. In the postdepression years, when she was a young woman raising my older sister and my father had escaped rural North Carolina for Maryland, gardening was an essential source of food, although raising the food gave her pleasure. As a girl I couldn't have cared less about gardening.

My mother, however, motivated my reluctant participation, if not my interest, by telling me what my task was: "We need to pick the string beans [or whatever vegetables were ripe] before it gets too hot," she'd say. "But I'm reading," I'd counter. "The book will be here; the beans [or other vegetable] won't be good if they sit through this hot day," she'd say. So before 9:00 a.m., my skinny brown form, her short sturdy one, and the tall thin shape of my mother's fellow gardener, her sister Lillian (Aunt Lil), would capture the ripe vegetables. Working in the garden involved a ritual of dress that I was reminded of when I read Paule Marshall's *Praisesong for the Widow* where Aunt Cuney dressed specifically for her trek with the small Avey, although it was not a garden visit. Aunt Lil and my mother always wore long cotton dresses (never jeans or slacks), ankle galoshes for protection against dirt and the possibility of a snake (never tennis shoes), and wide-brimmed straw hats topped off with a narrow ribbon that hung on their necks. The straw hat was the only part of the uniform that I wore. Aunt Lil carried large round deep pans that were strictly reserved for vegetable tasks, and my mother carried a hoe.

Back at the house with our pans brimming over with fresh produce, my mother, aunt, and I began whatever process a particular vegetable required. Stems had to be removed from turnip greens, mustard greens, or collards, and their outside, tough leaves discarded. String beans had to be snapped, tomatoes washed, and on and on. Whatever was not destined for dinner that evening would be conserved either by canning or, when it became fashionable, freezing. Both of these acts also required processes that my mother and aunt performed. A row of zinnias grew in the garden, where their upright and tightly gathered red or pink or goldish colored blooms offered a wonderful counterpoint to the predominant greens of the vegetables. Their beauty comforted me, minimally, from the labor of gardening.

Numerous shrubs grew around our two-story, white house and my mother maintained them. What I remember is her trimming them because she preferred to control their natural wildness. We had a Rose-of-Sharon and a gardenia bush that sat on the east and west sides, respectively, of the porch. I loved the gardenia blooms' heavy perfume as it filled the porch at night. A few rose bushes, azaleas, crepe myrtles, and "hedges," as we called them, were in other parts of the yard. We had silver maples, a weeping willow tree, and a chinaberry tree draped in moss. (In my mouth, chinaberry was "chaneyberry.") I played with the moss; it was the bed for my dolls or sometimes their long, fashionable hair. After the most severe hurricane of my growing up years, however, Aunt Lil and my mother decided the silver maple and the chinaberry tree could have crushed the house in the storm, so these trees were taken down. No moss adorned the other trees around us, and none reappeared after the demise of the chinaberry tree. I don't recall how I learned the names of the shrubbery or trees at an early age; perhaps I knew them because my mother identified them by their names.

My mother's houseplants disinterested me as much as the garden. She watered and repotted, as necessary, begonia, geranium, fern, snake plant, and wandering jew, which I always heard as "wandering dew." It wasn't until I began to read about plants after my undergraduate years that I knew the plant was a wandering *jew*! These familiar shrubs, trees, and houseplants defined the borders of my small world, and the vegetables provided food, but their importance on any level was unremarkable to me.

Whatever it is that entices us to follow the practices of our parents and relatives most probably directed my love of plants as an adult. Sidney Poitier in *The Measure of a Man* says that human beings have a "sensitivity panel . . . of connected sensitivity remembrances all passed along through the blood." He suggests that traits may lie dormant over generations and then suddenly lay claim to a member of a family. My love of plants sprang unanticipated and fully developed. Once my husband, young son, and I moved into a house with a yard, plants were immediately essential to the space, and I began to buy them. I chose those with visual appeal, without knowing what care they required. My love of plants includes growing vegetables, but I have never, technically, had a garden in the southern sense, that is, a plot of land solely dedicated to producing vegetables and fruits. Over the years, however, I have grown tomatoes, peppers, eggplant, okra, and herbs.

Strangely, I did not seek my mother's advice about plant care. I sought the library and books about houseplants, for I love books as well as plants. I found in them many of the specimens my mother had raised as well as the methods of care I remembered her practicing. However, I could not walk to the back of my subdivision yard and dig dirt in which my plants would thrive as my mother had done on her property. My yards have all offered inhospitable soil. None of the premixed varieties have surpassed my memory of the dense, moist feel and fecund smell of my mother's patch of special plant soil. As an adult, I've learned that the deep brown-black soil of that area was the result of natural composting. Long before my birth that area had been the site of the woodpile for the wood-burning stoves that, also years earlier, had cooked the food and warmed the house during the winter months.

My mother's plants were, in fact, "house" plants only incidentally, when she brought them inside to survive the cold weather. They were more properly "porch plants." My mother did not coddle her plants or shrubs. Only occasionally do I recall her making plants a part of her conversation. Her attention was placed on the garden, perhaps out of necessity, because the demands of the vegetable garden could not be ignored if she wanted its produce.

Unlike my mother, I am a confessed and shameless coddler of my plants and shrubs. They are my intimates, and I am emotionally attached to them and to their care. I surprised myself once when I cried because my mate, well intentioned though he was, severely crippled the naturally long, spiraling branches of the forsythia along our yard's border by closely trimming them. Coddling has not meant that I have embarked on a scientific approach to plants. I have not performed complicated methods of propagation, for example, but I have read about the execution of such methods and do engage in simple methods of propagation. I know only a few of their Latin names, but I did complete a Master Gardener class. I have not traveled to southwestern China to collect and to observe rare species as Jamaica Kincaid details her experiences in *My Plant Book*. But when I travel, however, I am receptive to the flora. The plant life in the Caribbean seduced me. When I spent four weeks in Guadeloupe, croton was not a houseplant but a shrub of several feet; the stately antherium covered hillsides, and caladium grew wild. I saw my first allemanda there and immediately loved it. I had myself photographed amid its compact, trumpet-shaped brilliant yellow blooms as I later had myself photographed in southern Germany amid the perfume of lilac bushes that were taller than I was. I found allemanda in nurseries in North Carolina and grew it during the summer. Unfortunately, it does not survive our winters except in a greenhouse. My love of plants is nearly indiscriminate; I love almost all of them, but not quite.

Any lover of plants knows that a small degree of coddling is rewarded at least trice over, although some houseplants will live and look pretty without it. But I like to think that the emotional attachment that drives care reveals itself indirectly in the beauty of the specimen, in the vibrancy of color, in the size of blooms, and in the overall lushness of the plant. My plants reward my care with healthy hues of green and whatever markings distinguish their particular leaves. The blooming ones reward me with their distinctive pinks or reds or whites. My Christmas cactus, for example, blooms profusely, although early, the week before Thanksgiving. The salmon pink, elongated blooms look like furious, ruffled shrimp. Minimum care is required for the cactus, yet its annual costume of color is always extravagant. African violets, on the other hand, need more than minimal care, although they are not difficult to grow and do reward with frequent blooms. My niece gave me a violet for Valentine's Day in 1991. "I'd like to keep it," she said, "but it would die." That flower is now twelve years old, and I have a few violets that are older, whose circumstances of acquisition went unremarked.

Plants have an emotionally stabilizing effect for me, and perhaps for others, too. They calm by their presence and lure a frantic mind back to safer space. They must be more than a passing fashion and serve more than a superficial decorative purpose in our malls, restaurants, hotels, and in most of our public spaces. Their beauty affects us in ways that defy articulate explanation. For example, I find the bareness of my campus office without plants is alienating. Each fall when I return from summer for the new semester, I can't settle and work there without cut blooms or plants. As soon as possible I purchase a floral bouquet until transplanting a few potted plants from home is convenient. I am convinced that plants must be a necessary extension to our humanity and to the sustenance of our spirit.

Over the years, plants have come to mark numerous significant events in my life. When I had recuperated from my first ever surgery, I posed in the backyard with two split-leaf philodendrons. One of them was donated to a library, but the other one is now taller than I am. Most of the azaleas and rhododendrons in the backyard were planted when I knew that my first husband's multiple myeloma, one of the three kinds of bone cancer, had finally won its seven-year battle with him, and he had only a few months left to live. While he was in the upstairs bedroom during the weeks before his final hospitalization, I spent many afternoon hours shoveling dirt to create holes for the small bushes that I tugged from their black containers and planted in the backyard. My husband could sit up in bed and watch my labor. As his strength dwindled, almost literally before my eyes, I mounted my own battle against death through the promise of life symbolized in plants. They were, as I later came to think of this time, *my* therapy and salvation. I did not consciously choose specimens to commemorate this period; the beauty of the pictured bloom on the plants' tags was enough. When my husband died, someone sent an elaborate dish garden to the house that a creative florist had instead arranged in a shallow basket. Amid the confusion of that time, the sender's card was lost, but I have coaxed the barely four-inch schefflera from the arrangement to its present five-feet height. It is also now twelve years old and a strong, well-branched, healthy little tree. Not all of the plants I have owned, loved, and coddled have lived, but the longevity of plants is one of their surprising and marvelous qualities.

In my home and in the yard, too, my plant collection continues, slowly, to grow and also to reveal itself to me. Their revelations, in fact, are part of their appeal. "OK, what do you require?" I silently ask. In time, they tell me. One type of coreopsis, for example, a low-growing landscape plant with a yellow upturned bloom in early summer, told me it was as hard to control as a wayward teenager and required the entire backyard. I had to practice tough love and have it removed. The peony prefers independence; it requires only sun and my affection. How can one not love and be amazed by a peony bush? Its rapid red stalks emerge from earth and ascend in April, all prepared to support its deep rose lush blooms amid waxy green leaves in May. I cut vases of them, one for my house, one for my friend Gracie, and one for my mother. The calla lilies, too, are also independent and sexy! Photographers and painters confirm the elegance and appeal of their blooms because their images are almost as frequently seen as the rose. My calla lilies are yellow. Early in my relationship with the man who became my second husband, he brought me an incredibly lovely arrangement of hosta leaves and white calla lilies when he did not know how much I loved them. Well, reader, *I married him!*

Plants both in the house and outside have become remarkable to me and inseparable from me. My mother has long ceased being surprised at their inclusion in my life and has never assumed responsibility for being my model. But often, when I am tending my plants, and they are enabling my spirit, I think back to my childhood reluctance in her garden, and laugh.

A Very Good Year

— HERMINE PINSON

I n my fourth-grade photo, which is somewhere in one of the innumerable boxes I've packed over the years and put in attics or garages, I wore a burgundy plaid cotton dress, a white Peter Pan collar, and a bright orange sweater, in fact, my favorite one. Two lopsided pigtails stood out from my head like lambs' horns. I smiled from ear to ear according to the photographer's directions to say "cheese." My two front teeth slightly turned in toward each other, which made them look as if they hadn't quite settled. They were new to my face.

I took that picture in 1962, a year of several indelible experiences whose impact I'm still discovering over forty-five years later, although I already know that to render this experience with clarity and insight would be like trying to fish bare-handed.

It was three years after my family moved from Beaumont, Texas, to Nashville, Tennessee, where my father and mother set up house so he could complete his studies at Meharry Medical College to become a doctor while she supported his efforts by teaching in the public school system. It was the year I bonded with a group of remarkable girls and discovered my own propensity for language and performance. It was the last year I thought the national news didn't affect my life on my street in my house. It was the last year before the deadly series of assassinations of public figures in the United States started with the killing of President John F. Kennedy and ended with the killing of Dr. Martin Luther King Jr .

For me, the sound of 1962 is not Ray Charles's chart-topping "I Can't Stop Loving You" or Gene Chandler's "Duke of Earl," although our babysitters sat by the radio or danced in their socks to these songs. I hear "Let us Break Bread Together." Kathleen Battle's gorgeous rendition of the simple but deeply moving spiritual sounds my early years in Nashville and our furnace-heated house on Scovel Street. Of course, the song predates Ms. Battle's recording of it, but her supple soprano with its perfect rendering of southern inflections and full vibrato unlocks a door to the time the Fisk Jubilee Singers sang spirituals in close harmony in the Fisk Memorial Chapel to an attentive audience of students (young women, their hair done in demure pressed curls and wearing their best dresses and pearls and young men in thin neckties), professors, families from the community, listening and nodding in recognition and affirmation of communion and community. My mother and father sat with their then four (soon to be five) children, she in her white gloves, content to listen to music she had grown up loving. Here more than anywhere else, she was engaged and content. It was as if we in the chapel all loved each other in a way we all implicitly understood.

In 1962 my world was bounded by my house on Scovel Street, my elementary school on Todd Boulevard, and Otey's Grocery Store, the John Calvin Presbyterian Church, and Fisk University on Jefferson Street. School days, girl scout shoes, book satchels, long waxed linoleum corridors, peanut butter and jelly sandwiches, the *Flat & Scruggs* early morning show on weekdays, the *Twilight Zone* on Friday nights, Hoss and Little Joe on Sunday's *Bonanza*, and *The Ed Sullivan Show* before bed filled my world. We were, after all, the first TV generation: the straightening comb once every two weeks in Mrs. Durden's close kitchen, careful play on Saturday so as not to sweat our hair back for church Sunday, and in spring grandmother-made organdy dresses with bowed sashes the color of red maples. My parents admired the opera singer Leontyne Price, who people said had conquered the Western world with her marvelous voice. They admired the Reverend James Lawson, Martin Luther King, and John F. Kennedy, so I did too, without knowing anything about them except Miss Price sang beautifully and she, along with the men, was the hope of the black community and the nation. Grown-ups excitedly argued among themselves in living rooms, barbershops, and churches across the city and the nation about what "integration" meant and whether it was a needful thing. I did know that I was "Negro" and Negroes were not always treated fairly by white people in America. You didn't see them in charge of things on TV, and when one did appear it was newsworthy enough to call neighbors and friends to remark upon it. But the injustice of segregation or even the occasional eruptions of institutionalized violence in the form of police arrests of protesters didn't rend the fabric of our lives or seriously disrupt the day-to-day rhythm of life in our all-black community of mostly wood frame houses, churches, schools, stores, gas stations, funeral parlors, nightclubs, and juke joints. My girl classmates and I wanted to wear pencil-thin skirts, mohair sweaters, and bouffant hairdos like the big girls who wanted to be like the singers of Motown, Martha and the Vandellas, or Diana Ross and the Supremes. I didn't know enough to want to be kissed by a boy. I still held my big sister's hand when I crossed a busy street. I certainly didn't understand the implications of living a segregated life.

My parents had been undergraduates and sweethearts at Fisk before marrying and starting a family. By the time I came along, the second of eventually five children, they had managed to get through the familial milestones of christenings, first teeth, first steps, first grade, chicken pox, vaccinations. They had also lived through birth of rock 'n' roll and rhythm and blues (by my ninth year, my mother still had her poodle skirt), the end of the Korean War, and the effects of *Brown v. Board of Education*, which commenced the modern push for black social, political, and legal parity in the South. To be in the South was exciting but also stressful, because if you were black, no matter how enlightened you perceived yourself to be, you could not escape the day-to-day indignities that defined the place to a greater or lesser degree. When my parents married in 1951, blacks were still sitting in the back of the bus in Nashville, Tennessee, and Beaumont, Texas; they still would not be served in certain stores or restaurants, if they demanded to try on the clothes or sit down at the tables. They could not be sure whether the policeman who stopped them was a fair man or an affiliate of the Klan or White Citizens Council. My parents brought the stress of these experiences home with them, even if they had decided early in their marriage not to train their children to hate or fear "white folks." They wanted to be one of the progressive-thinking-and-acting couples they associated with. They once went to a fundraiser ball that featured Sidney Poitier and Harry Belafonte. On the other hand, it seems they were psychologically bound by outdated notions of marriage that said the wife's place was in the home, and the husband was provider and last word on everything.

Between the external pressure of racism and the internal conflicts that sprang from being two explosive, strong-willed, creative people, their tensions often combusted into raging arguments. As early as the age of three, I could remember the sound of raised voices and the occasional tussle while I listened from the relative safety of the bedroom where my mother had placed my older sister and me.

As we grew, my siblings and I heard fragments of dialogue, "I'm a man and this is my house!" "You're not my father, and I'll do as I damn well please!" We knew better than to ask questions about arguments the night before. That was "grown folks' business." Their arguments started over any number of things. Maybe, as he sometimes tried to explain, he had stayed out late to play cards or to blow off steam with other young doctors or stopped by the Del Morocco to catch Jimi Hendrix and the King Kasuals. Maybe, he was worried about a patient and so sat with him through the night. For my mother's part, maybe she'd discovered a lipstick-stained handkerchief in my father's pocket when she was washing his clothes or perhaps that same handkerchief was scented with another woman's perfume. Or maybe Mother refused to back down when my father said she should not risk her safety to stand on the picket line or maybe he tried to chastise her about staying out past what he thought was a decent curfew for his wife. Maybe the moon was full, and maybe there was no moon at all.

My parents weren't always uncivil to each other or to us. They were capable of turning their attention to the business of family and teaching their children the meaning of doing well. They were no strangers to joy or beauty, and often during periods of tranquility they shared their beauty and knowledge with us. From my father who enjoyed fishing, we learned the pleasures of going down to the river's edge to catch a fish or to bask in the rhythm of nature or to sit in the backseat on road trips and take my father's "common knowledge" quizzes to ward off boredom while passing through small towns at three in the morning, all of us in the car together going someplace far away.

From my mother was the gift of literature and music: fairy tales, children's ditties, Aesop, Dr. Seuss, Dave Brubeck's "Take Five," or Nina Simone alone with her piano and her splendid rage, something my mother, a gifted pianist, well understood. We went as a family on sightseeing trips to Hadley Park or the Parthenon at Christmas to buy a Christmas tree in the temporary forest of potted trees, dwarfed by the formidable and classic lines of the Parthenon that had somehow landed like a space alien on a low hill in Nashville. When my father sang along in his slightly flat bass with Glenn Campbell, I wanted to believe he was the "lineman from the county" and my mother was the one he longed for. Sometimes, especially early on, their friends—young doctors, schoolteachers, secretaries, and graduate students—would come to our small stucco house on Scovel Street. They shared potluck dinners, wine, whiskey, and stories about difficult professors, difficult cases, and the developments in the student-led civil rights movement, which had effectively integrated downtown lunch counters two years before with the leadership of students like John Lewis, Dianne Nash, and the Reverend James Lawson. Some had sat at the lunch counters; some had marched the picket line; some were planning to take the nonviolent classes that were held in the basement of Jubilee Hall on Fisk's campus. My mother wanted to volunteer. Amid this excitement, we, ostensibly the "next generation" of freedom fighters, were called into the living room briefly to greet the guests, before being banished to our beds.

"My, my you're a big girl! How old are you?" asked a handsome intern in glasses.

"I'm nine and I can sing Gloria Lynne's "I Should Care." Wanna hear it?" I said, stalling for time to gaze at these glamorous grown-ups with their perfume, cigarettes, pipes, and clinking wine glasses. I wanted to see these adults, to listen to their stories, to be part of their ritual of sharing and laughter because the other one, the secret ritual of violence, shattered things to the point where we had to start all over again, picking up the broken pieces of our lives, moving back to normal.

Home was home and school was another thing. I think my mother took pride in the fact that we didn't miss school. Perhaps it was a way for both my parents to convince themselves that things weren't so bad, that they were really no different from any other parents trying to steer their children through certain racial and class-determined land mines. In school, I could get attention by obeying the rules and being smart, so I began to equate studying hard and getting good grades with organization and perfection. While the grown-ups worried about sit-ins or picket lines at major department stores such as Harveys and Cain-Sloan, we focused on what we could control in our world, and that wasn't very much. I was among the "smart" ones who could read, write, and figure a little better than the rest. But we weren't especially close, and artificial divisions disappeared almost entirely on the playground when we played jump rope or a hand-clap or circle game. We were obedient children, mostly being seen and not heard, until the spring of 1962 when a new girl came to the school.

Though I think she entered in the spring of our third-grade year, my memory of Oprah doesn't become vivid until the fall of that year, when we entered Mrs. Duncan's fourth-grade class. By this time, the whole class had taken notice of her, because she turned in her homework assignments early, even if we weren't asked to do so, and she knew enough Bible verses that Mrs. Duncan called on her often to say the morning devotional. Curiosity and not a little envy soon turned to overt devotion and emulation among the girls, especially the ones used to getting called on by the teacher to read and recite, and to take messages to the office. When we got to know Oprah better, we discovered she was on a mission to do the best she could and to trust in the Lord, but she also liked to laugh and do the things girls do. Deborah Bright and I were among the girls who responded to the urgency and conviction of Oprah's encouragement to do better, to be better, to believe and trust in God. What we did from moment to moment mattered. We mattered. To my nine-year-old mind, the idea of being good and letting that be my goal every day sounded like a solution to the problem of worrying about what tomorrow would bring or trying to control my home life. Now, at nine years old I didn't have a formal plan of conduct, but my goals were simple then and being good was easier to imagine than to do. Sometimes this philosophy had unexpected consequences. When I tried to apply it to ballet, my attempts at precision must have looked to my teacher Mrs. Love like rigor mortis because she tried to bend my stiffened arm for a more natural look. For better or for worse, being good and doing well were my raison d'être.

Several girls in the class and I formed an all-girls group that stuck together in our beliefs and expressed our regard for each other by our fierce devotion to these simple principles. Once, for example, when Mrs. Duncan left the classroom on an errand, the fiercest girl in the class and a peripheral member of our group got into a nose-bloodying fight with one of the boys. Our group resolutely turned our chairs away from the fracas, upon Oprah's insistence that we "do our work," no matter that the fight pushed us closer and closer to the margins of the room, until our desks were pushed hard against the blackboard. Our desks bunched in futile defense against the encroaching bodies of loud spectators, but we continued to copy Mrs. Duncan's neat script. At least, we were exercising some control over our environment. Anyone peering in through the window would have thought we were a room of schizophrenics or subjects of a bizarre experiment in which half the room responded to certain "stimuli" with abandon while the other half practiced fastidious control, noses pressed almost against the blackboard.

When my parents' disagreements threatened to turn the house upside down, I tried to follow Oprah's example of single-mindedness and purposefulness. I thought my close self-monitoring would somehow make them stop focusing on their differences to the exclusion of the daily order of things, but I cared too much about the combatants, and I couldn't read or write with a jumbled stomach and my heart in my mouth.

I depended on Oprah's sense of urgency and conviction. Her remarkable talent for spelling (she was usually the last one standing in a spelling bee), her memorization of seemingly endless numbers of Bible verses, the straightness of her posture, the set of her mouth, with the slight upside-down smile on her chin, all these things fascinated and, indeed, uplifted me and I think encouraged our group, as a whole. Envy was subsumed in concentrating on the work. This was not the case with classmates outside our band of believers. On the playground away from the watchful eyes of Mrs. Duncan, who held Oprah up to the class as a shining example, others, especially the boys, teased her and told her to her face she was crazy and so were we for going along with her. The boys tried to give her nicknames that usually didn't stick, because she seemed oblivious to them and if she could not avoid them, she faced them down and talked them away. Perhaps it was her stern, righteous demeanor or the way she spoke to them, as if she knew with all her heart and soul Jesus was coming again. Her energy and resolve (with us standing beside her) usually caused the most brazen boy to backpedal, while pretending not to be intimidated. To be Oprah's friend was to believe with her in an all-powerful God who righted wrongs and looked out for little black girls. Oprah was on her way to Canaan land, and if you didn't go, she'd leave you in the dust of your own sins. Her conviction was somehow linked in my mind with my mother's recording of *Porgy and Bess* and Robert McFerrin's Porgy singing in his deep baritone, "Oh Lord, I'm on my way. I'm on my way to Canaan land." It was buoyant and precious and hopeful in the way Porgy, in spite of his own crippled status, was traveling down the road to find his true love Bess, as surely as Dorothy traveled down the yellow brick road to find the wizard. Porgy was going a long, long way to get to some place better, to find his Bess. Oprah knew the way to Canaan land for little black girls with parent troubles or sister-and-brother troubles or teacher troubles.

Maybe one day I bragged to the group about my powers of memorization and recitation. I don't exactly remember the occasion, but Oprah challenged me to memorize "Invictus." When we talked years later, Deborah Bright-Johnson, a girl I had known since first grade, reminded me that Oprah had challenged her to memorize the poem, as well. This was not Mrs. Duncan's assignment, but one made by our peer, our leader. I boasted that I could memorize the poem in no time. I could not contain my excitement. I felt as relevant and present as daylight. Oprah's challenge to me was a gift and a goal. I didn't know anything about William Henley, didn't know he was white or that he was blind or that he'd written the poem while recovering from a serious illness. To me the poem was about faith in beating the odds, about not simply surviving, but prevailing in the face of mountainous obstacles. The poem's first line incited no fear because I remembered Langston Hughes's poems celebrated people the color of night.

> Out of the night that covers me
> Black as a Pit from pole to pole
> I thank whatever gods may be
> For my unconquerable soul.

Bracing words for little middle-class black girls who for all practical purposes were invisible to the wider world. No Disney-sponsored *That's So Raven* sitcoms featured little black girls and Diahann Carroll's *Julia* was still a few years away. We were only beginning to see more black dolls on the market. In 1962, Barbie's costumes and hair color came in all varieties, but not her skin tone.

I didn't tell my parents of my peer-assignment. I wasn't trying to keep it a secret, but I also didn't want to share it until I had mastered it, so I didn't tell them until I was ready to recite the poem, which took a couple of days. Memorizing the poem invigorated me, not in the way an Easter speech at church or a part in the school play would make me nervous or apprehensive. I had been asked to commit a poem to memory, if for no other reason than to demonstrate my power of recall, commitment, and will.

The day I memorized it, I waited with sweaty palms and a galloping heart for my mother to get home from work. It just so happened that my father was home that day, and I asked them to sit and listen to me recite a poem. They both looked surprised and pleased at my self-motivation and asked if I would recite outside, so out we went to the backyard. I remember the yard being unkempt with bald patches where we often played and a fence with missing staves where we had created an easy entrance to our neighbor's yard, but it was green and fragrant with new growth. My mother and father and Primila, my oldest sister, sat on the concrete steps of the back porch, holding their knees.

"Go on! We're ready," they said.

I stood with my hands at my sides and recited the poem. As I spoke, the words took on a personal significance that resonated in the conviction of my delivery. When I finished, everyone clapped as if I had just given a concert at the Fisk Memorial Chapel.

"When's the program?" my mother asked.

"Yes, we didn't know anything about the program," my father said.

"There's no program. I just did it because Oprah asked me to do it," I said.

At that moment, I might have looked exactly as I had in my class picture, because I had chosen to wear my burgundy plaid cotton dress with my bright orange sweater, knee socks, and leather lace-up shoes, and I was smiling, showing those teeth which did not yet match my face.

"Oh! How nice!" my parents said, while looking a little puzzled. Adults were accustomed to children dutifully reciting Easter or Christmas speeches chosen for them by their teachers. They were not accustomed to children giving themselves such work to do. Later in the week, I took a moment when Mrs. Duncan left the room to recite the poem for Oprah. I wanted to impress her because more than I believed in and trusted any adults then, I trusted her. Oprah was pleased that I had accomplished this feat and proven my commitment to being as strong and as smart as I could be. Not long after that she invited our little group to her house. We arrived after church and sipped punch and munched on sandwiches and cookies. Then, Oprah asked us all to take a long walk in the woods with her.

The woods near the Monroe home on Clay Street in North Nashville were appealing this time of year (I think it was mid-spring). The writer in me wants there to have been wild grass, skunk cabbage, and bluets. The writer in me wants to remember the sun passing its fingers of light through trees as we walked, giving us a sense of peace and quiet. What's true is I was fully engaged, and the other girls were too, because in spite of our differences in personality and taste, this green space induced a kind of self-forgetting. It was a place to skip and chatter and be girls together. I was tickled to be there. At the same time, I knew this was a special gathering. We never had one like it again; even if we had birthday parties or parties at the Recreation Center, we never had one like that one. And even if sentiment has gilded this memory, making the trees greener and the light brighter, what's really important is being out there in that space granted us all time to breathe and matter to each other in the moment, to talk about those things we were interested in. We were content to be.

I was gaining a sense of self-awareness and self-possession, and my mother noticed. One day I heard her talking on the phone to one of her sisters.

"I don't know what's gotten into her. Since she's taken up with her classmate, she wants to read the Bible. She says she wants to be saved, but there's something else I can't put my finger on."

I had actually asked my mother if I could be saved, to which she smiled and answered, "You are already saved; you've been saved since you were two years old, and your grandfather christened you in the Presbyterian Church."

"But I want to be dipped in the river, washed clean," I answered, thinking the more dramatic ceremony was somehow more authentic and more lasting.

"Let's wait and see. If you still want to do it in a year, we'll see," was all she said. She smiled and shook her head as she returned to folding clothes.

Just when I was beginning to see myself as someone separate from my family, someone who thought separate thoughts and felt separate feelings, Oprah moved away. She was gone by the beginning of our fifth-grade school year. I didn't communicate with my school friends during the summer, so I didn't know who to ask for her address, even if I had thought to write her a letter. She had been the animus of our group, though we couldn't have articulated it then. Her absence impoverished my social life at school and also my imaginative life at home. I think the other girls felt it too because we drifted back into our former loose social groupings of twos and threes. Deborah Bright and I grew closer that year, not speaking of Oprah but persisting in our own way in our pursuit of the right thing to do and be, but I must say in spite of my best efforts, I was a little lost. For a while I acted out my disappointment and grief by deliberately doing things to alienate my friends and family. By the fall of my fifth-grade year Dr. King had already given his "I Have a Dream" speech in Washington, D.C., in what has now become known as the "March on Washington," and President Kennedy was assassinated in November of 1963. We students were lined up in the corridor and told to be still and be quiet, while the teachers gathered around TV sets to get the latest developments of the news. I was discovering that the world was a hostile place, and there were people in the world who cared nothing about being good or kind, who in fact craved blood. None of this stopped the ongoing personal wars of my parents. I couldn't control what they did, and I couldn't talk about it, but I could use the new curse words I'd learned on the playground. One day, walking home from school with my friends, I deliberately used every curse word I could think of in as many combinations as I could think to use them. Deborah and the other girls asked me to stop, then walked ahead of me, rather than endure my foul mouth. At home, my new sense of relative personal autonomy had equally mixed results. One day my mother had to leave the house suddenly, so she didn't have time to get a babysitter. She put Primila, my then eleven-year-old sister, in charge and told us to do our homework and sit on the couch until she returned. I had other things in mind besides sitting on the couch and decided instead to don my best Sunday dress with blue flowerets on a flared skirt. I was like the little girl with the curl when she was bad. Round and round the house I danced in my finery and said horrid things to my brothers and oldest sister, who were offended by my imperious manner and demonstrated their displeasure by chasing me around the house, which caused me to tear and stain my beautiful dress. My mother arrived home to a great commotion and a house that looked as if it had been ransacked. I was acting the part of the distressed princess in what was left of my dress.

"But Mama" was all I had a chance to say, as my brothers and sister recounted how I was the instigator. What could I say in my defense? I was wearing the evidence. My mother wasted no time in disabusing me of any notions that I was a distressed princess.

"Young lady, you march in your room and take that dress off. I don't know what's gotten into you, but I will not tolerate this behavior. Get me that strap. Yes, that one!"

By the time Oprah moved back to Nashville, my family and I had moved, first to Mississippi, then to Houston, Texas. That was also the last time I saw most of the girls in our group. For a while I missed our camaraderie, not that I had shared confidences with Deborah or Oprah or any of my school friends, nor do I know how much they shared with each other, but in 1962 we gave each other ourselves with a purity of heart that is the measure of innocence: love, faith, loyalty, yes, and willingness to believe together, against all naysayers, in a dream of our personal best, not always in the attainment of it, but in the pursuit of it. Oprah and those little girls back in Nashville were the first to give me a sense of myself as powerful and capable, and for that I will be forever grateful.

Of the girls who were part of our group, I've kept in contact with Deborah Bright (now Bright-Johnson), who still lives in Nashville and is a successful executive with the telephone company. Deborah, of the big eyes, long bangs, ponytail, and broad smile, as bright now as it was when we were in school together, keeps up with some of our classmates, many of whom have gone on to have busy careers and families. Once during my freshman year of college back at Fisk University, I saw one of the fiercest members of our former group leaning against a car at a hamburger stand. She was the one who would get into fistfights with the boys and declare how tough she was, as she wiped her bloody nose. She looked weary for all her eighteen years. We spoke, but she didn't recognize me or seemed not to do so. I've seen Oprah sporadically over the years, never long enough to ask her in-person about our girls' group, but once when I wrote her a letter and reminded her of our hike in the woods near Clay Street, she wrote me back to say she remembered our fourth-grade class. Our girlhood is literally a lifetime removed from the women we've become. Young people, especially those reared in the South, address me as Professor or Ma'am, and people at poetry readings ask me what inspired me to become a poet. I tell them about getting a diary in the fifth grade. I tell them about loving Dr. Seuss at three years old or discovering Emily Dickinson and Langston Hughes in third grade. I don't usually tell them I was once an ashy-legged girl with new permanent teeth who memorized "Invictus" on Oprah's dare. Now, Oprah leads thousands of women and men from all walks of life and from all over the world in her role as television icon. Proof of her influence is the school for girls she founded in South Africa in 2006. Perhaps she sees in these young South African girls' energy and idealism her younger self, fiercely committed to making a difference in the world, to living by her principles and helping others to realize their potential. I cherish the memory of all the girls in my fourth-grade class: Deborah Bright (Johnson), Foncetta Darden, Annie Davis, Monica Fenton, Deborah McKell, Vanessa Reese, Cassandra Claiborne, Oprah Winfrey, Bessie Smith, Franchetta Stokes, Lynn Vaughn, Anita Witherspoon, and those whose names I have forgotten. As with any place, the Wharton Elementary School I attended exists only in what I remember of it. The building is still there, but the name has been changed. Still the Wharton I knew and the girls I laughed and cried and learned with in 1962 shaped me, lifted me up, strengthened my confidence in my abilities, and led me to discover the power of words and my lifelong fascination with them. I discovered too the necessity of perseverance in the face of obstacles and to take the high road even when it's not feasible or popular. I haven't always taken the high road; often I've come up miserably short of my mark, but when the odds were against me, I have used my childhood experience as a touchstone to motivate me one more time or one more 'gain, as we said back in the day.

In 2004, in the first twenty-four hours after I had major surgery for the removal of a malignant brain tumor, I was unaware of my inability to control my emotions or my thoughts, a consequence of being administered significant doses of powerful steroids and antiseizure medication. I recall singing out loud and (when my husband Don had gone home for a change of clothes) calling for someone to hold my hand during that long first night. I don't remember when they moved me to my room, but when they did, one of the first things I did was to call a group of young Residents together to tell them of my fourth-grade class and my friendship with Oprah, as if my former relationship with her would somehow make them work harder to assist in my recovery. I felt vulnerable and incomplete, as if the neurosurgeons had excised more than the tumor, as if they had taken my memories and my humanity, as well. Perhaps I was doing a reflexive exercise in memory retrieval. The Residents took notes and left when I had finished what must have seemed to them to be a delusional story, at best. I don't know what I was trying to communicate, but surely in my desperation, I wanted them to know how precious life, my life, was to me. Steroidal psychosis, yes, but the very act of remembering affirmed my life, confirmed I was still among the living. I don't know what this anecdote proves, except my experience as a girl of faith has stayed with me, for better and for worse, all my life. Maybe the very idea that we were pursuing something that started from our own inner visions made all the difference in the world. We were children pursuing a state of grace, no matter the outcome.

In Octavia Butler's *Parable of the Sower*, an intriguing and prophetic futuristic novel about life in these United States, the main character, Lauren Olamina, says, if "God is change," then we can "shape change" and in so doing shape our destiny. Her concept sounds innovative, but at heart she's saying what William Henley said all those years ago—"I am the master of my fate / I am the captain of my soul." Words to carry with us on the road to Canaan.

A Sanctuary of Words

Bury the Thought

—KARLA FC HOLLOWAY

One little girl wears her Easter bonnet. Its long velvet ribbons reach the tops of her overalls. Her hat indicates a special occasion, but her jeans reveal it as ordinary. The women talk quietly back and forth—mostly about the babies they carry. He's got teeth already? The men are mostly silent auditors, but all of us stretch our arms out to steady the latest walker in the group. Our conversation, even for those who just listen, helps time pass. We don't really know each other. But we are all in the same line.

The talk goes still when the gates open. We reach down and grab walking, teething babies, and hold the still-carried ones tighter as we approach the guardhouse. When it's our turn, we go inside. First, we empty our pockets into a plastic bowl. Drivers' licenses, change for the candy machine, keys . . . We know the routine, my husband and I. Then we walk through the detector. If you have boots on, you have to take them off and walk through in your socks because metal in the heel sets off the alarm. My asthma inhaler is the only odd thing in the bowl. "Is it mace, Ma'am?" "No." I tell them—again. They ask that question each time I visit. There is no institutional memory. Invariably, I begin to cough and need to use it. Also routine. My asthma always flares on visiting days.

If asked, we would say that we are normal folk caught in a horrific circumstance. But in public discourse about prisons, inmates, and their families, we are insisted into a pathology and characterized as the answer to what went wrong. To me, the Easter bonnets, the clucking sounds over drooling infants, and the private chatter about churches and schools feel quite unlike the ugly, failed families sketched in public narratives.

Sometimes there are grandparents in line. We all move aside to let them pass first—embarrassed at their being there with us. Neither their walkers nor their canes are allowed to go through the detector. And so they move slowly and carefully, holding on to its walls, their deliberate steps mournful and measured. As we move closer to the gate, our steps slow too, and our pace becomes like theirs. Then we are like our elders—a moving display of grief.

In the visiting area, the little girl in the Easter hat is hoisted high by her big brother. The ribbons dangle over his face and she giggles. The talk starts up again, but not with the others. Now we are focused on our own. Babies are held and rocked by fathers and boyfriends and brothers. Mothers, like me, are hugged for a very, very long time.

We lingered over our hugs, my son and I. In my preparations for our visit, I always put on the perfumed cream he liked on me when he was a child. It is the same scent my mother wore. And he always noticed. You smell like Grandmommy, he tells me. The newly walking baby totters over to our table and grabs hold. We turn him gently around and only momentarily watch him walk back before turning back to each other.

During the weeks when those visits were my weekend ritual, I could not think too long about them. I remember one particular day when my thoughts drifted to my son—which was ordinary for me—and then to the events that brought him to prison and then to those that were likely to be a part of his day. But I could not bear to stay in that mindful space. On that day, before I could catch my words and draw them back, I heard myself say aloud "bury the thought."

Most of the time, I thought of his absence like death.

I recall musing only briefly at that moment, in a way probably ordinary to English teachers, at the symbolic irony in my words. It made me shudder to recall my child to a metaphor about death. But then, given my preoccupation at the time, it may not have been unusual. I had, for many years, been working on a book about African American death and dying. I wrote on weekdays and visited my child on weekends. The irony ended in June 1999 when the two moments collapsed, and my researched narratives about the experiences of African Americans with violent death and dying outside of their generational time became my life's story as well. Our son was shot and killed in an attempted prison escape.

It was a long time before my writing claimed me back. Eventually it became a way to hold my son, to embrace him once again. I have thought of writing as a sanctuary—a discovery space, and, it seems, a redemptive one as well. In the years since his death, as pieces of his life and death story work themselves into my books, as a reluctant reader in *BookMarks—Reading in Black and White*, or as one of the too-soon-dead black children in *Passed On—African American Mourning Stories*, my memories of him gain a texture and claim a shape that does not leave it to grief to mold his remains. These days, in the time I spend with words I consider more carefully the spirit work they do, their proffer of authority, and their invention of sanctuaries beyond those fashioned of bricks and mortar. My writing him back into my words folded him into a sanctuary of my own making. Words like a womb. They are, finally, the remains of those days.

The Death of the Mother

—EUGENIA COLLIER

Ll her life she had feared death. Of the myriad fears which directed her life and ours, this was the most powerful. Among my earliest memories the clearest and most terrifying are the death scenes in which she wept and prayed and called us to her bedside for tearful good-byes. To this day I have no idea what malady afflicted her. She never specified what, if anything, hurt, and she never saw any doctor. There were only these episodes, which we called "having a spell."

She was in her early thirties then. The Great Depression was at the full, and we lived with Daddy's family in a big house on Madison Avenue, which she hated. By the time I was seven, the death scenes had gradually diminished, and when we moved from Grandma Lewis's house to a home of our own, they stopped altogether. But death still lurked nearby, shadowing her days. Every sickness in the family was a sickness unto death. Every cold was pneumonia; every cough was tuberculosis; even a bad sunburn was potentially fatal. Yet no physician was ever called. She had a deep fear and distrust of doctors, despite the fact that my father was himself a doctor. Sickness was not to be healed but yielded to. Death was not to be resisted but accepted.

As the years passed, my father became the focus of her death-fixation. She insisted that he had heart trouble. When I left home for college— Howard University, forty miles away—she demanded that I come home on weekends, because my father did not have long to live. Once when I was invited to spend the weekend with a dormitory-mate she was especially adamant: if I wanted to spend my time with some stranger when my dying father wanted to spend his last days with me, whom he missed so dreadfully, then I should go ahead. Of course I went home instead, having no way of knowing that my father would live for another thirty years. Eventually she added diabetes to the illnesses assigned to my father. Yet he was seeing no physician, following no diet, taking no medicine. He never said anything about his condition one way or another, but then he seldom said much about anything, being generally withdrawn and silent. To her, his illness was real.

In his last nine years my father really was ill. I have never been certain of his diagnosis, for she managed his illness with the same possessive vigor that she managed everything else. By his sixty-fifth birthday he had regressed to childishness, a retrogression that continued for the nine years he had left to live. She did take him to Johns Hopkins Hospital for diagnosis, but I had no clear idea of what was wrong. When I called his doctors to ask for information, they told me that their records were confidential and they could talk only with my mother. So that was that. According to her, in addition to the undefined heart trouble, he had atherosclerosis, Paget's disease, and Huntington's disease. The diabetes apparently got lost in the shuffle.

As my father deteriorated, she orchestrated the death scenes. She summoned me out of class during the day and out of slumber at night to attend my father's deathbed. No doctor, of course, was ever called—only me. I went to out-of-town conferences bowed down with guilt. Suppose it was real this time. Once when I went to Ocean City for a weekend with friends, she called at 3:00 a.m., and I took the next bus home, frozen with fear for my father's life. When I got to her house, my father, bathed and powdered, lay upon fresh sheets smiling happily, glad to see me. She had cleaned the house in anticipation of the funeral. She had not, however, called a doctor.

My brother was perhaps the one most victimized by her preoccupation with death. She had never wanted children, having been the oldest of nine and having spent her childhood babysitting and washing diapers. She did not welcome her first pregnancy and as far as I could ever discover, had no prenatal care. Probably because of her fear of hospitals, she had her baby at home, attended by a doctor who was a friend, a neighbor, and, I have been told, an alcoholic. The birth was long and arduous. Slender and narrow-hipped, she could not bring the child forth. Beyond all sense, her body could not relinquish its complete control over her boy-child. By the time it was over, the baby, my brother, had suffered brain damage which resulted in cerebral palsy.

Both she and my father were convinced that the baby would soon die. Overwhelmed with an irrational guilt that lasted for the rest of their lives, they decided that as long as he lived they would take care of him, serve him, and meet all his needs. Because of his impending death, there was no need for him to learn to function in this world. He would never need to work or, in fact, do anything at all for himself. Their love was a cocoon from which no chrysalis need ever emerge. They named him Maceo after my father and referred to him as "poor little Macie." Even into his fifties, my brother was, to them, poor little Macie, even when they realized—probably with a shock—that he was going to outlive them.

When my brother was four months old, she became pregnant again. Embarrassed at being pregnant so soon and convinced that this time both she and the baby would die, she made desperate and futile attempts at abortion. A photograph of her, taken the day before my birth, shows an unsmiling face with dark-ringed, tragic eyes. Unbidden and unwanted, I was born prematurely, less than a year after my brother, weighing a little over three pounds. It was again a home birth, with the same alcoholic doctor. Because of her preoccupation with death, nobody ever said that there was any concern that at three pounds, I might not survive.

Not wanting children anyway and now faced with two children who brought much responsibility and little joy, she had a "nervous breakdown." This is a blurred chapter in family history. Nobody ever talked about it. Postpartum depression would not be recognized or named for many decades. She must have felt that only she was suffering the emotions that buffeted her like tornado winds. For all her life she considered it shameful to need help for emotional or mental problems. Only "fools" needed such help. Even in my adulthood, the ultimate put-down she would hurl at me during an argument was, "You need to see a *psychiatrist!*"

Once, struggling to survive a crumbling marriage and a crumbling life, I timidly ventured to tell her that I was undergoing therapy with a clinical psychologist. I had left my husband. The children and I were staying at her house until I could make other plans. The therapist urged that I tell my parents that I was having treatment. That was more difficult than he knew. When I told my father, his response was to continue chewing on his cigar and reading his newspaper. He never looked at me. He pulled his silence around him like a blanket against the cold. I went to the kitchen, where my mother was preparing dinner. I told her. She said only, "Don't we have enough fools in the family now?"

So she went through the stormy time following my birth with no treatment and with disdain rather than support—at least in her perception—from her in-laws, whom she regarded as enemies. Nor, apparently, was there much support from my father. Their respective responses were, as ever, from opposite directions: she met crises with emotional excess; he, with emotional withdrawal.

I can only conjecture about my disastrous first months. I cannot imagine that I had any sense of security and love. I think that my parents became resigned to my birth when they realized my value as a potential caregiver for my brother. He did not sit up until I did; he learned to walk when I did. I could understand his speech before anybody else, and I became his interpreter. When he fell, I would run up to him and he would pull himself up by grasping onto me. My parents told me that God had sent me to take care of my brother. As we grew, they let me know that if they died before he did, it would be my duty to take care of him as they had. My mother resisted my marrying, and when my family and I moved from the apartment in their house after seven tumultuous years, she made me feel as if I had betrayed them. When my marriage ended after twenty years, she never forgave me for refusing to sell my house and move in with them so that when they died—an ever-present possibility—I could take care of Poor Little Macie in his own home.

Nobody, of course, asked him what *he* wanted. He never asked me or anybody to take care of him. From the beginning he had great strength and determination which, if aimed toward alleviating his physical problems and making a way in this world, could have worked miracles. Instead, he grew up with no therapy for the cerebral palsy, no exercise program, no effort to wring the best from his body. My mother fed on his dependence. On the few occasions when they went out, he used no walker but instead leaned on her. She permitted him to go nowhere without her, even in his adulthood.

She squelched any budding friendship. She denounced me whenever I suggested a therapeutic program. In her old age she used to say, half-seriously, "I don't know what he's going to do when I die. I guess I'll just have to reach up out of my coffin and pull him in with me!"

I believe that her smothering possessiveness did extend beyond death. When she had been in her grave for nearly a year, I had a dream that was horrifying in its vividness. My brother, living alone in the house they had shared, had rented out portions of the house and, even though he had put himself into a wheelchair rather than seek physical therapy, he was building a life for himself. In a dream she came to my bedside and began shouting at me, "You're not taking care of Poor Little Macie!" She jumped on me and began to beat me with her fists. I would not hit her back, but I tried to hold her down to prevent her from hitting me. She was getting the best of the struggle. I awoke disoriented and trembling, my heart about to burst through my ribs.

Some dreams are dreams and some are visions.

Childhood was a bitter experience. I never felt that I had any parents. I felt that they were Maceo's parents and I was some kind of servant-companion. I felt unloved and therefore unlovable. When I was about three or four years old, she would take me downtown with her so that I could tell our address in case she fainted. I would sit obediently in the chair where she put me while she shopped, and I fantasized that she had abandoned me and that when I found my way home they would have moved. Even in adulthood, when I looked in the mirror, I saw something ugly.

I think now that she resented me for being "normal" when her son had been damaged, for in her family sons were more highly valued than daughters. And for most of my life, I had more than a touch of survivors' guilt.

The lessons of my childhood were devastating. I learned that the world—my world—demanded the utmost of caring and sacrifice from me, but that I myself was not worthy of being loved. My value was utilitarian rather than intrinsic. I learned that I was an outsider, ever alone. It took a lifetime of silent anguish and seven years of therapy from a wise and compassionate psychiatrist to unlearn those bitter lessons.

After my father died at seventy-four, her preoccupation with death focused again on herself. She insisted at different times that she had heart trouble, rectal cancer (a result of my brother's birth fifty-some years before), emphysema, and a shrinking left eye. At my insistence she took a test for cancer, and when the results were negative, she said that tests are not always accurate. I took her to an internist, who found that she had low blood sugar and a sluggish thyroid, but no heart trouble. The doctor prescribed thyroid medicine, which she refused to take, and recommended that she see a psychiatrist. She was highly insulted and would not go back for follow-up. She did not return to that doctor until I took her years later, when senile dementia had erased the memory of that day.

Increasingly she enacted death scenes. She and my brother lived alone now, but I was only five minutes away. She would call most often two or three hours after midnight and demand my presence, even though I would have to brave the dangers of night in a crime-ridden city. When I asked her whether she had called the doctor, she would say, "Of course not. I wouldn't disturb him at this time of night!" I got so that I would say, "Well, call me back after you've talked with the doctor." But there would be no further sleep for me. Suppose this time it was real. Eventually I disconnected the phone at bedtime.

The danger of immediate death was most acute when I planned to go out of town. As surely as the sun rises, she would have an attack. I stopped telling her when I was traveling; but an uneasiness clouded my times away. Suppose this time it was real.

Once I was convinced that the time had come. My son Phil, then a teenager, and I had just returned from swimming at the YWCA. I had needed release in physical activity, because I was deeply worried about my longtime friend Bert, who would undergo a cancer operation in the morning. Bert had sent her friend out to buy her a lottery ticket in the hope that she would awaken from her operation and find that she was a millionaire. But the inevitability of pain and the possibility of death were real. As Phil and I entered the house, the phone rang, setting off the nerves I thought I had soothed. "Come quick! I'm dying! I'm dying! Come now!" It was my mother, having an attack. I called an ambulance (nobody, apparently, had thought to do that) and started out the door. Phil pulled on his jeans over his wet trunks and hurried after me, ready to give strength and support.

Not until we were on our way did I realize that it is rather unusual for a dying person to make her own telephone calls, especially to someone who has no medical knowledge and thus no ability to ward off death.

When we got to her house, neighbors were there, putting cold cloths on her brow, fanning her, and offering words of comfort. She was moaning and praying to God to spare her. My brother was in his room, staying out of the way. The ambulance arrived, and the young attendants expertly shifted her from the bed to the stretcher and whisked her into the ambulance. With all her moaning, she had the presence of mind to ask not to be taken to Provident, a black-run hospital, but since it was the nearest facility—just down the street—she had to make do. Following close behind the ambulance, its sirens screaming, I was in torment.

In the emergency room they found nothing wrong.

Her vital signs were fine. She was in great shape for her age. They sent in someone from Psychiatry—a young white woman about the age of my students—who talked with her for a few moments and then explained to me in one-syllable words that you would use with a child or a mental defective that physical symptoms were a way of channeling negative feelings. I knew that, and I knew more.

As we left, I walked ahead to the car. Phil, striding silently with me, probably had no idea how grateful I was for his quiet presence. Walking behind with a neighbor who had accompanied us, my mother said loudly enough for me to hear, "Genia is mad with me." She didn't know. If I had said one word to her, all the anger of all the years would have come tumbling out, and ultimately, despite her age and our sacred relationship, despite my own physical passivity and the fact that she had always been stronger than I, I was ready to leap upon her and pummel her to the very ground.

All her life she had feared and courted death.

The call from the nursing home came one sunny October morning as I prepared to go to school. She had taken a turn.

I sat alone by her bedside and watched her body take deep, slow breaths. Her eyes were closed, and her essential *being* seemed already far away. They had taken out the various tubes that had kept her functioning for weeks. They had taken off the strips of gauze that had secured her hands to the bed in order to keep her from tearing out the tubes. She was beyond fear now. She was in God's hands.

I watched alone. I had called my brother, who was notifying relatives. Following the family tradition of protecting him from unpleasant realities, I had not even considered that he should be with me at her bedside. I have since come to realize that he is a man, not the perpetual child that the family considered him. I watched alone. The nurses were kind but remote, having lived this experience many times. The doctor eventually came and told me that there was nothing to do but wait. She might remain in this condition for many hours. If I wanted to go teach my classes, he said, I should do so.

I watched alone. The thoughts that I am recording now were vague feelings, engulfing me like an amorphous cloud of emotion. I was overwhelmed by the reality of death. By the power of death, which nothing could deter. Nothing. I felt completely alone, estranged even from her. In this defining hour, I still felt like a family servant. Maceo's mother was about to pass.

I watched alone. My grief was my own, with no resonance from anyone else's. I felt crushed by the responsibility of what was to happen next, by the unanswered question of what was to happen to my brother, and by the extreme ambivalence of my own feelings. What was I supposed to feel? What *did* I feel? Some find succor in the arms of others. My succor lay in teaching my classes.

When I returned to the nursing home, it was over. Death, with whom she had flirted for so many years, had prevailed. She had died alone.

Not until I saw her peaceful in her coffin, her hair a soft white halo around her serene face, did I realize something that she had never known—that she was, even at age eighty-seven, a beautiful woman.

The road to this point had been long and rocky. She had always been so ill-tempered and fear-ridden that we never realized the point at which she crossed the boundary line from neurosis to full-blown dementia. She became increasingly forgetful. She began repeating herself, asking the same question over and over, forgetting that she had already asked it and that you had already answered. Her fears became, for her, actuality. She had always feared that someone would break into her house at night. When I was a child, if I didn't lock my bedroom door, she would tell me, "You're going to wake up and find some big black nigger standing over you." Now, in her dotage, she saw a face peering into her second-story bedroom and called the police. She explained that the man had been standing on a ladder. No ladder was ever found, nor could one fit among the thick, unbroken bushes beneath her window. And anyway, it would have been a gutsy second-story man who would carry around a fifteen-foot ladder at 3:00 a.m.

She was convinced that people were stealing from her. She fired the cleaning lady, being unshakably convinced that the woman was stealing money. She thought that people were in her house plotting against her. Voices from the radio in another room were voices of people planning her murder. She thought that someone had left a baby in her house, and when she couldn't find the baby, she thought that someone had killed it. She would scream out of her upstairs window to passersby that she was being held prisoner, and she would beg them to call the police. Sometimes she would call the police herself.

The household was chaotic. Even in her dementia she still ruled. She prepared bizarre meals and sometimes forgot to prepare meals at all. She and my brother both became frighteningly thin. When I realized what was happening, I arranged for a homemaker from a social agency to cook for them. However, my mother decided that the homemaker was planning to kill her. Somewhere she found a thick board, with which she broke out a basement window and then assaulted the homemaker, who fled and, of course, never returned.

She had long since forgotten who I was. She thought that I was her cousin Yetta, with whom she had grown up. She expected me to remember long-past events and broke my heart by asking, "Yetta, how are your parents?" At first I corrected her, insisting, "I'm not Yetta, I'm Genia." But an instant later I was Yetta again.

All the while, I was taking her for medical treatment, but physicians could only give her tranquilizers and medicine for the thyroid. They said she probably had Alzheimer's, for which there is no cure.

She began leaving the house, saying that she was going home to Washington, where her people lived. After nearly sixty years in Baltimore, she was still a stranger. My brother, now unable to walk alone, had to call neighbors to find her. Sometimes she would go out in her underwear. Once or twice she stood on the corner and shouted at passing cars, accusing the drivers of stealing her things. We knew that she was beyond my brother's control. His life was hell. But she had ruled for so long that we both shrank from the scenario that would surely occur when we would have to put her in a nursing home. More important, regardless of her mental state, the law said that she could not be confined against her will unless she broke the law and was sent to jail. That was, of course, unthinkable. She had never trusted me enough to give me her power of attorney, and although I had applied for guardianship, the process was taking forever. I dreaded the coming of summer that year; because I knew that as soon as school closed, I would have to find a way to have her committed.

Sometimes things have to hit bottom before they start the long trail up. In June my brother had to go to the hospital suddenly and unexpectedly, and there was no choice but to get her into a nursing home somehow. She would never have gone with me alone, but my Uncle Nelson's widow, Mamie, whom I will always bless, was with me, and Mamie's presence made her feel that it was all right to go. We told her that it would be for only a few days until Maceo came back. I wept when I left her in those grim, urine-scented rooms. I knew she would never see her home again.

The nursing home did not end the problems. She adjusted well, having less and less awareness of her environment. But she was a wanderer. She went all over the building, clad in a peach bathrobe and carrying a patent leather purse. One evening she got another patient to set off the fire alarm, and in the confusion she slipped out the back door. For hours nobody could find her. The nursing home notified the police and then notified me. I won't try to describe the agony of those hours. As I waited immobilized by fear, I saw with terrible clairvoyance all the violence that could happen to a helpless, addled old woman in a peach bathrobe, carrying an empty patent leather purse. Eventually she boarded a bus, and the bus driver notified the police, who met her at the end of the line and took her back to the nursing home. She had thought she was going back to Washington, to her people. Thereafter, the nurses kept her tied to a chair. That was, for me and certainly for her, another kind of agony.

We could do nothing but watch her slow slide downhill. Body and mind collapsed completely, and her last two or three months were spent in a strange slumber from which she never awoke.

I understand her better in death than I did in life. Her overwhelming presence and the tension which it always elicited kept me from seeing her clearly. She lived a tragedy that engulfed us all, even succeeding generations. She was a neurotic, born of a neurotic family. My father, like hers, was a mild man incapable of coping with a wife whose extreme emotions guided the family into destructive paths. Consequently their parenting was characterized by unintentional psychological abuse and neglect, and the result was children who were seriously impaired. Her neuroticism and my father's inability to cope gave our family a distorted contour. Ours was a strange, upside-down family in which the mother was harsh and aggressive and the father gentle and submissive, in which sickness and disability were encouraged and ability looked upon with suspicion and hostility, in which death infused life and life clung to death.

Yet, in spite of everything, they set me on a path that has led to riches of the spirit. For I inherited the best of both parents: my father's gentleness and my mother's strength. From the expectation that I would serve others, I learned sensitivity to the needs of others. From my position as outsider, I learned the value of warm relationships. From my loneliness I learned the joy of reading, and from my inwardness I experienced the satisfaction of expressing myself in writing. From my own profound needs, I learned compassion.

Once, shortly after her death, I cried out to my therapist, "She was a terrible person! She should have died long ago!" Then, shocked by the vehemence of my own outburst, I wept in grief for her suffering and death, for her joyless life, and for the mother-daughter relationship that we had never had. That was, for me, the beginning of forgiveness, and in forgiveness is healing.

The irony of it all is that her problems could have been so easily alleviated if medical science had been as advanced as it is today or even if she had had the insight to avail herself of its knowledge in her time. Women did have their babies in hospitals, even when she was having hers, and a Caesarean or even a simple episiotomy could have saved my brother and the rest of us a lifetime of misery. I believe also, in the light of current knowledge, that a major portion of her problem was physiological. Her thyroid problem, had it been diagnosed and treated earlier, could have been prevented from hot-wiring her emotions into dangerous extremes. More important, she, her siblings, and their quarrelsome mother, from what I know of them, appear to have suffered from depression, which is a hereditary physical dysfunction. A combination of psychotherapy and medication could have changed their lives and the lives of their ruined children.

I believe, too, that much of her life was tainted by racism. She and her family of origin bought too easily into the American myth of black inferiority. Light-skinned and wavy-haired, they thought that white was right, and they hated being lumped in with "those other Negroes." Blackness was shameful. Although she was proud when some black person achieved something commendable, of which white people would approve, for the most part she had only disdainful things to say about black people. Her conversations were peppered with observations like, "She is dark but intelligent" (a high compliment) or, "How could you expect him [a dark-skinned person] to have any sense?" I believe that racism reaches into the depths of our most intimate selves. If we accept its tenets, as she did, our whole vision of ourselves and our world will be distorted. Our lives could have been so different if we could have been proud of what we were.

This measure of understanding has come gradually, its path strewn with pain. "I'll be in therapy forever," I once groaned and had no faith in my therapist's quiet assurance that I would not. The therapy did end, ended forever, but as the years passed, the understanding continued to increase and even accelerated.

Epiphany came in a dream. I used to have a recurring nightmare. I thought that I was back in the house to which we had moved when I was seven. In the nightmare the house was dark, haunted. I was a child again, and something dreadful was about to happen. I awoke terrified. A few nights ago—I had spent that evening revising this piece—I dreamed again of that house. But this time the house was bright and sunny, its hardwood floors gleaming in the sunshine. I was in my parents' bedroom, where a real fire—not the artificial log they had really had—was crackling in the fireplace. There was no furniture, for in the dream we—my brother and I—had planned to sell the house but instead had simply preserved it in the years since our parents' death. I was profoundly happy, for the house was suffused not only with sunlight but also with our parents' spirits. Loving, joyful spirits. I said that I would move back into the house. I would furnish it as I chose, with my own beloved possessions. I was profoundly happy. I awoke bathed in joy and peace.

And that morning I knew—to the depths of my being, I knew—that my lifelong struggle with my mother had finally ended.

As I recall my mother's last years, two incidents emerge, demonstrating the poles of our troubled relationship.

Thinking to give my brother some relief, I tried to enroll my mother in an adult day care center. It looked like a good program, which might slow her mental deterioration by providing activities which might engage her. She seemed at first willing to try it. But when she found that her income was high enough to require her to pay for the service, she bristled and refused to join. "Everything I have is for my sick son," she declared. "My daughter doesn't need anything."

I flinched as if from a blow. She had summarized our entire relationship.

The other incident occurred sometime later, after I had become, to her, Yetta. I was taking her across town to an outpatient clinic, tense and miserable as I had always been in her presence. She was chatting away to Yetta, and I was trying not to hear. Then suddenly, in a flash of lucidity, she interrupted herself. "You're not Yetta," she said in wonder. "You're Genia! You're my daughter!"

I clutched the wheel.

"You're my daughter! You're Genia! Why did I think you were Yetta?"

I muttered something, I don't remember what. I paused in an intersection to make a left turn.

"How did you feel when I thought you were Yetta?"

I couldn't answer her right away. It was the first time she had ever asked me how I felt about anything. My eyes misted. I made the turn. Then I smiled. "I knew that one day you would remember."

At the clinic she beamed and told everybody about having found her daughter. She was proud of me. For a little while she was happy.

Later I took her to lunch. She loved eating out and had little chance to do so anymore. I took her to a quiet place on a sunny corner, where she could watch the cars come and go. For her, I had already begun to recede into Yetta again. The doctor had repeated what he had said before, that she could only deteriorate. Watching her profile as she turned to gaze out the window, I envisioned what she was going to have to endure, of which she had no inkling but I did. And if I could have done anything to spare her what was to come, even if it meant giving her years of my own life, I would have done so.

In the midst of all my dark memories of my mother, that day glows, an iridescent pearl of redemptive love.

A Remembrance

—SONIA SANCHEZ

The news of his death reached me in Trinidad around midnight. I was lecturing in the country about African American literature and liberation, longevity and love, commitment and courage. I could not sleep. I got up and walked out of my hotel room into a night filled with stars. And I sat down in the park and talked to him. About the world. About his work. How grateful we all are that he walked on the earth, that he breathed, that he preached, that he came toward us baptizing us with his holy words. And some of us were saved because of him. Harlem man. Genius. Piercing us with his eyes and pen.

How to write of this beautiful big-eyed man who took on the country with his words? How to make anyone understand his beauty in a country that hates Blacks? How to explain his unpublished urgency? I guess I'll say that James Arthur Baldwin came out of Harlem sweating blood, counting kernel by kernel the years spent in storefront churches. I guess I'll say he walked his young steps like my grandfather, counting fatigue at the end of each day. Starved with pain, he left, came back. He questioned and answered in gold. He wept in disbelief at himself and his country and pardoned us all.

When I first read James Baldwin's *Go Tell It on the Mountain*, I knew I was home: Saw my sisters and aunts and mothers and grandmothers holding up the children and churches and communities, turning their collective cheeks so that we could survive and be. And they settled down on his pages, some walking disorderly, others dressed in tunics that hid their nakedness. Ladies with no waists. Working double time with the week. Reporting daily to the Lord and their men. Saw his Black males walking sideways under an urban sky, heard their cornbread-and-sweet-potato laughter, tasted their tenement breaths as they shouted at the northern air, shouted at the hunger and bedbugs, shouted out the days with pain, and only the serum of the Lord (or liquor) could silence the anger invading their flesh.

When I first saw him on television in the early sixties, I immediately felt a kinship with this man whose anger and disappointment with America's contradictions transformed his face into a warrior's face, whose tongue transformed our massacres into triumphs. And he left behind a hundred TV deaths: scholars, writers, teachers, and journalists shipwrecked by his revivals and sermons. And the Black audiences watched and shouted amen and felt clean and conscious and chosen.

When I first met him in the late sixties, I was stricken by his smile smiling out at the New York City audience he had just attacked. I was transfixed by his hands and voice battling each other for space as they pierced, caressed, and challenged the crowded auditorium. I rushed toward the stage after the talking was done. I rushed toward the stage to touch his hands, for I knew those hands could heal me, could heal us all because his starting place had been the altar of the Lord. His starting place had been an America that had genuflected over Black bones. Now those bones were rattling discontent and pulling themselves upright in an unrighteous land. And Jimmy Baldwin's mouth, traveling like a fire in the wind, gave us the song, the marrow, and the speech as we began our hesitant, turbulent, and insistent walk against surrogates and sheriffs, governors and goons, patriarchs and patriots, missionaries and 'ministrators of the status quo.

I was too shy, too scared, too much a stutterer to say much of anything to him that night. I managed to say hello and a few thank-you's as I ran out of the auditorium back to a Riverside Drive apartment, as I carried his resident spirit through the coming nights, as I began to integrate his fire into my speech. No longer slavery-bound. No longer Negro-bound. No longer ugly or scared. But terrifyingly beautiful as I, we, began to celebrate the sixties and seventies. Opening and shutting with martyrs. A million bodies coming and going. Shaking off old fears. Laughing. Weeping. Hoping. Studying. Trying to make a colony finally into a country. Responsible to all its citizens. I knew finally as the Scriptures know that "the things that have been done in the dark will be known on the housetops."

The last time I saw Jimmy Baldwin was at Cornell University. But it is not of that time that I want to speak, but of the next to the last time we spoke in Atlanta. An Atlanta coming out from under serial murders. An Atlanta that looked on him as an outsider attempting to stir up things better left unsaid.

A magazine editor motioned to me as I entered the hotel lobby at midnight, eyes heading straight for my room, head tired from a day of judging plays. He took me to the table where Jimmy was holding court. Elder statesman. Journeying toward himself. Testifying with his hands and mouth about his meeting with professors and politicians and preachers. He had listened to activists and soothsayers and students for days, and his hands shook from the colors of the night, and the sound of fear fell close to his ears each day.

We parted at five o'clock in the morning. I had seen Atlanta through his eyes, and I knew as he knew that the country had abandoned reason. But he stayed in Atlanta and continued to do his duty to the country. Raising the consciousness of a city. And the world.

I was out of town, traveling to the Midwest on flat lands with no curves, the last time he visited Philadelphia. He had come to speak with poet Gwendolyn Brooks at the Afro-American Historical and Cultural Museum. One of my twins, Mungu, walked up to Jimmy that night, shook his hand and heard his male laughter as he introduced himself. They hugged each other, then my son listened to his Baldwinian talk cast aside the commotion of the night. The next day Mungu greeted me with Jimmy's sounds, and he and his brother Morani thanked me for insisting that they travel to the museum to hear Mr. Baldwin and Ms. Brooks.

Today, home from Trinidad, I thank James Arthur Baldwin for his legacy of fire. A fine rain of words when we had no tongues. He set fire to our eyes. Made a single look, gesture endure. Made a people meaningful and moral. Responsible finally for all our sweet and terrible lives.

From: Sanchez, Sonia. *Wounded in the House of a Friend*. Boston: Beacon Press, 1995. 31–34.

The Night I Stopped Singing like Billie Holiday

— TOI DERRICOTTE

I had the CD on in the car, and I was enjoying her voice, talking to Richard about the difference between Billie Holiday early and late, and I was thinking about which song of hers I could learn and sing when I read with the drummer in D.C. Just before he got out, I asked him, "You never heard me sing like Billie Holiday, did you?" "No," he said, "but I heard someone describe it." "What did they say?" "Well, Ben Shannon said it was the first night of class and that you closed your eyes and sang a cappella and that there had never been anything like it."

Driving home with the top of the car open, feeling that wonderful softness and openness of the night, I was deciding whether I should turn down my street and go into the gated parking lot or just turn up Billie and keep driving—over one or two of the beautiful yellow bridges of Pittsburgh, so perfectly architectural, like the large scale bridges of New York—the Brooklyn and George Washington—but small scale, doable. The bridges would be nearly empty on a summer night like this, so that you would have the feeling that you had the bridge all to yourself. Imagine it: a bridge all yours like a beautiful woman on such a night.

During the movie, for some reason, I had put my hands under my arms and felt my own body—that beautiful fat curve under a woman's arm as it becomes part of the breast, the soft full crease—and I liked it, as I might like feeling that in another woman's body. Then, when I pulled my hand out, I could smell myself on myself. After two years of suffering over a breakup, I was beginning once again to have an odor. That meant the sexual juices in me were starting to come to the surface again, that I would attract and repel like some flower.

Then a terrible premonition right before I turned into my driveway, that if I opened my mouth and started singing I wouldn't sound like Billie Holiday. For years that sound had exuded out of me, as if she was in there just waiting for me to open my mouth. Always there was the strain. Some part of me clamped down on top of what was coming up to make Billie happen—I thought maybe even Billie had had that slight squeeze at the top of her voice—but something had changed and, when I started to sing, I *didn't* sound like Billie. I don't remember ever hearing *me* sing, but I think it must have been *me* singing *me* before—characterless, without her phrasing, as if my body had forgotten what was most natural for it to do, as if, as much as I don't want it, now I had my own voice and, like it or not, I couldn't go back. It was as if the only way I could be Billie was by not being me. I sounded like any person that has an okay voice but nothing special. Before, even if I wasn't as good as Billie, at least I sounded like her. And there was an aching try that someone listening could feel, like the pain that made her turn a phrase into something sweet, short, and unforgettable. Now my phrasing was off, like *anybody* trying to win a Billie Holiday contest. The twinness of us had broken, and I sounded like her stranger.

I couldn't sing when I was young. The people in my family would say, "Sing solo," then, "So low we can't hear you," and "She can't carry a tune in a bucket." I started listening to her when I was fifteen. My boyfriend, who listened to jazz all day in his dark room in a powder blue cashmere sweater, had introduced me. Cleaning house or doing homework, I listened to "Deep Song" and "You're My Thrill" over and over, moving the needle back, standing close to the phonograph so I could catch it. I couldn't get "You're My Thrill" right because I couldn't make my notes slide. I didn't have the flexibility. But "Deep Song" was perfect, not too many notes and slow. I would listen to it for hours until I fit my voice over hers like the clothes on a paper doll. Years later I read an interview that she gave right before her death and, when they asked what her favorite songs were, she said, "'You're My Thrill' and 'Deep Song.' People don't know them, but one day they will." We had the same taste. That convinced me even more that we had pieces of each other's soul.

I had known she was on drugs and that she was beaten up by men. I knew that she had been molested when she was a girl and that she had been in prison. I hadn't said it to myself yet, but I too had been beaten up by a man, by my father, and I too had been molested. But it wasn't the similarities in our lives that made me love her; it was the pure blood, as if her voice took away our bodies. There were feelings that were never expressed in my house. I wasn't sure those parts of me existed until I heard her sing.

I knew I'd never meet her, and never wanted to. It wasn't Billie Holiday that I felt close to, it was that voice that cried out of her, bodiless. I wasn't alone, perhaps like when you pray, or make love, or the way babies look into the eyes of their mother.

I think I saw her once. It was at the Flame Show Bar on John R. Maybe I peeked in the door on my way home from school and saw her at the microphone. It was dark and smoky and she was so weak she could hardly stand. Maybe I made it up. I was walking home from school when I saw the headline in the paper that she had died in the hospital with eight fifty-dollar bills taped to her thigh. In the small clips that exist, when her singing stops, the sweetness evaporates. She is coarse, illiterate, and clumsy. The nuance, the brilliant articulation is gone, and she speaks like the most recalcitrant streetwalker.

At my next reading, I decided to read for joy and to close with my favorite Billie Holiday song. I was terrified, but I remembered another time I had been afraid at a reading and a voice had come into my head, "Just open your mouth," it said. And I realized that the meaning is not in words, the meaning is in sounds. When we speak the sounds—concentrating on every up and down, concentrating on the mouth, the tongue, the roof of the mouth, on the breath, on making each individual sound sing—then all the nuances, all the meaning that the sound holds, will be conveyed, even to the poet, even if she's forgotten what she felt so long ago when she wrote it. It is the sound, not the words, that holds the emotional meaning. We must sing poems, for we write by our hearts singing.

I made the poems sing that night and, at the end, I sang a Billie Holiday song. Afterward, no one told me I sounded like Billie, but many said I had a beautiful voice. When I had announced at the reading that I was going to sing, even my mother who was there—and who has always hated my voice—almost stood up and pleaded, "No, don't sing!" Even she couldn't believe my voice. She thought I had been taking voice lessons.

My voice still had a squeeze in it, as if I was strangling something, and that *did* sound a bit like Billie—the way she asked men to beat her up before a performance so that she would remember the pain—but it was open at the throat, and something that was me came up, and Billie didn't interfere.

Afterword: Rites, Rituals, and Creative Ceremonies

A Social History of the Wintergreen Women Writers' Collective

—SANDRA Y. GOVAN

Each year since 1987, twelve to fourteen African American women poets, scholars, fiction writers, essayists, and general readers have gathered together high in the secluded Blue Ridge Mountain haven of Wintergreen, Virginia, for an annual retreat. In May 2007, we celebrated our twentieth year of meeting to cultivate, energize, sustain, or simply support the creative spirit. We pray and eat together, play and work together, read together, tell stories, and relax together. In a constantly malleable (one or two new women are invited every year) yet essentially consistent community, we annually reaffirm a connection to the spirit within us and to the cords of sisterhood that bind us into a community.

Summoned to the first Wintergreen gathering by Joanne Gabbin in September 1987, the original group of ten women who comprised that first collective retreat were Joanne Gabbin, Nikki Giovanni, Paule Marshall, Trudier Harris, Daryl Cumber Dance, Opal Moore, Mary T. Harper, Sandra Y. Govan, Carmen Gillespie, and Catherine Rogers. Gillespie and Rogers were Joanne's graduate students at James Madison University. We came largely from the surrounding areas of Virginia or North Carolina, able to drive to stunningly beautiful Wintergreen because it was not too far to go to rejuvenate spirits in need of solace—spirits wearied by the "white noise" of our jobs. By meeting early in the fall semester, the demands of teaching, department and committee meetings, or community service at our respective institutions had not yet become too burdensome or onerous. Then too, the cost of the retreat was extraordinarily reasonable—under $150 for two and one half days, including meals, for the first thirteen years.

Initially, we all loved the fall meeting time. The South's lush deep-green tree canopy had begun the gradual slide to reddish gold; silky sweet September seemed a beautiful month to get away. The weather stayed warm in the low country and the drive up the road through the slowly rising foothills to the mountains seemed pleasant, whether one approached Wintergreen along I-77 to I-81 North (or I-81 South or I-64 East), or followed US 29 north from Greensboro, straight up through small-town Carolina and Virginia. However, September on the mountain proved unlike September in Charlotte or September in Richmond, Radford, Harrisonburg, Christiansburg, or Chapel Hill. For our first three years, September on the mountain always presented surprises.

During our first year, for instance, after leaving the warm comfort of our respective homes, we found ourselves winding our way up the switchback and hairpin turns on the mountain road through layers of ever-thickening clouds and increasing cold. Before the weekend ended, we coped with unanticipated snow and watched, with that mixture of fear balanced against perverse delight, a large brown bear tramping through our backyard and raiding the trashcans! The heedless collective stampede to the windows to see the bear out there caused the smallest of our group (me) to be thrust aside and nearly trampled in the rush to see a real bear! (No grudges were held, however, as mass hysteria is a recognized social phenomenon.) The unexpected September snow presented another opportunity for adventure. Could the serious power-walkers among us actually make it to the crest of the mountain on Saturday morning despite the falling snow? Were they that hardy, that daring? Would they accept the challenge, defy the weather? I can honestly report that they did precisely that. Returning victoriously from their hike were stalwart walkers Daryl, Joanne, Paule, and Trudier. Their determination to make that trek despite the snow subsequently confirmed walking the mountain together as a major segment of what was to become a regular Saturday morning ritual for future Winter-green gatherings.

Our second September on the mountain, 1988, brought with it a penetrating cold rain, followed by snow, and then an exceedingly dense fog. Shoveling snow in Chicago had always been problematic for me but shoveling snow with Sylvia Hicks from the steps of our house at Winter-green, heavy dense December-style wet snow—the kind that makes firm snowballs—somehow acquired the status of play or an adventure of sorts. However, the truly harrowing adventure that year occurred in conjunction with dinner when, in order to keep our reservations and not be charged a cancellation fee, we wound our way down the mountain in the fog to eat in the resort's Copper Mine restaurant. We dined elegantly, laughing and regaling each other with stories; after dinner, we proceeded to caravan in just a few cars (with a few select drivers) for the return trip back to our house up high on the mountain. Therein lies the tale.

While we sat in the restaurant and ate, the dense white fog intensified; it settled thickly on the mountain's ridges and in its hollows like an old heavy quilt sinks in upon a sleeper. Getting back up the mountain in the dark, and in that fog, was a matter of skill, intuition, or magic. There was no way to truly see the road nor the tight turns marked by un-illuminated, knee-high, hand-carved road markers; the driver had to virtually intuit the right direction. Fortunately, I rode in the car with the redoubtable Trud-ier Harris, she of keen eyesight and unerring direction. Folks riding with Joanne, our host and former lead driver, undoubtedly held their breaths on the way back up because Jo had already missed at least one crucial turn on the way down and taken us all in a giant circle. But Nikki Giovanni and Virginia (Ginney) Fowler had the scariest adventure. Unable to see at all and too slow leaving the restaurant to join our caravan, Nikki put Gin-ney out in front of her low-slung two-door red sports car with a fading flashlight to search for the minuscule road signs and/or the correct turns. Picture this: pole-slim Ginney out scouting the trail in the thick white fog, inching along a winding road walking oh so carefully in front of a mov-ing vehicle. Meanwhile, Nikki was driving ever so slowly, creeping along just behind her. Evidently, however, they had neither skill, instinct, nor the right juju between them, for the two wound up inching back to the main lodge for the night, unable to find their way to our house on the mountain-side. When they finally called to announce they were safe but staying put, our fears were relieved and we all laughed uproariously. Somebody said, I disremember precisely who, "The whole thing was most likely a plot for Nikki to avoid losing another Bid Whist game."

Hurricane Hugo, who came in September of 1989, ended our fall gath-erings. Following Hugo's fantastic charge from the South Carolina coast up through mid-North Carolina and up the center of Virginia, a ram-page which prevented all but two of our most intrepid and daring (read "foolhardy") sisters, Joyce Pettis and Karla Holloway, from making the harrowing drive across wind-whipped and rain-lashed terrain, through storm-shredded towns fearing the threat of possible tornados in Hugo's wake, the general consensus of the group was that we ought to move our annual retreat to a time more auspicious and accommodating, a time more acceptable to the gods of mountain weather and the Muses that hover over the often mist-shrouded peaks. Thus notwithstanding the May graduation exercises at one university or another that occasionally interfere with the coming of one or two, the annual Wintergreen Retreat or Wintergreen Women Writers' Collective has been held every spring since 1990.

Those first few years set the tone for subsequent Wintergreen gather-ings and established a loose framework for events that became our rites, rituals, and ceremonies. Some customs remained the same over time while others subtly evolved or changed. To wit, there was, and remains, the annual subtle challenge to see who will climb up the mountain first and thus reserve (read "claim") a favorite bedroom space—the master-suite with the one bedside telephone. The snacking and munching—fresh fruits, chips, salsa, nuts, crackers and cheese—begins almost immediately upon arrival. Food quickly became an integral part of our Wintergreen experi-ence; subconsciously I think we recognized even our snacks as a neces-sity for reaffirming the importance of body, ritual, and community—for the healing of individuals in our community, to borrow from Malidoma Patrice Somé's book about ritual. Over time, another arrival rite became the slight tension accompanying the inevitable wait. Who else is coming? Where are they coming from? When will they get here? Have they left from wherever in time to make it up the mountain and to "our house"—for seven years the Smith House—before dark? Will they be lost somewhere on the highway, winding the wrong way around some other mountaintop in the Blue Ridge range, having driven west when east was the direction they should have gone? Or, will they arrive at the Mountain Inn front desk check-in at long last, tired to the bone, then receive an unreadable map in teeny-tiny print from guest services, and thus still be wandering around the mountain, searching for an unlit sign announcing Devil's Knob Loop and Fawn Ridge Drive or Blackrock Drive and Peddler's Edge? There was a huge sense of relief when the lost souls finally arrived, and then preparations could begin for dinner.

During the first two years, preparations for dining meant getting dressed just a bit more formally on Saturday night to wind our way back down the mountain to eat in the Copper Mine; those first two years Joanne usually cooked on Friday and we ate in-house. But after the fog of '88 prevented two of us from finding our way back up to our house, we determined to prepare all of our meals in-house from then on—not just Friday and Saturday dinner but Saturday and Sunday morning breakfast too. (At our first breakfast [1987] in the Copper Mine, prior to everyone's departure, Nikki had archly proclaimed that as a bona fide urban woman, she did not do nature. Yet later that day, as Mary Harper and I stopped at Virginia's Natural Bridge to take in the splendor of this natural architectural marvel, we chanced to espy Ms. Nikki emerging from her car, apparently attempting to do [some] nature after all.)

Following the Friday arrival rituals of hugging, squeezing, squealing, laughing, exclaiming over the lost souls who joined us at last, come the Friday night rites! Friday nights are set aside for serious sister bonding. Nothing intrudes upon this process—no TV, no radio, no newspapers, no news bulletins highlighting the horrors besetting the outside world. For three days, we remove ourselves from a Western sense of space and time. The rhythms conflicting the outside Western industrial/technological complex, the values of that nihilistically modern fast-paced world, are put on hold to allow us time to embrace, subconsciously, the ancient communal values of collectivity found in eating, talking, playing, singing, sharing, and reflecting on events in our lives, in our respective creative orbits. On Friday nights for the past fifteen years, we created our own particularized rites and rituals that serve to revitalize our spirits. Generally speaking, following the dinner that Joanne orchestrates, the Friday Night Rites involve games. There are a few bridge players among us but gin rummy, spades, hearts, penny poker, and of course, the grand dame, Bid Whist, happen each and every Wintergreen Friday night. In the early years, the wolfing and braggadocio that accompanied these Bid Whist games acquired the status of legend over time. Who ran Boston on whom? How many Bostons were run? Who made enough books to get to Philly? Who sold how many "wolf tickets" her hand could not support? Who reneged!? Which bold soul demanded the kitty, claiming she could make a "six low," downtown when the hand she was dealt held crap and the kitty held no aces? What lucky sister got dealt a roadmap, then pulled three aces from the kitty? Dependence upon one's partner in such a game is vitally important; some partners, like my partner Daryl C. Dance, whose quiet skill in 1988 prompted a poem, always have your back. Others are less reliable. Players with reputations for trash talking during a game include Nikki G., Val Gray Ward, newcomer and guest, Elaine Crocker, and even bubbly mild-mannered Joanne. Solid Bid Whist players with a reputation for graciously trouncing opponents include Daryl C., Opal Moore, and me (though candidly I have been known to wolf after the whooping). We do occasionally play other games—Scrabble once, Monopoly once I think, and an African game, Wari, played with seeds in a pod that Daryl introduced in 1993; but Bid Whist, though the wolfing has subsided among the newest Wintergreen women, is clearly the game of choice. However, I for one miss, as my partner said, the legendary rivalries and battles of yesteryear. From now on, I will be rested and the challenge will be proclaimed.

Following the games comes the singing, then more eating, more talking, more sharing. and more stories—anything to extend the communal sisterhood bonding that occurs—anything to avoid going to bed! At earlier Wintergreens, after the card games the daring would leave the house to sit at midnight in the outdoor hot tub attached to the Smith House back deck. There we would sit in the dark, soak, and talk until, bitten by bugs, we would retire. Typically, in the modern Wintergreen, the early birds call it a night somewhere between 10:00 p.m. and 1:00 a.m.; the night owls among us (Ethel Morgan Smith, Opal, Toi Derricotte, Hermine Pinson, Janus Adams, Linda Nelson) hang until 3:00 or 4:00 a.m., and then retire. These are not the morning people who arise bright, sunny, and annoyingly chipper on Saturday morning, ready for the rituals we've established to mark this day.

Note: A rite more recently established is that Friday evening following dinner has become the time we mark achievements, victories, or celebratory moments. We have cheered and applauded Opal Moore's winning a Fulbright to teach in Germany in 1993 and another fellowship to study with Wole Soyinka in summer 2002; Ethel Morgan Smith's move from Virginia to West Virginia and her Fulbright to teach in Germany; Joanne Gabbin's winning of an Outstanding Faculty Teaching Award for Virginia at James Madison University; Daryl Lynn Dance's birthday; my own recognition as a Bank of America Teaching Excellence Finalist in 2001; Deborah McDowell's winning of a Woodrow Wilson Fellowship; Trudier Harris's 1994 winning of a fellowship to spend two months writing in Bellagio, Italy; Trudier Harris's 2002 winning of the huge bronze Eugene Current-Garcia Award as Alabama's Distinguished Literary Scholar, an award conferred by the Alabama College English Teacher's Association (ACETA) and the Alabama Writers Symposium. We also celebrated with a quite funky, quite risqué wedding shower (replete with utterly shameless hussy gifts which, to quiet the recipient, were saturated with overtones of sexual adventures most of us fantasize about) for Trudier's fall 2001 marriage. This is the time when we note new book contracts and/or new publications (in 2002, Janus Adams graciously gave us all copies of her 2000 book, *Sister Days*), announcements of impending projects (Daryl Dance's fabulous *Honey Hush* [1998] took shape first at a Wintergreen), new book projects, and conference planning sessions. The energy that went into the Furious Flower African American Poetry conference (1994) was first channeled at Wintergreen; Joanne's plans for an upcoming Furious Flower were discussed at the 2002 Wintergreen.

Our Saturday rites and rituals follow an entirely different pattern. In the morning, we form ourselves into three disparate groups: the seriously athletic, the low-impact body-toners, and the utterly comfortable couch potatoes. The seriously athletic rise early; often they are galvanized by Trudier's truculent Saturday challenge: "Joanne, ain't you ready yet? Oh, piss! You were going to be the first one up this morning. Come on, Daryl, let's go; she can catch us." And just as they hit the outside door and stop to do their stretches, a cheery Joanne bounds down the stairs and heads out to join them. The power-walkers must be out before breakfast to hike their four or five miles before the roads become too hot or clogged with weekend resort traffic.

Occasionally the weather even cooperates; a Saturday spring morning can dawn gorgeous—sixty-five degrees early in the day with a promise of actual summer heat to follow! After breakfast, the power-walkers are joined by the tennis players who all tramp off to the courts. The active tennis players include, in various years, Trudier, Joanne, Daryl, Ethel Morgan Smith, Mari Evans, Nikki Giovanni, Marilyn Mobley, and Sonia Sanchez— though perhaps Sonia should have gone with the body-toners because when she played at tennis, jumping to return a serve cost her a broken foot. Those in the body-toning group prefer low-impact water aerobics to high-impact exertions. Following breakfast we head for the resort's pool complex to enjoy first a massage (for me and sometimes Daryl or Trudier), then our workout in a far more cushioned environment, performing our stretching, bending, stomach crunching, and stride jumps and jumping jacks in a heated pool. The pool people group, with its "Floating" membership, dependent on who comes any given year, regularly includes me, Daryl, and Daryl Lynn, Maryemma Graham, Opal, Carmen, Toi, and sometimes Joanne; new additions are Linda Nelson, Elaine Crocker, and Marilyn Mobley. After we exercise some of us sit talking in the indoor warm therapeutic hot tub with its gentle jets playing across newly toned muscles; the wilder women brave the brisk outdoors and the sharper jets of the deep, hot, outside hot tub. And then comes the best moment of the early afternoon—relaxing in the dry heat sauna, baking all the toxins out of our bodies, sweating out all those awful impurities, cleansing now in order to imbibe more toxins and ingest additional impurities with the late afternoon chips with soda or the wine and assorted desserts following dinner.

On Saturday mornings the couch potatoes, after cleaning the kitchen, either sleep, or sit and read, or sit and write following Saturday breakfast. The still adventurous yet more fragile among us, those carefully nursing straining muscles and failing joints (Eugene Collier and myself), may sometimes also take a less strenuous walk, weather permitting. Once, fully attired in our broad brim sunhats and shades, Eugenia and I slowly trekked together up and down one low grade right to the mouth of the resort's

Nature Preserve. Later that day, the Wintergreen of 1998, an accommodating Trudier Harris traipsed back with me through that gorgeous wooded preserve so I could get the true feel of it like the Girl Scout I used to be. Following the increasing sound of a talking brook, we clambered over a narrow, boulder-strewn trail blazed with bright yellow paint splashed on fallen logs, and across a wooden plank bridge until we found the source of the brook's roar. I had said to Trudier earlier that I wanted to put my hands into one of these brooks; now was my chance. I went down on my hands and knees, stretched an arm until I could cup the water, tasted it, and felt the peace of contented satisfaction descend. My friend T. was right there, to put her arms around me, holding me steady so that I could rise.

If, however, any single ritual has become the heart and soul of Wintergreen, it is the Saturday night rite of "the readings." Following dinner and the K.P. chores of clearing the table and loading the dishwasher, folks settle in for the readings. When it's cold out, the great-room fireplace is lit. Folks take their seats in the open room's pillow-stuffed couches or dining-room chairs. Sometimes a designated reading seat, the high-back oak rocker near the best lamp, is chosen; at other times people read from where they're seated. Sometimes the poems, stories, fragments of a larger essay are meant to be "workshopped" with feedback from the group; sometimes the poems, stories, and other genres are simply meant to be shared in the safety of the group. At all times, whether the reading is intense, revealing, clinically detached, poignant, tragically sad, or hilariously funny, the reading is followed intently and heard with respect. Sometimes the reader wants and needs critical feedback; other times the reader simply wants a supportive audience with whom to share. All who read receive encouragement. Not everyone reads at Wintergreen. A twenty-minute time limit has been established and if all read, we'd be there all night. Some who have read in previous years grant the newcomers the experience. (In letters or e-mails after the fact, newcomers generously praise this acceptance, their feeling of utter comfort and support in this zone.) Sometimes folks try out new works for upcoming projects; sometimes folks test new ground—moving from poetry to fiction or poetry to personal essay to creative nonfiction. Sometimes the poets just take control and move us emotionally from level to level, descending or climbing, holding back or breaking out our tears and/or our laughter as we follow where their words lead.

I cannot close this history without mention of two Wintergreens deserving special note, a yearly Wintergreen ritual requiring specific attention, and two Wintergreen Women who are mo' special indeed.

The tenth-anniversary Wintergreen began May 17, 1997. The gathering that year was so large that it required two houses. Present for the tenth-anniversary celebration, and the surprise honoring of founder Joanne Gabbin, were Nikki Giovanni, her mother Yolande Giovanni, her sister Gary Giovanni, and Gary's friend Linda Dixon. Staying in the house with them were Opal, Ethel, Val Gray Ward, and Gloria Naylor. They all camped out in the Taylor house—which I dubbed the "Smoke House" because everyone there could light up unapologetically. Staying in the Strand house were the Dances, Daryl C. and daughter Daryl Lynn; the Gabbins, Joanne and daughter Nayo; Trudier Harris, Eugenia Collier, Toi Derricotte, Mari Evans, Karla Holloway, Deborah (Debbie) McDowell, Maryemma Graham, and me. The Bid Whist game that year proved the stuff of folklore. In her college days, Debbie had been humbled by "pros" who apparently dared her to ever play again; but she vowed that "if Joanne can play," then she could too. As for Ms. Gloria, well, it turned out her Bid Whist skills were rusty at best. Seems she thought she could just lay out the kitty and pick only what she wanted for her hand! She also believed that taking the bid with a "five" meant she only had to turn five books total! However, she and Jo made a good team after all. After fumbling a shuffle then dealing the wrong direction, the two actually managed to win their bid and the game. The tenth anniversary was also one of the competitive Scrabble years. Daryl took game with a huge one-point word to dethrone Debbie and finish up as champion.

However, the tenth anniversary was memorable for far more than its games. This was the year we saw the beautiful Dorothy Holden's handmade quilt from which our eventual Wintergreen T- shirts came. This was the year Joanne was upstaged as events moved swiftly beyond her control. Following a truly scrumptious meal, prepared by chefs Nikki and Gary Giovanni, the Wintergreen women moved into action. Trudier Harris presented Jo with a plaque dedicated to our "Effervescent Founder"; Daryl presented her with a beautiful potted plant, and Opal read the poem "Green in Winter," which she wrote to commemorate the occasion. Then every Wintergreen Woman presented Jo with a single yellow rose as a gesture of homage accompanied by a personal testimony on how much Joanne, as Wintergreen founder, meant to each. Of course, Jo broke down; she had to be prompted to stop crying through each presentation. It was my job as emcee to guide the show and to staunch the flow of tears. I failed the second charge. The next night the unstoppable Joanne had us celebrate each other. Debbie read from her memoir, *Leaving Pipeshop*. Trudier was recognized for her editorial role in *Call and Response*, Daryl for *Honey Hush*, and Toi for *The Black Notebooks*. Val was cheered for surviving a brain tumor, Opal for her move to Atlanta and Spelman College, Daryl Lynn for her success in graduate school, Nayo for attaining a new job and new independence in Greensboro, North Carolina. And Eugenia Collier was applauded for retiring at last and for her celebratory poem, "For All My Former Lovers." Without question, our tenth anniversary was a superb Wintergreen moment.

Another wonderful Wintergreen moment came the year we varied our routine and left the mountain. In 2000, the Wintergreen Collective was held in Williamsburg, Virginia. We changed our rhythm to accommodate an early Wintergreen Woman, Joanne Braxton, of the College of William and Mary, as she orchestrated the "Memories of the Black Atlantic" conference. Our part was to give a public reading. Trudier Harris, Opal Moore, Daryl Dance, Pinkie Gordon Lane, and I read that night. Introduced by Jo G. with our own individual haiku, we brought down the house. Opal and Pinky read some extraordinary poetry; Daryl read from her work on her family genealogy; Trudier read from her Chapel Hill newspaper column on Blacks accepting ourselves as "Southerners," not just saying we're "from the South" but reclaiming a heritage; and I read the apparently hilarious "Confessions of a Serial Reader: My Life of Crime." For the first time ever we had "groupies," audience members requesting autographs—first time for me anyway. The next day established Wintergreen rituals took hold. There was the long fast Saturday morning walk for the power-walkers (with a slower, more gentle walk for the less athletically fit), the afternoon spent talking, reading, and dining.

The careful reader will have noted recurrent allusions to dining or food throughout this account. While we at Wintergreen are not strict Epicureans, we take a certain gustatory pleasure in both the presentation and consumption of a splendid well-prepared meal. At Wintergreen, we have had plenty. Breakfast and dinner are our two communal meals. Our breakfast menus have included quiche, soufflé Govan, egg casserole, French toast, pancakes, cheese eggs, muffins, biscuits, bagels, grits, home fries, oatmeal, various savory sausages, regular bacon, turkey bacon, fresh fruits of all kinds (strawberries, bananas, and melons abound), assorted juices and coffees. With the assistance of some willing sister, I have done most of the Saturday morning breakfasts for years; 'tis the only meal I am comfortable cooking and it's good solid food. Our exquisite dinners, however, are usually prepared by culinary artists. We have supped on such scrumptious fare as roast turkey, roast leg of lamb, honey-baked ham, expertly fried catfish, flounder stuffed with crabmeat, grilled salmon, jambalaya, gumbo, candied yams, corn on the cob, corn off the cob, new potatoes, potato salad, barbequed chicken in a bourbon sauce, stuffed shrimp (with crabmeat), garlic shrimp, hot sauce shrimp, various greens, chef salads, carrots cooked in orange juice, and of course, the wine to accompany the meal. When Ethel Morgan Smith was a regular, she supervised table aesthetics. No plastic, no paper plates or napkins, no chintzy glasses for Ethel, ever. She always brought beautiful cloth napkins in varying shapes or textures and usually lit dinner candles.

As one might surmise, dinner conversations have been rich, full, varied, passionate, and sometimes explosive—given the mix of wine, artistic sensibilities, history, and personal memories. We've had vociferous debates during or following dinner on Spike Lee films, the "cosmic loneliness of black men," racism (of course), slavery (of course), violence in America, angry kids making rap records, Black on Black violence, and at the 2002 Wintergreen, the virtues (or lack of same) of spanking. That heated conversation began mildly with a proposed salute to "old-fashioned mothers" who knew how to discipline children without "timeout," but as some allowed they could not on principle toast to those mothers, the conversation rapidly broadened to issues of abuse, of brutality in the home, of a supposedly identifiable "pathology" distantly related to the violence of slavery (yes, that was addressed!), to the deeper meaning of Black comedians universally signifying on the Black mother's ultimate claim of parental authority, "I brought you into this world and I can take you out." That particular conversation required a referee and traffic flow monitor to make sure everyone who wanted to speak got heard.

After twenty years of coming to Wintergreen, missing not one time, I must say I see changes. Though US 29 North is now straighter and more direct, as it no longer winds through Danville or Lynchburg, it seems a longer drive to me. Carmen changed from graduate student at James Madison University to Emory University PhD; now teaching at Bucknell University, she also produced two children. Vanessa Dickerson, our once naive, noncooking yoga-stretching little sister, has published her book and gone on. Others of us, while maintaining an active physical fitness regimen, are also showing signs of time's flight, marked sometimes by the graying of hair, the replacement of joints, the increasing consumption of bottled water instead of Coke and Pepsi, or perhaps marked more acutely by a failure to put the correct number of cards in the kitty, thereby causing a misdeal, and thus forfeiture of the game!

Other Wintergreen Women have grown up under our watchful eyes. I speak, of course, of those two special young women, Daryl Lynn Dance and Jessea Nayo Gabbin. These daughters of Wintergreen grew up with us, spending their teen years around us and maturing into wonderful women. At one time, a quiet compassionate teenaged Daryl Lynn served as my personal fashion consultant, assisting me with the purchase of a Wintergreen bathing suit, slowing down to walk with me, and graciously sharing reading materials with me. She has spent several birthdays at Wintergreen, yet never once grumbled at having to share her mother, on her birthday, with the rest of us. Daryl Lynn has also moved into full-fledged participation, engaging in our conversations and sharing her work at a Saturday night reading. Although she may yet write the "Mommy Dearest" Wintergreen insider's tale, Jessea Nayo Gabbin has been my young "cut buddy," my present southern niece, and my gallant rescuer who has had my back. In 2001, health issues threatened my record of perfect attendance at Wintergreen. My left shoulder joint had disintegrated to the point of bone grating on bone; it was "frozen." I could not move it without intense pain. I would not be able to drive myself up the mountain. Trudier Harris was driving from elsewhere and needed to pick up her former student and first-time Wintergreen Woman Lovalerie King at a Charlottesville airport. So Nayo drove south from Greensboro to pick me up in Charlotte and the two of us climbed back into her Honda, and took off back up 29 North all the way to

Wintergreen. The companionship was terrific, the pain level manageable, and as Joanne had said, I might as well "hurt some at Wintergreen" among women who loved me than "hurt alone at home." She was right. I was rejuvenated immediately by the warmth of the Wintergreen connection, the Wintergreen spirit emanating from all of my Wintergreen sisters. Though I could not cook nor play Bid Whist that year, my niece Nayo and the others made sure I was well fed, comfortable, cared for, and properly pampered with a regular laying-on-of-hands.

When you come right down to it, that is what being a Wintergreen Woman is truly all about. Our rites, rituals, and creative ceremonies, from the obligatory games to the walks and the readings and the meals we share, are solely intended to heal each other, to support each other, to restore our souls to a creative equilibrium, and to rest or repair our spirits. Or as Daryl says, to see to the "greening" of those spirits. Wintergreen has been a wonderful, unique experience for the past twenty years. I am privileged, honored, and glad to have been a part of the Wintergreen Women Writers' Collective since its inception.

Poetry Reading
A Coda

—OPAL MOORE

"I want to bring you wintergreen."

"Excuse me," I said.

"I want to bring you wintergreen." The woman made her smile even bigger. It was the end of the poetry reading. We had come to Barbados for our twentieth-anniversary meeting and Carmen, unable to join us there, had arranged for us to join in a poetry reading with a group of local poets. Our hosts were offering us sandwiches and punch, and everyone was milling about. The woman had materialized out of the crowd, and the darkness.

"I want to bring you wintergreen," she said. "People today, they forget the healing properties of the wintergreen. We still use it here. In Barbados. We still do some of the things in the old ways here, you know?"

Finally, I understood. This woman with the great smile wanted to bring wintergreen to the Wintergreen Women. I laughed. Yes, *of course*, that would be *wonderful*. But we were staying at the opposite end of the island. It was a tedious drive, I warned. I told her the name of the house. "I know it. I know where you are. I will come," she said.

They come.

On the long drive back to our rental house, I considered the woman, her offer of wintergreen, and the balmy night air brought back to me

the opening two words of a poem I had written ten years earlier to commemorate our tenth gathering at the Wintergreen Resort in the mountains of Virginia. The poem celebrates the fruitfulness of an idea—that
each year women will choose a time and place, lay aside their routines,
obligations, and other loves, to affirm each other in their being, encourage their ideas, inspirations, inventions, celebrate their triumphs. That
what had begun as a single weekend retreat was now a necessity, a balm,
a ritual cure for the myriad isolations that mark and mar our modern
lives, a tradition. In our tenth year, we were no longer a group of women
who retreated to a resort once a year at a place called Wintergreen. We
were the Wintergreen Women Writers' Collective. We *were* Wintergreen,
and so we determined to bring Wintergreen down from the mountain to
the ocean.

> *They come*
> *the women in their white gather on the mountain.*
> *they dream of ocean,*
> *their crossing is a cosmogram.*

The poem imagines a ritual of healing and renewal. It is ambivalent
in its references to wintergreen as an agent of healing and as a naming of
the women themselves, and in describing the properties of the leaf and the
properties of the women gathered.

On a visit to Brazil in 1995 I learned of the annual celebration of the
African Orisha, Yemanya. The tour guide described the beauty of the celebration of the Orisha and its importance to the people of Brazil. To honor
the goddess of the seas, Brazilians by the thousands each year end come
to the edge of the ocean and offer Yemanya white flowers and beautiful
jewelry to flatter her, "because the Orisha loves beautiful things," and ask
her for favors. To make a wish, the supplicant must float a paper boat full
of white flowers and other gifts upon the water. The tour guide, a lovely
twenty-three-year-old Brazilian woman, assured us that the beauty of the
ritual must not be missed, that we must return to Brazil in December to
witness it, bring our offerings to Yemanya, and make a wish.

In my poem, I make a wish:

The women bear jewels, crystal beads strung together
or pearls, or petals of white flowers,
offerings to lay among the waves
of her voluminous skirts.
they make ritual joy.
it is a summoning.

they have prepared themselves for this—
shed their hard shoes, rinsed their faces and the soft folds
of winter feet in water chamomiled.
they eat mint leaves, and laughter,
make songs to welcome themselves back
from the wilderness and wars.

Her simple gift, an offering of wintergreen. I was delighted, for the sheer poetry of it and the surprise. The gesture was what mattered, not whatever it was that she would actually bring. I knew this because I still remember, in a physical way, the old women of my childhood who kept coins and single bills tied in handkerchiefs, or knotted in the sleeves of their white dresses. They gave careful gifts. And I recalled how it felt to wait for the giving, and how it felt to receive something so small, flesh-warm, so full of the act of giving itself. Indeed, in Barbados they were doing things "in the old ways." These were the ways of women, the ways of self-healing, of women carrying to one another small gestures of goodwill, of caring, of intuition, of knowing the myriad small coin offerings required to carry us daily from sun rise to sun fall. The annual retreat that gave birth to the Wintergreen Women had begun with such a gesture. The poem "Green in Winter" is a memory of our healing properties, of our crossings.

I want to end this closing notation with the story of how Ms. Applewhaite came to our house at the water's edge bearing a simple sprig of wintergreen, of how we stood with bare feet in the warm Caribbean sea and crushed its leaves lightly between our fingers to release the pungent oil, how the scent kept with us for hours or a day. Or that she brought us long-forgotten remedies for achy joints or stuffy noses. Too bad that didn't happen. She brought a bottle of rubbing alcohol. The label announced that the green color was because of, I guess, a tincture of wintergreen, with a little help from artificial coloring, I'm sure.

I laughed again. So delighted that she had come such a long way, that her gift was what it was—a reaching out to women connected to her by the water of history that surrounds the island of Barbados and the stories of how women take care. She sat in the kitchen, drank tea, and talked with some of us about various subjects. She left as a Wintergreen Woman.

the women carry mint in their mouths.
they have written her name upon their hearts
as upon a fold of paper, a conjuration of air
and light and jeweled breath of secrecies
and song. and this is the beginning,
this fluid warmth, and they
are the jeweled petals tossed upon her oceans,
the eternity she has foretold.

here upon the mountain dreaming of ocean,
they are the joining,
they are the waking green
of winter.

CONTRIBUTORS

Emmy Award winner, author/historian, publisher/producer, and creator of Backpax children's media, **Janus Adams** has been engaged by history and culture since childhood. Her Master's in Pan-African Culture is the nation's first graduate degree in Black Studies. Adams has authored nine books including the *Glory Days* trilogy on African American history. In cooperation with McDonald's Corporation, her "McDonald's Presents Glory Days" project yielded more than three million copies. Her *Glory Days-in-Concert* has been performed on Nashville's Music Square with Phylicia Rashad and *Take Six*'s Joel Kibble. *Glory Days: A Tradition of Achievement*, a documentary history of African American women, is in development for PBS with breakthrough filmmaker Julie Dash as Director. A frequent lecturer and on-air guest, her column is now in its twelfth year and her commentaries are heard on NPR. As producer/host she has launched programming for CBS, News 12, NPR, Pacifica, PRI, and PBS. Her CD, *A Day for Soup and Other Morsels*, inspired by personal experience, offers "food for thought" to caregivers of loved ones with dementia. She is a member of the Women's Media Center's Advisory Board.

Elizabeth Brown-Guillory is a playwright, performing artist, and Professor of English at the University of Houston (UH) where she has won the Cooper Teaching Excellence Award, the College of Liberal Arts and Social Sciences Teaching Excellence Award, and (two-time winner of) the English Honor Society's Sigma Tau Delta Distinguished Professor Award. Brown-Guillory teaches graduate and undergraduate courses in African/Diaspora literatures, women writers, American ethnic literatures, playwriting, and American dramatic literature. Her books include *Their Place on the Stage: Black Women Playwrights in America*, *Wines in the Wilderness: Plays by African-American Women from the Harlem Renaissance to the Present*, *Women of Color: Mother Daughter Relationships in Twentieth Century Literature*, and *Middle Passages and the Healing Place of History: Migration and Identity in Black Women's Literature*. She frequently publishes essays, book chapters, reviews, and interviews in major journals and critical anthologies.

Eugenia Collier, a native of Baltimore, is a writer and critic. She taught English at colleges and universities in the Baltimore-Washington area until her retirement in 1996. She has published scholarly and critical articles as well as stories, personal essays, and poems in numerous periodicals. With Richard A. Long, she coedited the anthology, *Afro-American Writing*. Her stories are collected in *Breeder and Other Stories*. Her work is motivated by her love for African American literature, drama, and culture.

Daryl Cumber Dance, a native of Charles City County and a graduate of Virginia State College and the University of Virginia, is Professor of English at the University of Richmond in Richmond, Virginia. She has also taught at Virginia State College, Virginia Commonwealth University, and the University of California at Santa Barbara. She is the author of *Shuckin' and Jivin': Folklore from Contemporary Black Americans* (Indiana University Press, 1978), *Folklore from Contemporary Jamaicans* (University of Tennessee Press, 1985), *Long Gone: The Mecklenburg Six and the Theme of Escape in Black Folklore* (University of Tennessee Press, 1987), *New World Adams: Conversations with Contemporary West Indian Writers* (Peepal Tree, 1992), and *The Lineage of Abraham: The Biography of a Free Black Family in Charles City, Virginia* (1998). She edited *Fifty Caribbean Writers: A Bio-Bibliographical and Critical Sourcebook* (Greenwood, 1986), *Honey, Hush! An Anthology of African American Women's Humor* (Norton, 1998), and *From My People: 400 Years of African American Folklore: An Anthology* (Norton, 2002).

Toi Derricotte, cofounder of Cave Canem and a Professor of English at the University of Pittsburgh, has published four books of poems: *The Empress of the Death House*, *Natural Birth*, *Captivity*, and *Tender*, winner of the 1998 Paterson Poetry Prize. Her literary memoir, *The Black Notebooks*, was a recipient of the 1998 Anisfield-Wolf Book Award, the Black Caucus of the American Library Association Nonfiction Award, and was nominated for the PEN/Martha Albrand Award for the Art of the Memoir. It was also a New York Times Notable Book of the Year. She has won numerous awards, including the Lucille Medwick Award from the Poetry Society of America, the Distinguished Pioneering of the Arts Award from the United Black Artists, a Rockefeller Foundation Fellowship, a Guggenheim Fellowship, two poetry fellowships from the National Endowment for the Arts, and two Pushcart Prizes. Her essay "Beginning Dialogues" was published in *The Best American Essays 2006*. Toi Derricotte has also taught in the graduate writing programs at New York University, George Mason University, and Old Dominion University.

Camille Dungy is the author of *What to Eat, What to Drink, What to Leave for Poison* (Red Hen Press, 2006), a finalist for the PEN Center USA 2007 Literary Award and the Library of Virginia 2007 Literary Award. Dungy has received fellowships from organizations including the National Endowment for the Arts, the Virginia Commission for the Arts, Cave Canem, Bread Loaf, the Dana Award, and the American Antiquarian Society. Assistant editor of *Gathering Ground: A Reader Celebrating Cave Canem's First*

Decade (University of Michigan Press, 2006), Dungy is Associate Professor in the Creative Writing Department at San Francisco State University.

Mari Evans, educator, writer, and musician, resides in Indianapolis. Formerly Distinguished Writer and Assistant Professor, African American Resource Center, Cornell University, she has taught at the main campus of Purdue University and at Purdue University in Indianapolis, Indiana University, Northwestern University, Washington University in St. Louis, the State University of New York at Albany, the University of Miami at Coral Gables, and Spelman College, Atlanta, over the past twenty years. She is the author of numerous articles, four children's books, several performed theater pieces, two musicals, and four volumes of poetry, including *I Am A Black Woman, Nightstar*, and *A Dark and Splendid Mass*, published in 1992. She also edited the highly acclaimed *Black Women Writers (1950–1980): A Critical Evaluation*. Her work has been widely anthologized in collections and textbooks, and her poems have appeared in several languages including German, Swedish, French, and Dutch. In 1998, she published *Singing Black: Alternative Nursery Rhymes for Children*. Her poetry is a superb distillation of the black idiom, capturing tones from the exquisitely humorous to the hauntingly poignant. It also reveals a skillful grasp of craft that shows to advantage the elegance and dignity that pervade her lines.

Nikky Finney was born by the sea, in the small fishing and farming community of Conway, South Carolina. Daughter of a civil rights attorney and an elementary school teacher, Finney has been writing for as long as she has memory. Poetry has been her favorite language forever: lavishly visual, plain-as-day lyrical, and passionately portrait-yielding. Finney received a Bachelor of Arts degree in English Literature from Talladega College in Alabama. While in graduate school, at Atlanta University, she dedicated herself to the crafting of her first body of original narrative work. In 1985, Finney published her first book of poems, *On Wings Made of Gauze*. In 1995, Finney published *Rice*, a collection of stories, poems, and photographs. *Rice* won the PEN American Open Book Award in 1999. Finney's 1998 volume of short stories, *Heartwood*, was written to assist adult literacy students across the country. Her latest poetry collection, *The World Is Round*, was published in 2003, and won the 2004 Benjamin Franklin Award for Poetry. She is editor of the anthology *The Ringing Ear*, a rich contemporary collection of one hundred poetic Black voices published by the University of Georgia Press in 2007. Finney is Professor of Creative Writing at the University of Kentucky. During the 2007–08 academic year she is the Grace Hazard Conkling Writer-in-Residence at Smith College in Northampton, Massachusetts.

Joanne Veal Gabbin is the Executive Director of the Furious Flower Poetry Center and Professor of English at James Madison University. She is the author of *Sterling A. Brown: Building the Black Aesthetic Tradition* (1985), which was published in a new edition by the University Press of Virginia in 1994. She edited *The Furious Flowering of*

African American Poetry (1999), and *Furious Flower: African American Poetry from the Black Arts Movement to the Present* (2004), and she wrote a children's book, *I Bet She Called Me Sugar Plum* (2004). Gabbin has published essays in *Wild Women in the Whirlwind*, edited by Joanne M. Braxton and Andree Nicola McLaughlin, and *Southern Women Writers: The New Generation*, edited by Tonette Bond Inge. Her articles have also appeared in *The Dictionary of Literary Biography*, the *Zora Neale Hurston Forum*, *The Oxford Companion to Women's Writing*, the *Langston Hughes Journal*, *Callaloo*, *The Oxford Companion to African American Literature*, and *Black Books Bulletin*. As director of the Furious Flower Poetry Center, Gabbin has organized two international conferences for the critical exploration of African American poetry and produced two Furious Flower video and DVD series. Gabbin is also the founder and organizer of the Wintergreen Women Writers' Collective.

Carmen R. Gillespie is an Associate Professor of English at Bucknell University. She is a scholar of American, African American, and Caribbean literatures and cultures, and a creative writer. Her articles and poems have appeared in numerous literary journals and anthologies. Her book, *A Critical Companion to Toni Morrison*, was published in December 2007. She currently has a contract for another book publication on the life and works of novelist Alice Walker. In 2005, Gillespie was the recipient of an Ohio Arts Council Individual Artist Fellowship for Excellence in Poetry. She has been a Fulbright scholar and a Cave Canem Fellow, and has received awards from the National Endowment for the Humanities, the Mellon Foundation, the Bread Loaf Writer's Conference, and the Fine Arts Work Center in Provincetown. She is fortunate to share her life with her husband, Harold Bakst, and daughters, Chelsea and Delaney.

Nikki Giovanni, poet, writer, activist, and educator, was born in Knoxville, Tennessee, and grew up in Lincoln Heights, an all-black suburb of Cincinnati, Ohio. She and her sister spent their summers with their grandparents in Knoxville, and she graduated with honors from Fisk University, her grandfather's alma mater, in 1968; after graduating from Fisk, she attended the University of Pennsylvania and Columbia University. She published her first book of poetry, *Black Feeling Black Talk*, in 1968, and within the next year published a second book, thus launching her career as a writer. Early in her career she was dubbed the "Princess of Black Poetry," and over the course of more than three decades of publishing and lecturing she has come to be called both a "National Treasure" and, most recently, one of Oprah Winfrey's twenty-five "Living Legends." Her autobiography, *Gemini*, was a finalist for the National Book Award; *Love Poems, Blues: For All the Changes*, and *Quilting the Black-Eyed Pea* were all honored with NAACP Image Awards. *Blues: For All the Changes* reached number 4 on the Los Angeles Times Bestseller list. Most recently, her children's picture book *Rosa* became a Caldecott Honors Book. Giovanni's spoken word recordings have also achieved widespread recognition and honors. Her album *Truth Is On Its Way*, on which she reads her poetry against a background of gospel music, was a top 100 album and received the Best Spoken Word

Album given by the National Association of Radio and Television Announcers. The author of some thirty books for both adults and children, Nikki Giovanni is a University Distinguished Professor at Virginia Tech in Blacksburg, Virginia.

Sandra Y. Govan is a Professor of English at the University of North Carolina at Charlotte. In 1994, she became the Coordinator/Director of the Ronald E. McNair Postbaccalaureate Achievement Program and remained in that position until July 2001. In 2001, Govan was a Finalist for the Bank of America Teaching Excellence Award. Govan's primary research interests are African American literature and culture, American literature, and popular culture, particularly science fiction. Most of her publications have been scholarly articles on such figures as Harlem Renaissance writer/artist Gwendolyn Bennett and Langston Hughes; she has also written about black science fiction writers Octavia Butler, Samuel Delany, and Steven Barnes. Throughout the 1990s she contributed scholarly essays to *Erotique Noire*; *Sexual Politics*; *Langston Hughes: The Man, His Art, and His Continuing Influence*; *Notable Black American Women*; *Notable Black American Men*; *The Oxford Companion to African American Literature*; and *The Oxford Companion to Women's Writing*. In addition, she contributed personal essays to *My Soul is a Witness: African American Women's Spirituality* and to *Father Songs: Testimonies by African-American Sons and Daughters*. Govan is a founding member of the Wintergreen Women Writers' Collective.

Maryemma Graham is Professor of English at the University of Kansas and founder/ director for the Project on the History of Black Writing. She has published extensively on American and African American literature and culture and has directed numerous national and international workshops and institutes on literature, literary history, criticism, and pedagogy. Her most recent books include *Fields Watered with Blood: Critical Essays on Margaret Walker* (2001) and *Conversations with Margaret Walker* (2002). She is currently completing *The House Where My Soul Lives*, the authorized biography on Margaret Walker.

Kendra Hamilton is an award-winning writer living in Charlottesville, Virginia. She holds an M.F.A. from Louisiana State University. Her personal essays have appeared in *BrightLeaf: New Writing of the South and Southern Cultures*; her poetry has been published in *Callaloo*, *Shenandoah*, the *Southern Review*, *River Styx*, *Obsidian III*, and the anthologies *Bum Rush the Page: A Def Poetry Jam*, *The Best of Callaloo*, and *The Ringing Ear*, an anthology of Afro-Southern poetry. One of only twelve Southern writers invited to the Spoleto Festival USA's forum on the Confederate flag, Hamilton has been featured on C-SPAN's *BookNotes* and has made several national radio appearances, including one in 2002 with former NPR anchor Bob Edwards. She is active with the Cave Canem collective, a workshop/retreat for emerging African American poets. She is a frequent collaborator with artists from the disciplines of performance art, theater, and visual arts—most recently concluding work on *Water Table*, a massive installation on the intersections of race, landscape, and culture featured at the 2004 Spoleto Festival USA.

Trudier Harris grew up in Tuscaloosa, Alabama. She is the author of numerous books, including *From Mammies to Militants: Domestics in Black American Literature*; *Saints, Sinners, Saviors: Strong Black Women in African American Literature*; and *Fiction and Folklore: The Novels of Toni Morrison*; and she is coeditor of numerous anthologies, including *The Oxford Companion to African American Literature*; *Call and Response: The Riverside Anthology of the African American Literary Traditions*; and *The Literature of the American South: A Norton Anthology*. She is currently the J. Carlyle Sitterson Professor of English at the University of North Carolina, Chapel Hill.

Karla FC Holloway is Arts and Sciences Professor of English and Professor of Law at Duke University. She is the author of nearly forty essays, including "Cruel Enough to Stop the Blood: Global Feminisms and the U.S. Body Politic" (meridians 6.5), "Accidental Communities: Race, Emergency Medicine and the Problem of Polyheme" in the *American Journal of Bioethics*, and "Private Bodies/Public Texts: Literature, Science, and States of Surveillance," which appeared in *Literature and Medicine* (2007). Her books include *Passed On: African-American Mourning Stories* (Duke University Press, 2002) and *BookMarks—Reading in Black and White* (Rutgers University Press, 2006). Her current project is on privacy and bioethics. She has won numerous national awards and foundation fellowships including the Rockefeller Foundation's Bellagio Residency Fellowship and residency at Harvard University's Du Bois Institute. Holloway's public essays on ethics, race, and culture have appeared on National Public Radio.

Lovalerie King is Assistant Professor of English and affiliate faculty in Women's Studies at the Pennsylvania State University, University Park. Her areas of expertise include African American literary history, African American culture and legal discourse, black women authors, and black feminist thought and theory. She is the author of *A Students' Guide to African American Literature* (2003), *Race, Theft and Ethics: Property Matters in African American Literature* (2007), and *The Cambridge Introduction to Zora Neale Hurston* (2008). She has coedited *James Baldwin and Toni Morrison: Comparative Critical and Theoretical Essays* (2006) and *New Essays on the African American Novel: From Hurston and Ellison to Morrison and Whitehead* (2008). She has contributed numerous essays, reviews, and articles to journals, essay collections, and literary and cultural reference volumes. Her ongoing projects include an autobiography and a coedited project examining the relationship between African American cultural production and legal discourse. She is a member of the Pennsylvania State University English Department's American Women Writers Workshop and serves on the Advisory Board of the Pennsylvania State University Center for American Literary Studies. She holds a B.A. from Michigan State University, an M.A. from Emory University (with certification in Women's Studies), and a Ph.D. from the University of North Carolina, Chapel Hill (with a major in African American Literature and a minor in theory).

Paule Marshall, née Valenza Pauline Burke, was born in Brooklyn, New York. Formerly a researcher and staff writer for *Our World* magazine, located in New York City, Marshall traveled on assignment to Brazil and to the West Indies. Once her literary career had been launched, she contributed short stories and articles to numerous magazines and anthologies and began lecturing at several colleges and universities within the United States and abroad. The recipient of several prestigious awards, including the John D. and Catherine T. MacArthur Fellowship, Marshall continues to write and to teach. She is a Professor of English and creative writing at Virginia Commonwealth University and resides in Richmond, Virginia. While clearly influenced by the literary giants (black and white), Marshall attributes her love of language and storytelling to her mother and other Bajan (Barbadian) women who, sitting around the kitchen table, effortlessly created narrative art. In her informative essay "From the Poets in the Kitchen," the author explains the process as a transformation of standard English into "an idiom, an instrument that more adequately described them—changing around the syntax and imposing their own rhythm and accent so that the sentences were more pleasing to their ears." Her first major works are: *Brown Girl, Brownstones*; *Soul Clap Hands and Sing* (a collection of novellas), *The Chosen Place, The Timeless People*; *Praisesong for the Widow*; and *Daughters*.

Marilyn Sanders Mobley is the Vice President for Inclusion, Diversity and Equal Opportunity at Case Western Reserve. She was Provost at Bennett College for Women and Associate Provost for Educational Programs at George Mason University. She was an associate professor of English and the founder and first director of the African American Studies Program (1992–98) in the College of Arts and Sciences. A Toni Morrison scholar, Dr. Mobley is past president of the Toni Morrison Society and now serves as a member of its advisory board. Mobley is the author or editor of numerous articles and the book *Folk Roots and Mythic Wings in Sarah Orne Jewett and Toni Morrison: The Cultural Function of Narrative*. Her article "Labor Above and Beyond the Call: A Black Woman Scholar in the Academy" was published in *Sister Circle: Black Women and Work* (under her former name of Marilyn Mobley McKenzie and edited by Sharon Harley and the Black Women and Work Collective). She currently has two other projects—a book-length study tentatively titled *Spaces for the Reader: Toni Morrison's Narrative Poetics and Cultural Politics*, and *The Strawberry Room: And Other Places Where a Woman Finds Herself*, a volume of essays about a woman's journey from personal and family trauma to spiritual recovery. She is the proud mother of two adult sons—Rashad Mobley of Greenbelt, Maryland, and Jamal Mobley of Atlanta, Georgia.

Opal Moore is an Associate Professor in the Department of English at Spelman College, Atlanta, where she teaches creative writing, a fiction writing workshop, and courses in contemporary African American literature. Her fiction and poetry have appeared in journals and anthologies, including *Callaloo*, *African American Review*, and *Honey, Hush! An Anthology of African American Women's Humor*, edited by Daryl Cumber

Dance. Her other interests include the representations of ethnicities in children's and young adult literatures; she has published a number of articles on this subject in journals and collections, including *The Black American in Books for Children: The Role of Illustration in Multicultural Literature for Youth* (1997). Her collection of poems, *Lot's Daughters* (Third World Press, 2004), is a meditation on black women in portraits. She is currently completing a new series of poems, "Children of Middle Passage," written in collaboration with visual and performance artist, Arturo Lindsay.

Linda Williamson Nelson is an Associate Professor of Anthropology and Africana Studies at the Richard Stockton College of New Jersey. She earned the bachelor and master degrees in literature, before completing a Ph.D. in anthropological linguistics, thereby melding the close examination of language and culture with the nuances of literary studies in her analysis of oral and written narratives. Before joining the Anthropology Program, she was a professor of writing for over twenty years; during that time her scholarship focused on writing pedagogy. Her published articles and book chapters in anthropology are concerned with culturally constructed meaning in oral and written narratives, especially pragmatic presuppositions, narrative co-construction, and dialectal code switching. Her recent coauthored book, *Telling Our Lives: Conversations on Solidarity and Difference*, explores the trajectories of the lives of the three authors, who represent varying locations with regard to academic disciplines, ethnicity, religion, and sexual orientation. They share origins in the working class or below. The analysis of their triadic discourse brings theory to experience as the authors examine the relationship between their embodied knowledge and their teaching and research commitments. In addition to her publications, Nelson has read her work at conferences in the United States and abroad. Since her recent field research in Jamaica, she is currently working on an analysis of Jamaican women's life stories.

Joyce Pettis is retired Professor of English at North Carolina State University, Raleigh, where she taught graduate and undergraduate courses in African American literature. She is the author of *Toward Wholeness in Paule Marshall's Fiction* and is currently working on a study of celebration and festivity in African American and Black Caribbean fiction. She has published numerous articles, including "Reading Ann Petry's *The Narrows* into Black Literary Tradition," in *Recovered Writers/Recovered Texts*, edited by Dolan Hubbard (University of Tennessee Press, 1997); "The Marrow of Tradition: Charles Chesnutt's Novel of the South," *North Carolina Literary Review*; and "'She Sung Back in Return': Literary (Re)vision and Transformation in Gayl Jones's *Corregidora*." Additionally, she serves on the editorial board of the *North Carolina Literary Review*, is a former associate editor of *Obsidian II: Black Literature in Review*, and evaluates manuscripts on African American literature for several university presses.

A native of east Texas, **Hermine Pinson** is an Associate Professor of African American Literature at the College of William and Mary. Her short fiction and poetry have appeared in anthologies such as *Common Bonds* and *KenteCloth*. Pinson is the author of two collections of poetry, *Ashe* and *Mama Yetta and Other Poems*. She is also the author of a play, *Walk Together, Children*. Her latest work, *Changing the Changes in Poetry and Song*, is a CD produced in collaboration with Yusef Komunyakaa and Estela Conwill Majozo.

Sonia Sanchez is one of the most deeply moving and committed poets to emerge from the Black Arts Movement in the late sixties and seventies. A poet, activist, playwright, editor, and teacher, Sanchez has significantly influenced African American literature and culture by the urgency of her sustained and powerful voice. From 1969 to the present, she has authored eight books of poems including *Homecoming* (1969), *We a BadddDDD People* (1970), *A Blues Book for Blue Black Magical Women* (1974), *homegirls & handgrenades* (1984), *Under a Soprano Sky* (1987), *Wounded in the House of a Friend* (1995), *Does Your House Have Lions?* (1998), and *Like the Singing Coming Off the Drums: Love Poems* (1998). A recipient of numerous awards including a National Endowment for the Arts Award, the 1985 American Book Award for *homegirls & handgrenades*, the Governor's Award for Excellence in the Humanities for 1988, and the Peace and Freedom Award from the Women International League for Peace and Freedom for 1989, she recently received the Pew Fellowship in the Arts for her outstanding literary achievement. Sanchez has lectured at over five hundred universities and colleges in the United States and has traveled extensively, reading her poetry in Africa, China, Europe, Canada, and the Caribbean. She is a faculty emerita at Temple University.

Ethel Morgan Smith is the author of *From Whence Cometh My Help: The African American Community at Hollins College*. She has published in national and international journals; and she has been a Fulbright scholar in Germany, a resident at the Rockefeller Foundation in Bellagio, Italy, a DuPont scholar, a visiting artist at the American Academy in Rome, and a visiting scholar at the Women's Research Center at Brandeis University. She is an Associate Professor of English at West Virginia University.